Shakespeare in the Theatre: Peter Hall

SHAKESPEARE IN THE THEATRE

Series Editors Bridget Escolme, Peter Holland
and Farah Karim-Cooper

Published titles

Patrice Chéreau, Dominique Goy-Blanquet

Cheek by Jowl, Peter Kirwan

Trevor Nunn, Russell Jackson

The American Shakespeare Center, Paul Menzer

Mark Rylance at the Globe, Stephen Purcell

The National Theatre, 1963–1975: Olivier and Hall,
Robert Shaughnessy

Nicholas Hytner, Abigail Rokison-Woodall

Peter Sellars, Ayanna Thompson

Forthcoming titles

The King's Men, Lucy Munro

The Other Place: The RSC and Studio Theatre,
Abigail Rokison-Woodall and Lisa Hammond-Marty

Shakespeare in Berlin, 1918–2018, Holger Schott Syme

Shakespeare in the Theatre: Peter Hall

Stuart Hampton-Reeves

THE ARDEN SHAKESPEARE
LONDON • NEW YORK • OXFORD • NEW DELHI • SYDNEY

THE ARDEN SHAKESPEARE
Bloomsbury Publishing Plc
50 Bedford Square, London, WC1B 3DP, UK
1385 Broadway, New York, NY 10018, USA
29 Earlsfort Terrace, Dublin 2, Ireland

BLOOMSBURY, THE ARDEN SHAKESPEARE and the Arden Shakespeare logo
are trademarks of Bloomsbury Publishing Plc

First published in Great Britain 2019
Paperback edition first published 2021

Copyright © Stuart Hampton-Reeves, 2019

Stuart Hampton-Reeves has asserted his right under the Copyright,
Designs and Patents Act, 1988, to be identified as author of this work.

For legal purposes the Acknowledgements on pp. vi–vii constitute
an extension of this copyright page.

Series design by Dani Leigh
Cover image: Judi Dench as Titania and Oliver Chris as Bottom in
A Midsummer Night's Dream, directed by Peter Hall at the Rose Theatre
(© Robbie Jack/Corbis/Getty Images

All rights reserved. No part of this publication may be reproduced or
transmitted in any form or by any means, electronic or mechanical,
including photocopying, recording, or any information storage or retrieval
system, without prior permission in writing from the publishers.

Bloomsbury Publishing Plc does not have any control over, or responsibility for,
any third-party websites referred to or in this book. All internet addresses given
in this book were correct at the time of going to press. The author and publisher
regret any inconvenience caused if addresses have changed or sites have
ceased to exist, but can accept no responsibility for any such changes.

A catalogue record for this book is available from the British Library.

Library of Congress Cataloging-in-Publication Data
Names: Hampton-Reeves, Stuart, author.
Title: Shakespeare in the theatre: Peter Hall / Stuart Hampton-Reeves.
Other titles: Peter Hall
Description: London, UK; New York, NY: The Arden Shakespeare, 2019. |
Series: Shakespeare in the theatre | Includes bibliographical references and index.
Identifiers: LCCN 2019016259 | ISBN 9781472587077 (hb) |
ISBN 9781472587091 (epub) | ISBN 9781472587107 (epdf)
Subjects: LCSH: Hall, Peter, 1930-2017–Criticism and interpretation. |
Shakespeare, William, 1564-1616–Stage history–1950- |
Theater–Production and direction–History–20th century. |
Theater–Production and direction–History–21st century.
Classification: LCC PN2598.H2 H36 2019 | DDC 792.02/33092–dc23
LC record available at https://lccn.loc.gov/2019016259

ISBN: HB: 978-1-4725-8707-7
PB: 978-1-4725-8708-4
ePDF: 978-1-4725-8710-7
eBook: 978-1-4725-8709-1

Series: Shakespeare in the Theatre

Typeset by Integra Software Services Pvt. Ltd.

To find out more about our authors and books visit
www.bloomsbury.com and sign up for our newsletters.

CONTENTS

Acknowledgements vi
Series Preface viii

Introduction: Speaking Shakespeare 1

1   Nostalgia and Politics at the Shakespeare Memorial Theatre 13

2   Nation, Culture and Authority at the Royal Shakespeare Company 49

3   Authority in Crisis at the National Theatre 89

4   Protest and Politics at the National Theatre 109

5   Death and Sexuality after the National Theatre 131

6   Playing Shakespeare in America 149

7   National Stages 163

List of Productions 190
References 193
Index 200

ACKNOWLEDGEMENTS

I am very grateful to the librarians at the Shakespeare Centre Library in Stratford-upon-Avon, the National Theatre Archive in London, the Harry Ransom Centre in Austin, Texas and the Performing Arts section of the New York Public Library, without whom none of this work would be possible. I am particularly grateful to Ian Moore from the Sound and Vision Reference Team at the British Library, who arranged for many of the audio recordings of Peter Hall's productions to be digitized so that I could listen to them. These are now available for anyone with a reader's pass to access in the reading rooms without an appointment. I have benefited from discussing this work in seminars and more casual conservations with too many people to list, but I thank Bridget Escolme, Paul Prescott, Pete Smith, Paul Edmondson, Robert Shaughnessy, Robert Ormsby, Jaime Marshall, John Russell Brown, Michael Cordner, Geoffrey Wheeler, Andrew Jarvis, Stephen Purcell, Peter Kirwan, Tony Howard, Carol Chillington Rutter and Darren Tunstall. David Jones and Chris Green have been invaluable sources of information about the Perse School. I am indebted to Richard Wilson, the Sir Peter Hall Professor of Shakespeare Studies, for inviting me to the Kingston Shakespeare Seminar where I was able to present some of this research. I am also grateful to Frank Whately at Kingston for reading an early draft of the last chapter and to Stanley Wells, a meticulous and authoritative observer of Hall's work from the beginning, for his thorough and helpful comments on the manuscript. Peter Holland commissioned this book and has been a remarkably patient and perceptive editor whose detailed notes have also made this a better book. Margaret Bartley, Mark Dudgeon and Lara Bateman at Bloomsbury, and Atalanta Willcox have been equally patient and I am grateful to all my editors for giving me the opportunity to work on this book: they have done their best to make it as good as it can be, but all the mistakes are my own. This project began life as a chapter on Peter Hall in the book *Great Shakespeareans Volume XVIII: Brook, Hall, Ninagawa, Lepage*, edited by Peter Holland, which, like this study, discussed Hall's productions in chronological order. I stand by that work as a concise history of Hall's Shakespearean career, but the argument of this book is different and I have reframed and extended most of the passages in that chapter for this work, as well as writing extensively about many productions which are not mentioned at all in that chapter.

I never met Peter Hall, who died in 2017 as I was nearing the completion of this book, but I did correspond with him briefly at the very start of this project when he offered to fact-check my work, so I gained a small insight into the generosity and openness with which he treated scholars.

All quotations from Shakespeare's plays are taken from *The Arden Shakespeare: Shakespeare Complete Works*, revised edition, eds Ann Thompson, David Scott Kastan and Richard Proudfoot (London: Arden, 2011).

SERIES PREFACE

Each volume in the *Shakespeare in the Theatre* series focuses on a director or theatre company who has made a significant contribution to Shakespeare production, identifying the artistic and political/social contexts of their work. The series introduces readers to the work of significant theatre directors and companies whose Shakespeare productions have been transformative in our understanding of his plays in performance. Each volume examines a single figure or company, considering their key productions, rehearsal approaches and their work with other artists (actors, designers, composers). A particular feature of each book is its exploration of the contexts within which these theatre artists have made their Shakespeare productions work. Thus, the series considers not only the ways in which directors and companies produce Shakespeare but also reflects upon their other theatre activity and the broader artistic, cultural and socio-political milieu within which their Shakespeare performances and productions have been created. The key to the series' originality, then, is its consideration of Shakespeare production in a range of artistic and broader contexts; in this sense, it de-centres Shakespeare from within Shakespeare studies, pointing to the range of people, artistic practices and cultural phenomena that combine to make meaning in the theatre.

Series editors: Bridget Escolme,
Peter Holland,
Farah Karim-Cooper

Introduction: Speaking Shakespeare

Peter Hall directed his first Shakespeare production in 1954 and his last in 2011. His career spanned more than half a century of innovation in theatre and, for much of that time, Hall was at its epicentre. His achievements as the founder of the Royal Shakespeare Company (RSC) and then the second (and to date longest-serving) Director of the National Theatre (NT) have been the subject of many studies, but his work as a director of Shakespeare has often been in the background, footnotes to his career as a maker of theatrical institutions. For the purposes of this study, the story of the RSC and the NT is part of the background to Hall's work as a maker of theatre. Some of his productions have been so significant that they have been the subject of scholarly articles, university dissertations and monographs, but many have never been studied in any depth. To date, no study has attempted to bring all of Hall's Shakespeare productions together and see them in a context which arcs from the post-war welfare capitalism of the 1950s through to the post-9/11 turn back to war and nationalism in the first decade of the new millennium. This book aims to do that.

Like many of his champions and his audiences, Hall grew up in a world being rebuilt and transformed after the Second World War. He was in his mid-teens when the war ended and he went straight from school into national service. Much of the country was in physical ruin, but there were other kinds of ruins to negotiate: Britain's empire was effectively over, but the rhetoric of empire survived. Structures of power were being questioned, especially as education improved for the working classes. For Alan Sinfield, Hall was a product of this social and cultural moment, an emblem of the welfare capitalism that promoted the role of the state in subsidizing art (Sinfield 1994). Technology and changing social habits were also changing the place theatre occupied in British society. The popular theatre, particularly vaudeville, was in a sudden, terminal decline, killed off by the new medium of television. Hall was prescient enough to realize that classical theatre was also at risk, that the commercial market for Shakespeare was shrinking and could only survive through a mixture of innovation and government support.

Much of Hall's work was self-consciously directed at trying to understand the nature of this transformation, its opportunities, and its dangers. He directed mainly modern plays and built his reputation directing Beckett, Anouilh and Whiting, but Shakespeare was a constant presence in Hall's life and work. He was fiercely loyal to Shakespeare, and over time his commitment to the text only increased, sometimes to such absurd levels that he was often accused of textual fundamentalism. Yet he also saw no contradiction in approaching Shakespeare as if he were a modern author and, as he told Irving Wardle in a private interview in 1966, his own engagement with modern drama helped him to see how Shakespeare could speak to modern audiences (Wardle 1966).

The Play Way

Although primarily a director of modern drama, Peter Hall had from the beginning a special relationship with Shakespeare. He had first encountered Shakespeare as a schoolboy, playing

Macbeth in a special classroom called the 'Mummery' at The Perse, a boys school in Cambridge. (For more on The Perse, see Mitchell 1976.) The Mummery had been established by Henry Caldwell Cook, a pioneering teacher who believed in teaching boys through the practical performance of Shakespeare's plays. His curriculum began with verse-speaking: he would beat out an iambic rhythm with a baton as the boys spoke the verse, drilling into them a strong sense of the pulse of Shakespeare's language. The boys then worked their way through the comedies, histories and tragedies. This was not, incidentally, a method for teaching boys about Shakespeare: Cook believed that such lessons taught them fundamental life skills. He called his method the 'Play Way', which is also the title of the book he published describing his methods. The boys' productions at the Mummery attracted attention and were sometimes reviewed in the press: in fact, Hall's first appearance in the press was when he starred as Hamlet in a Perse production, which was reviewed by *The Times Educational Supplement* (19 February 1949). Hall was not taught by Cook, who died before Hall enrolled at the school, but he was taught by two teachers, John Tanfield and Douglas Brown, who were disciples of Cook and became mentors to Hall, helping him start his career as a director. Hall was, then, educated in the Play Way, and at school starred mainly in Shakespeare plays, starting with a small part in *Richard II* before graduating quickly to Petruchio in *The Taming of the Shrew* and finally Hamlet.

The Play Way gave Hall a thorough education in verse-speaking, and throughout his career he devoted much of his time with actors to developing this, often using a baton in much the same way as his teachers would have done, beating out the rhythm line by line (for more on the Play Way, see Beacock 1943). Hall subscribed to the view, most famously associated with the early twentieth-century director William Poel, that Shakespeare included instructions in his text for actors. This was an idea he had developed at Cambridge, partly through his own intellectual efforts but mostly through acting for George 'Dadie' Rylands, a lecturer at Cambridge who also directed the Marlowe Dramatic Society (the Marlowe). John Barton, who was also in the Marlowe, schooled Hall in original pronunciation and together they acted in an undergraduate *Julius Caesar* that was spoken entirely with sixteenth-century accents. Hall put verse-speaking at the centre of his work and spoke frequently about it throughout his career. There are few interviews with him which do not touch on verse-speaking and textual fidelity at some point and he eventually put his thoughts into a short book, *Shakespeare's Advice to the Players*, which is the closest Hall ever came to articulating a theatrical method. 'Shakespeare', he wrote, 'tells the actor when to go fast and when to go slow; when to come in on cue, and when to accent a particular word or series of words. He tells the actor much else; and he always tells him *when* to do it' (Hall 2003: 13).

Hall was a textual purist: whenever he could, he worked with the Folio, and if working with modern editions he would eliminate as much interpolated punctuation as possible. Despite gaining a brief reputation for radicalism after directing (and helping to prepare the text for) the early histories in the 1960s, when he produced John Barton's savagely cut *Henry VI* plays as part of *The Wars of the Roses*, Hall was (as he would often say himself) militantly classical, with an unswerving belief in the integrity of the original texts. When he could get away without cutting a play, he did. When he needed a text prepared, he worked with a scholar to create a text which he felt was as authentic as possible. In the early part of his career, this was John Barton; later he worked with John Russell Brown and Roger Warren in the same way. Hall saw himself as part of a tradition that recognizes that what 'Shakespeare demands always works' because 'his notation is amazingly accurate' (Hall 2003: 14).

Hall's approach to the text was extremely conservative, in the sense that he dissociated himself, and his actors, from any act of interpretation which affected the form of the words. This method was simple enough to be taught to an actor in three days, at least that is what Hall boasted (Hall 2003: 13), although over his career he frequently struggled with actor training and complained frequently about actors' verse-speaking skills in later life. Hall taught actors to respect the 'sanctity' of Shakespeare's lines, discouraging them from adding in reflective pauses which, he wrote, 'destroy the basic energy and shape' of the line. Fragmenting lines into 'little naturalistic gobbets' made Shakespeare sound modern, but he complained that this 'plays hell with the meaning' (Hall 2003: 24). Actors who spoke verse as Hall taught them generally had a cool, clean, almost forensic way with lines that came to define Hall's style, particularly at the RSC. He took seriously Hamlet's advice to the players to speak 'trippingly' and many of his productions were fast as actors sped through lines, trusting the cues that Hall had taught them to recognize. Hall invested in actor training at the RSC, using a grant from the Gulbenkian Foundation to pump prime three years of verse training led by Michel Saint-Denis and later Cicely Berry. In his later career, without this resource, Hall was forced to train actors during rehearsals. He would stand in front of the cast, his head looking down at a copy of the text on a lectern, beating the iambic rhythm of the verse out with a baton. At its best, this method produced the crisp, clear performances that the RSC, under Hall, became famous for. At its worst, actors sounded stilted as they artificially paused at the end of each line, regardless of the impact this had on its meaning.

The paradox of Hall's work is that his textual fundamentalism underpinned some provocative interpretations of Shakespeare's plays. In the 1960s, he was even thought of as a radical for giving Shakespeare a strong sense of contemporary relevance. Hall rarely dressed his actors in modern dress, but he always worked with designers who had either a reputation for contemporary art or a radical eye, able to create simple but powerful sets which articulated Hall's ideas. For Hall, there was no contradiction. Shakespeare may tell the actor how to perform the play, he wrote, but 'he never tells him *why*'. Hall continued to explain that the 'motive, the *why*, remains the creative task of the actor' and, he implied, the task of the director (Hall 2003: 13). This emphasis on motive gave Hall considerable liberty to define what Shakespeare meant for the present. He came to Shakespeare with a reputation for directing modern drama. His 1955 *Waiting for Godot* introduced Samuel Beckett to British theatre, and he was also notable as the director of plays by Tennessee Williams, Harold Pinter, Jean Anouilh, John Whiting and others, all writers who in different ways articulated the modern condition. As the Managing Director of the RSC, Hall saw it as his mission to bridge the gap between Shakespeare's form and the needs of modern audiences. He never wanted Shakespeare to sound modern, or look modern, but he was passionate about bringing out the relevance of Shakespeare's plays to the present.

This rigorous approach to the text could be limiting, and some of Hall's productions could be pedestrian, unadorned interpretations of the plays, but Hall at his best treated rehearsal as a creative endeavour. There are many accounts of his rehearsals, including some which were taped or videoed for documentaries, and others that are preserved in diaries kept by attending academics. In all of them, Hall is a strong presence in the rehearsal room, always certain of his judgement, his actors frequently deferring to his expertise. Yet he was also creative and did not inhibit his company from developing their own ideas and interpretations. Hall later compared this to jazz playing (Hall was a proficient musician and had been something of a prodigy before discovering the theatre): 'if you play in a little jazz group and you don't actually observe the rhythm, you don't actually play together and breathe together, it doesn't work together,' he told one interviewer. 'On the other hand,' he continued, 'if you do it mechanically and absolutely rigidly, it doesn't work either. It's that sense that you have in good jazz of nearly breaking the rhythm, of nearly losing it – that's the thrill. It's the same with Shakespeare actually, absolutely the same' (Hall 2014: n.p.). This did not always work: for example, he started with a strong focus on religion and the nature of evil when he directed *Macbeth* in 1967, but as he worked with his lead actor, Paul Scofield, the performance went in a different direction, leading to a somewhat messy and poorly received production. On the other hand, Ian McKellen's account of working with Hall on *Coriolanus* in 1984 demonstrate the extent to which Hall was open to developing performances in a creative partnership with his lead actors.

A good example of Hall's working relationship with actors is the one he had with Dustin Hoffman, who starred in Hall's *The Merchant of Venice* in 1989 (Peter Hall Company, Phoenix Theatre London). Hoffman was a major film star who wanted to play Hamlet, a role Hall steered him away from because he did not think it suitable for Hoffman's talents. Hall used Hoffman as an example in *Shakespeare's Advice to the Players*, recalling that Hoffman at first struggled to adapt to Hall's methods. 'First comes the form and second comes the feeling,' Hall remembers insisting (Hall 2003: 17). The rehearsals were filmed as part of a documentary about Hall. More accustomed to film acting than to the stage, Hoffman brought an extraordinary commitment to his rehearsals, giving full-on performances for 6–7 hours. Nevertheless, Hoffman struggled with verse-speaking. He would spend an hour every morning practising iambic pentameter in front of the mirror until he had it right, but then fell apart in the rehearsal room. In the film, Hall can be seen asking an assistant to for help because 'we have a problem'.

The conflict between an actor who finds his interpretation through improvisation and a director who insists on fidelity to form before meaning is how Hall presents the relationship – a conflict that Hall, 'trying to keep the note of triumph out of my voice', wins in his account (Hall 2003: 17). Yet the film shows the two methods coming together, Hoffman using improvisation as a response to Hall's focus on text. Rehearsing Act 2, Scene 5, with Francesca Buller as Jessica, Hoffman struggled with the line 'yet I'll go in hate' (2.5.14). At first he delivered it like a vicar off to a tea party, affectionately stroking Buller's hair and gesturing feebly to the air. He then clutched her head and smiled with affection as he said, 'Jessica my girl' (15). It was amateurish: Hoffman had totally missed the point of the scene. Hall calmly interrupted: 'There's something about his hate', he said slowly, 'which we're not quite getting.' Hoffman tried again, this time coming like a Vice-figure to address the audience: 'But yet I'll go in hate' he started, snarling, staring at the imagined audience. Hall sat with a long cigar hanging from his mouth, looking unimpressed. Frustrated, Hoffman stopped on a line, unsure what to do with it. Hall reassured him, 'That was right': Hoffman closed his eyes, leaned back, saying, 'Yeah I know, just trying to get it.' He rocked for a few seconds, concentrating, mouthing words silently, and then he started on his own lines: 'Why am I going? I don't want to go. They don't want me because they love me, but even though I know they don't love me' – he jabbed with his finger, the pitch of his voice rising with aggression – 'I'll fucking go and I'll bring my own *fucking* hate. But yet they flatter me, but yet I'll go in hate to feed upon, they wanna *fuck* with me ... ' Hall blew cigar smoke and muttered, 'that's it, that's it'. Hoffman was improvising, Hall pushing him to match the feeling to the form.

Hall's twin focus on authenticity and modernity gave Hall the rare ability to move between establishment and anti-establishment worlds with ease. This is essentially how he managed to build the RSC from a provincial summer festival theatre to a government-funded, second national theatre which has endured through governments which would rather not fund any national theatres. Yet Hall is also something of a tarnished figure in both camps. When the study of Shakespeare became political in the 1980s and 1990s, the notion of originality and intentionality was put under pressure, any belief in the sanctity of the text was questioned, and the ideological politics of the RSC, and Hall's contribution to it, were probed with considerable scepticism. At the same time, Hall's abrasive interventions about the public funding of arts, combined with his championing difficult and challenging works (most infamously Howard Brenton's 1980 play *The Romans in Britain*, which led to a private prosecution for procuring an act of gross indecency), created many political enemies. Margaret Thatcher, who was prime minister for much of the time that Hall was Director of the National Theatre, was once heard asking her Arts Minister, 'When are we going to be able to stop giving money to awful people like Peter Hall?' (Hall 1993: 304).

This book brings together all of Hall's professional productions of Shakespeare, leaving out only his productions at Cambridge and immediately afterwards for the Elizabethan Theatre Company (which was essentially a Cambridge offshoot). They are presented in a linear way, following the chronological narrative of Hall's engagement with Shakespeare, starting with his comedies for the Shakespeare Memorial Theatre and ending with the two *Henry IV* plays. The productions in between are substantial both in number and achievement and include several which are, without question, seminal. I have consulted all documents relevant to these productions, some of which are easily available and others which have required more tenacity in tracking down. My aim in each chapter has been to see these productions in context, both in terms of the central themes of Hall's career and through the lens of the historical moment they were produced in. This is not a history of Hall's monumental achievements in founding the Royal Shakespeare Company and establishing the National's presence on London's South Bank. However, I have throughout endeavoured to use Hall's correct job titles as published in theatre programmes and other documents from the period. Despite being perhaps the most famous artistic director of his generation (and routinely referred to in this way in the media), Hall rarely held that title: he was Director of Productions at the Arts, Director Designate and then Director of the Shakespeare Memorial Theatre, Managing Director of the RSC (Trevor Nunn was the first person to use the title Artistic Director), Director of the National Theatre, Director of the Peter Hall Company and finally, in his seventies, Artistic Director of the Rose in Kingston.

This is a work of theatre history rather than an account of my own experiences as a playgoer. I was born after Hall's landmark productions for the RSC. My personal experience of his work starts with *Antony and Cleopatra*, which I saw in 1987 when I was 17, and I have seen many but not all of the subsequent productions discussed in this book.

Apart from Hall's 2011 *1* and *2 Henry IV* (Theatre Royal, Bath), I did not view any of them with the knowledge that I would one day be writing this study. As I have discovered many times during this project, memory is an unreliable record of theatrical experience, a fact that was brought home to me when I watched a video of Hall's 1992 *All's Well that Ends Well* (Swan), looking forward to reliving Judi Dench's performance as the Countess, only to find that she was never in that production. I appreciate that many readers will have seen productions and will have memories of them that this work may substantiate or diverge from. Performances varied from night to night and some of Hall's productions ran for two-to-three years in different theatres, sometimes with major parts recast during the run. Where possible, I've tried to give some sense of these differences, particularly where they led to significant changes in interpretation and reception. For example, David Warner's long scarf in Hall's 1965 *Hamlet* (RSC) has become a defining image of the production in theatrical memory, but Hall actually dispensed with it part way through the run. Audiences at later performances will have no memory of the scarf or, if they do, it will be a false memory shaped by the production's subsequent reputation. Theatrical performance is always an iterative creative process, at once ephemeral and elusive, but it leaves plenty of documentary evidence for the theatre historian to assemble and apply critical pressure to. Inevitably, scholarship and memory will sometimes collide.

Video recordings of Hall's work are surprisingly scarce and even those that are available, such as the recently discovered film of his 1959 *A Midsummer Night's Dream*, with Charles Laughton, are unreliable documents of the original stage performances. His major productions for the RSC and the NT were staged before the era of archival video recordings. Once he left the NT, Hall became an itinerant director, often working for theatres with no robust archiving procedures. Clips of some productions were made for television documentaries but otherwise I have had to rely on prompt books, production notes, theatre reviews and contemporaneous academic reviews for much of the detail in this book. Audio recordings do exist for many productions as far back as his 1959 *Coriolanus* and I have found these to be particularly helpful (often more so than the shaky, poor quality videos of later productions). Some of these were not available to me at the time of writing, as the British Library, where the tapes are kept, will no longer allow scholars access to the original tapes because of concerns about their preservation. Many are pristine recordings and are a good record of Hall's work, in some ways better than the hazy, out-of-focus static video recordings of his 1990s work at the RSC and in America. They have an intimacy and a clarity which those videos lack. This has helped me reassess the quality and vitality of much of that work. Hall's 1967 *Macbeth* and his 1975 *Hamlet* are remembered as failures, yet I was riveted by Paul Scofield's psychologically complex Macbeth and Albert Finney's daring, edgy Dane.

Given that Hall managed to win a review in *The Times Educational Supplement* for his schoolboy Hamlet, it is no surprise that his works were regularly reviewed in the press. Hall used the press with great skill in his early career, but like many manipulators he was often a target too: the scrapbook of his career is full of sycophantic interviews alongside scathing exposés. Even in his early days in Stratford, Hall had adoring followers and bitter enemies writing about him, minor culture wars about Shakespeare, the National Theatre and public subsidy often being fought through theatre reviews in ways which seem extraordinary to us today. Behind the press cuttings collected by the archivists is a web of old boys' networks, theatre and establishment gossip whispered in Pall Mall clubs and theatre bars, which are invisible to us now. This reached something of a climax in the 1970s, when Hall's regime change at the National Theatre sparked a war that spilled over into the press. This is important context, as evaluations of Hall's work were frequently coloured by such pettiness, but even so Hall was fortunate with his reviewers, both followers such as W.A. Darlington, Philip Hope-Wallace or Michael Billington, and his more trenchant critics, among them Irving Wardle, Gareth

Lloyd Evans and Kenneth Tynan. All write with precision and a keen eye for telling detail, and I have used them and other reviewers a lot to give a sense of what it was like to actually see these productions. Like all primary witnesses, their views may be prejudiced, but they supply a valuable sense of colour and life.

Each of Hall's productions gathered many reviews in national and local newspapers. Where these have offered important details, I have cited them, but on the whole I have privileged the mainstream press, partly because they are, in my view, more likely to have made an impression on Hall and those who followed his work, and also because this narrows down the witnesses to a group of journalists who tracked Hall through most of his career. I have also, where possible, read the whole newspaper article where the review appears. Press cuttings have the effect of extracting reviews from their original context: reading them in context has given me a better sense of the materiality of the moment within which they were written, or at least in which they were read. At times, I have developed a critical point out of some of these headlines: this is not to say that Hall's productions were directly inspired by such events, but in the spirit of cultural materialism, I am interested in the unintended resonance that theatrical meaning has within a particular historic moment. These are the narratives of power, authority, nation and culture which framed Hall's productions for their director, their company and their audiences.

1

Nostalgia and Politics at the Shakespeare Memorial Theatre

Peter Hall's years at the Shakespeare Memorial Theatre (SMT) in Stratford-upon-Avon cover a period of tremendous cultural change as Britain and the world emerged from the long shadow of war and austerity. The year that Hall joined the SMT, 1956, is often memorialized as a watershed in post-war culture. It was the year that Elvis Presley released *Heartbreak Hotel* to a young audience listening to Bill Hailey and watching James Dean at the cinema; it was also the year that the Berliner Ensemble visited Britain, inspiring a new generation of theatre-makers to think about the political potential of theatre. John Osborne's *Look Back in Anger* opened at the Royal Court, heralding a new wave of realism in British playwriting. There was, then, both optimism and rebellion in the air. Cities destroyed by the Luftwaffe were being rebuilt, food rationing had ended in 1954, and new technologies such as television, which had been suspended during the war and went mainstream in Britain after the coronation of Elizabeth II in 1953, were quietly transforming cultural lives. There was full employment in England for the first time in a generation and, with past generations decimated by war, it was the younger generation who set the pace of this new cultural revolution. Britain's military intervention in Suez that year, which triggered a brief reintroduction of petrol rationing, marked the difference between the generations. The investment in the British Empire as a concept was withering along with its territories: the tradition of playing the National Anthem before a theatrical performance was something that Hall and his generation eventually ended. It was the year of the angry young man, of rebels without a cause. Hall was at the heart of this cultural moment and contributed directly to it, in 1955, by introducing Samuel Beckett's *Waiting for Godot* to British audiences. By moving to Stratford, Hall distanced himself from these cultural currents. He went from directing hard-edged existential plays to surprisingly romantic Shakespeare comedies. As the modern world emerged around him, he embraced a provincial nostalgia for a pastoral world, a pre-war idyll.

Hall was twenty-six and had not directed a professional production of Shakespeare outside the Marlowe Dramatic Society and its offshoot, the Elizabethan Theatre Company (for more on Hall's undergraduate productions see Cribb 2007). After graduating from Cambridge, he had worked as an assistant to John Fernald at the Arts Theatre in the West End and took over from Fernald when he left the post (Rosenthal 2013: 40). It was here that he directed Beckett as well as Anouilh, Whiting and many other modern playwrights. The theatre was small and not lucrative, but with productions like *Godot* Hall could make an immediate impact and the post led to more lucrative commissions, such as the opportunity to direct the West End hit *Gigi*. He had big ideas about theatre and its place in the modern world. His choice of playwrights shows him looking to Europe and the avant-garde for inspiration. Television, which had become mainstream in British life following the televising of the queen's coronation in 1953, was quickly eroding theatre's traditional role. Hall thought British theatre too 'pre-war, safe and easy going': he ambitiously called for 'the stimulation that will attract fresh audiences' (Rosenthal 2013: 40).

Stratford was, on the face of it, an unpromising place for Hall to achieve such stimulation. Poorly connected to London, or anywhere, Stratford was sustained mainly by tourism and education. The SMT was nearly a century old and had grown from a summer festival to an endeavour that more closely resembled that of a repertory theatre. The theatre received no public subsidy and was proud of its independence. It still managed to attract stars – and make stars. Laurence Olivier, John Gielgud, Vivien Leigh and Peggy Ashcroft were all regular actors. Along with the Old Vic, Stratford was unquestionably one of the twin pillars of British Shakespeare performance, but its ability to attract high-calibre actors was under threat. A project to build the National Theatre was already underway, the first stone of the building that now stands on the South Bank laid in 1951 by Queen Mary as part of the Festival of Britain. The threat to the SMT was existential, something Hall grasped immediately. So did Glen Byam Shaw, who seems to have recruited Hall with the explicit intention of making the young director his successor.

The standard narrative of Hall's time in Stratford is shaped by the story of his efforts to shift the SMT into the space of public subsidy, to bring modern drama into its repertory, establish an ensemble company and stake a claim in London: in short, to change the SMT into the Royal Shakespeare Company, a second subsidized national theatre. Hall's work in the theatre tends to take a back seat in this story, but it was in the rehearsal room that Hall explored Shakespeare differently, sometimes chafing at modernity, at other times revelling in the spirit of youth in a way that seemed calculated to send up the Shakespeare performance style of the 1940s and early 1950s. He brought into the theatre artists, designers, directors, and composers who were not run-of-the-mill but well-regarded artists, including the Italian artist Lila De Nobili and the composer Raymond Leppard (now better known as a conductor). He maintained his interest in new writing, only devoting some of his time to Stratford before he took over as its director: of the seventeen plays he directed between 1956 and 1959, only five were for Stratford (Hall 1993: 435–436).

His Shakespeare productions were not, then, a retreat from modernity: on the contrary, Hall was using nostalgia and romanticism as a strategy for rethinking Shakespeare's role in post-war Britain. In her classic study of the performance of nostalgia in contemporary Shakespeare performance, Susan Bennett cautions against simplistically treating nostalgia as a paean to a lost world designed to support traditional worldviews: nostalgia, Bennett writes, 'might be best considered as the inflicted territory where claims for authenticity (and thus a displacement of the articulation of power) are staged'. This, Bennett argues, can 'enable re-memberings which don't, by virtue of the categorization, conjure up a regressively conservative and singular History' (Bennett 1996: 7). The exploration of the authenticity on the stage was, perhaps, a displacement of the battle for authenticity that Hall faced in his battles to protect the SMT's future against the rise of the National Theatre. He was simultaneously claiming Shakespeare and the past as a way of also claiming Shakespeare in the present. Hall's early work at the SMT stuck close to the romantic comedies: his productions of *Love's Labour's Lost, Cymbeline, Twelfth Night, A Midsummer Night's Dream* and *The Two Gentlemen of Verona* set out a stall that told a story about Shakespeare and modern England collectively. They are all primarily ensemble plays, allowing Hall the opportunity to explore Shakespeare as a dramatist who was both past and present. He also directed *Coriolanus* and co-directed *Troilus and Cressida*, with both discovering a sardonic and political edge that would re-emerge in the following decade as the political theatre of the Royal Shakespeare Company.

Love's Labour's Lost 1956 and *Cymbeline* 1957

The sense of nostalgia and youthful spirit which Hall created in his first SMT Shakespeare productions was at least in part personal. A decade before, just after the end of the war, Hall was soaking himself in the repertoire of the SMT. For three summers, from 1946 to 1949, he saw every play produced for the summer season multiple times. In his autobiography, Hall wistfully remembers cycling 100 miles to Stratford with a friend, camping in the rain and living off fish and chips (Hall 1993: 70). Two productions from 1946 made a particular impression on him: Peter Brook's beautiful *Love's Labour's Lost*, which was the big hit of the season, and Nugent Monck's *Cymbeline*, whose 'tangled complexities' entranced him (Hall 1993: 70). Paul Scofield also made his Stratford debut in 1946 and was in both productions. Brook and Scofield between them created a new energy in Shakespeare performance, inspiring not just the young Hall but a new generation of theatre practitioners, among them the director Tony Richardson, who felt 'stimulated and spurred on' by their work. Gary O'Connor argues that 'the impact and influence' of the season 'on future theatre and film people was inestimable' (O'Connor 2002: 58–59).

By looking backward, Hall was also looking forwards and setting out his vision for his career and Shakespeare's place in the modern world. It is surely no coincidence that Hall's first productions at the SMT were *Love's Labour's Lost* and *Cymbeline*, as if he were recalling that formative experience of seeing Scofield in 1946. Brook had a significant impact on the teenage Hall: his *Love's Labour's Lost* was both his first SMT production and the breakthrough work which established his reputation. Brook was twenty-one in 1946, only five years older than Hall, and already enjoying the career and reputation to which Hall aspired. Hall was following in Brook's footsteps when he chose *Love's Labour's Lost* as his first Shakespeare play to direct as an undergraduate at Cambridge and then again when he joined the SMT ten years after Brook's production.

However, he had other reasons for choosing his debut play. John Barton, still very much one of Hall's mentors, believed that Shakespeare performance could only be made meaningful for modern audiences by returning to the early comedies. At a debate in 1956 called 'Shakespeare and the Dramatic Critics',

Barton, a scholar who identified himself more as an actor, instead lambasted the current state of Shakespearean acting and proposed a new era of acting based on a solid foundation of Shakespeare's early comedies – with *Love's Labour's Lost* singled out. Recent revivals of the comedies, he argued, had highlighted the deficiencies in modern acting. The theatre was too reliant on plays with great roles and underestimated the extent to which those roles carried the performer. With the comedies, he insisted, Shakespeare had written material 'for performers of consummate skill in speech, timing, and movement'. They were ensemble plays, which demanded a high level of acting ability. Having castigated the work of the directors also in attendance, Barton finished by proposing that the early comedies are the right plays 'in which to train and develop a new generation of Shakespearean players' (quotes are from *The Times* 24 August 1956).

Whether Hall was in the audience or not, he would undoubtedly have known Barton's views and probably would have shared them. At this point in his career, Hall was still in awe of Barton and tended to agree with his trenchant opinions of Shakespearean performance and its future, even when Hall was himself the target. With hindsight, Barton was laying out a manifesto for what would become the Royal Shakespeare Company. Hall's first years at the SMT, and then the RSC, follow this blueprint almost exactly: of the seven plays he directed at the SMT, six were comedies. When Hall took over as Director of the SMT for the 1960 season, he announced a themed season of comedies with Barton as one of the directors. Although Hall worked with star actors at the SMT, including Charles Laughton and Laurence Olivier, most of his casts were young; a point remarked on in many of the reviews of his early work. Hall was putting Barton's vision into action: even as early as 1956, when he had only just arrived in Stratford, Hall was using his new celebrity status to push through their upstart version of a Shakespearean ensemble of new actors skilled in verse-speaking and the technical demands of Shakespeare's early comedies and histories.

Yet it is a measure of the complexity of the relationship between Barton and Hall that the production of *Love's Labour's Lost* which Barton probably had in mind when he castigated 'recent' revivals for the shortcomings of their actors was almost certainly Hall's, which had debuted a few weeks before. The production had attracted modest reviews, but Barton damned the production as a 'disgrace'. Hall agreed with Barton's assessment, and although the run attracted good audiences, he worried that he would not be asked back to Stratford (Fay 1995: 86). Hall's first professional Shakespeare production at Stratford should have been a momentous occasion, but he was still embarrassed enough by it thirty years later when writing his autobiography to dismiss the production in a few lines (Hall 1993: 145).

Barton was particularly critical of the stage design, which he thought 'camp and sugar-like' (Fay 1995: 86). Hall had been paired with James Bailey, a minor aristocrat with an undistinguished and soon-forgotten career as a costume and set designer. The set itself was a cramped collection of steps, towers and a semi-circular balcony which looked attractive but choked the playing space. The effect reminded the unnamed *Times* reviewer of a 'Grand Hotel terrace' (4 July 1956) which, as W.A. Darlington pointed out, jarred with those scenes set in the country (*Telegraph* 4 July 1956). The lighting plan helped neither Hall nor Bailey, a 'steady noontide light' which hardly changed throughout the production and made the stage look dull (*Times* 4 July 1956). Bailey's costumes (doublet and hose for the men, patterned dresses for the women) were colourful and varied, impressing Peter Forster, who remarked that they were 'sumptuous' and 'bright' (*Financial Times* 4 July 1956). Philip Hope-Wallace thought they suggested a 'full pack of Tudor playing cards' (*Guardian* 4 July 1956). But they were not practical. The female actors were lumbered with over-sized panniers under their dresses, giving their medieval looks an anachronistic eighteenth-century flamboyance. With all the main cast onstage, there was little room left for them to move. Judging by surviving photographs, the set design was very much of its time, a decent and competent example of mid-1950s British Shakespeare but lacking the freshness and modern eye of the director of *Waiting for Godot*. Hall learnt his lesson. He did not work with Bailey again (Fay 1995: 86), but more importantly, Hall grasped how crucial it was that he work with a designer who shared his vision. After *Love's Labour's Lost*, Hall's most important artistic relationship in every subsequent Shakespeare production was with his designer.

The production did not fulfil Barton's idea of a young cast learning their craft through an intense engagement with *Love's Labour's Lost* either. The members of the cast were mainly young actors, appropriate for a play that the SMT first announced as 'particularly youthful in spirit' with Peter Hall billed as 'the young director of the London Arts Theatre' who would be 'producing a Shakespeare play for the first time' (*Times* 26 June 1956). Yet they were a long way from the skilled actors Barton had in mind for his revolution in Shakespearean performance. Forster gave the most generous assessment when he wrote that they were 'a company of good young players who are not yet all good Shakespearean players' (*Financial Times* 4 July 1956). The performances were uneven. Harry Andrews, as Don Adriano, was roundly criticized in the press for missing the jokes, and Hope-Wallace thought that Alan Badel overdid Berowne's physical gestures such as his 'swan-prince walk' and 'unnecessarily rueful faces' (*Guardian* 4 July 1956). Clive Revill, as Costard, attracted more praise for his cheerful indifference (*Telegraph* 4 July 1956) but the actor who attracted most attention was Geraldine McEwan, who was only twenty-four and making her debut at the SMT as the Princess of France. *The Times* admired her voice which, despite a 'sublimated squeak,' 'royally dignifies her teasing mischievousness' (4 July 1956); Darlington wrote that she played the part with 'dignity and a touch of individuality' and for Hope-Wallace she was a 'pert and husky princess'. McEwan was the most significant actor from Hall's point of view: she was his first major discovery and the only one in the cast who went on to have a major role in the Royal

Shakespeare Company, although she rarely worked directly with Hall again. In fact, he worked with only a few of the cast again throughout his long career: this was not the nucleus of a new Shakespeare company, although Hall may have taken some satisfaction from Darlington's praise for the 'quality of the speaking' which, if a little too careful at times, was 'occasionally impressive' (*Telegraph* 4 July 1956).

Hall had not emulated Brook's success on his first outing, but he stuck close to the memory of the 1946 season for his next production, *Cymbeline*, in 1957. Hall was still finding his feet as a director and he did not need a second failure. Shaw took the trouble to write Hall a note of praise after *Cymbeline*'s opening night, praising it as 'a most skillful and beautiful production full of imagination, sensitivity and true romantic feeling' (Fay 1995: 92). For all its enthusiasm, Shaw's note hints that Hall found the production difficult. 'I realize you have suffered some agonies with this production,' he wrote, 'but I sincerely believe the best work is often the outcome of such tortures' (Fay 1995: 92). One of the agonies Hall faced was working with Peggy Ashcroft, one of his heroes. According to Fay, Hall had blocked out the entire play, determining every single movement for the cast (Fay 1995: 90) – a rookie mistake that was the result of over-enthusiasm and lack of professional experience. For all his fame and his already exhausting work schedule, Hall was still a young Cambridge graduate whose theatrical experience was broad rather than deep, semi-amateur rather than professional. Working with Ashcroft was a formative experience, as bruising as it was revelatory. Hall could not impose his directorial authority on her. He would instruct her to make a pre-scripted movement and she would refuse, insisting 'that move's wrong'. Eventually, Hall had little choice but to abandon his plans and work with the cast. 'I never give moves any more,' Hall told Billington, ' ... the actors must always feel they've invented it. She taught me to have the confidence to use their responses. It started a whole new method for me' (Billington 1988: 173). Judging by Shaw's note, Hall's experience of working with Ashcroft was more trying than Hall implies here, but it was a valuable lesson that he would not forget.

Hall had at least exercised more control over the design. Not content with being attached to an SMT stalwart, Hall used his wife's bohemian connections to bring the reclusive artist Lila De Nobili over from Paris to create the stage set. De Nobili was an artist rather than a set designer, and she approached the set for Hall in that spirit. She did not come into the theatre to oversee the painting of the backdrops: instead, she had the cloths laid out in a nearby village hall and painted every one herself. Hall observed her working, splashing paint everywhere and walking over the fabric as she did so. Her chaotic methods may have been another one of Hall's agonies, but he was reassured when the cloths were hung and the set assembled, De Nobili's random, formless painting magically transformed into a brilliant, dark and mysterious setting. Hall wanted an environment which brought together the different worlds of the play, fusing classical and renaissance, interiors and exteriors, into a single permanent set (Warren 1989: 27). Hall did not want the set to interfere with the play's pace as it moved from location to location (*Times* 26 August 1957). De Nobili gave him towers, archways, large stained-glass windows, staircases, a ruined abbey dressed with cobwebs, a grotto and a Renaissance-style room (Warren 1989: 28). Two large oak trees covered in ivy created a frame for the action, both cast from real trees near the theatre. Hall admired De Nobili's 'child's vision' and her ability to conjure these different worlds out of 'painted cloths and gauzes' (Hall 1993: 123). The setting was both colourful and mysterious. Hall remembered the set as 'an over-ripe autumn of browns, yellows and golds' (Hall 1993: 123). The *Times* reviewer wrote that the scenery created 'a haze of colour in the mind'. There were 'dark shadows' and 'glowing highlights' (Hall 1993: 123): Warren remembers mysterious lights glinting behind the stained-glass window (Warren 1989: 28). The *Times* reviewer was seduced and remarked that on a stage such as this, 'even the wildest of romantic tales will appear true' (3 July 1957). Not everyone was impressed: Darlington, writing in the *Telegraph*, worried that the production 'might expire under an overload of decoration' (3 July 1957) and Hope-Wallace dismissed it as 'pleasant but unremarkable' (*Guardian* 3 July 1957).

Hall approached the play as 'an adult and extremely sophisticated fairy story', as he explained to the Stratford Shakespeare Summer School when invited to speak to them about *Cymbeline* a few weeks after the play opened (*Times* 26 August 1957). He insisted that the play is 'first and foremost a romance' which was, above all, about 'sexual problems'. He viewed Imogen as an image of chastity, Iachimo as a man driven by an intellectual kind of desire, with Cloten, an angry young man whose lust is 'bestial and quite horrifying'. His production was, as *The Times* noted, a romantic production of a romantic play which fully embraced the play's romanticism and melodramatic flair (3 July 1957). For some reviewers, the production was carried by Ashcroft, who brought a light touch and warmth to Imogen. Clive Revill played Cloten as a 'pathetic ass' (*Telegraph* 3 July 1957) or, as Robert Speaight more generously observed, 'a cretinous Infante out of Velasquez' (Speaight 1973: 252).

Cymbeline attracted a particularly effusive review from Kenneth Tynan, who wrote in the *Observer* that 'my admiration for Mr. Hall's production is boundless' (*Observer* 7 July 1957). Tynan cheekily wrote a business card for Hall and Brook, proposing that 'these two young directors should at once go into business'. Tynan admired the way both directors had taken relatively obscure plays – in Brook's case, *Titus Andronicus* – and brought a strong unifying vision to them. He praised Hall for overlaying *Cymbeline* with a sinister, fairy-tale atmosphere which reminded him of the Brothers Grimm stories as if interpreted by Jean Cocteau. Hall made what Tynan regarded as the play's 'ludicrous anomalies' believable and compelling. Tynan, in his inimitable way, managed to mock Hall at the same time as praising him, spending more time writing about Ashcroft's distracting blinking than her performance. His tongue was a bit in his cheek when he flamboyantly declared his admiration for the production, but Tynan's review was an important milestone in Hall's emerging identity as a young director of Shakespeare. As Speaight put it, having made no mark with *Love's Labour's Lost*, Hall's work on *Cymbeline* 'did much to confirm his candidature' as the next major Shakespeare director (Speaight 1973: 252).

Twelfth Night 1958

With his next production, *Twelfth Night*, Hall found his voice and started to put into practice the vision for a modern Shakespeare playing company that he and Barton had imagined. Of these early productions, *Twelfth Night* is the one where we can see most clearly the Royal Shakespeare Company in embryonic form. For Hall, *Twelfth Night* is a play about youth, its pleasures, and its torments. 'I wanted to get back to its youth and to its comic heart,' he wrote in his memoir, 'so I chose a young cast' (Hall 1993: 146). They included many actors who would become stalwarts of the Royal Shakespeare Company, among them Dorothy Tutin, Geraldine McEwan, Patrick Wymark, Richard Johnson and Ian Holm. Here, at last, was Barton's ideal of a young company cutting its teeth on a Shakespeare comedy made real by Hall. Decades later, Barton remembered *Twelfth Night* as Hall's 'greatest production' (Fay 1995: 93). With *Twelfth Night*, Hall made his first major statement as a director that fulfilled his vision and laid the foundation for the RSC. Hall was fired up by his ambition to transform Shakespeare. 'Above all,' he recalled, 'I was convinced that Shakespeare demanded, as well as technical dedication, contemporary awareness if he was to continue to speak forcefully to the second half of the century' (Hall 1993: 156).

The contemporary theme of *Twelfth Night* was not immediately apparent, but the play's concerns with reconciliation and harmony, which Hall developed into a brilliantly realized theatrical fantasy in which both peace and regret were intensely felt, was a striking riposte to the critical political developments of the day. Growing tensions between Russia and the West over nuclear weapons dominated the year, and in Britain there had been considerable unrest over the country's defences. As Hall rehearsed *Twelfth Night* in early April, thousands of people marched from London to Aldermaston, where the Atomic Weapons Establishment was based (this historic event coincided with the creation of the Campaign for Nuclear Disarmament). Among those on the march was the theatre critic Kenneth Tynan (*Guardian* 5 April 1958), who had been an effusive champion of Hall's *Cymbeline*. The threat of war and nuclear annihilation was very much in people's minds, with the West announcing a substantial escalation of its nuclear arsenal that month: the Cold War had begun in earnest. Nostalgia for a different world, where the threat of destruction gave way to peace, was one way to counter this mood.

Hall and De Nobili created a rich, oak and bronzed Caroline world as an escape from these modern nightmares. De Nobili painted giant, Rococo pictures on gauzes which hung as backdrops and became translucent when lights were shone through them. Some scenes were bucolic, others depicted a walled Warwickshire garden, contrasting pastoral freedom with a bricked enclosure. For *The Times*, the scenography and lighting called to mind the art of the late baroque artist Jean-Antoine Watteau, who had also influenced Brook's *Love's Labour's Lost* (23 April 1958). De Nobili and Hall placed a wooden circular rostrum stage centre as a way of organizing the playing space, which was otherwise uncluttered to give actors room to perform. This inner circle became one of Hall's hallmarks and re-appeared in many of his subsequent Shakespeare productions until the end of his career.

Within this pastoral world, Hall portrayed a world ripe with burgeoning sexuality, perhaps picking up on the hormonally charged youth culture led by Elvis Presley, but also present in the Aldermaston march, where skiffle groups played to protestors. The production was notable for presenting unusually young and sexual interpretations of Olivia and

Viola. Geraldine McEwan played a skittish Olivia who wore her mourning lightly, and whose resemblance to Dorothy Tutin fuelled the erotic nature of her crush on the boyish, cross-dressed Viola. Hall remembers McEwan's Olivia as 'vain, a little ditsy, not to say silly' (Hall 1993: 146). The part had last been played on the Stratford stage in 1955, with Vivien Leigh acting opposite Laurence Olivier's Malvolio. Leigh had been in her forties and presented a conventional, matronly Olivia. McEwan's Olivia was noticeably younger: perky, as some reviewers remarked, 'bright almost to twittering point' (*Guardian* 23 April 1958), a 'saucy schoolgirlish Olivia' played with 'wide-eyed pert-nosed, breathlessly baby-voiced directness' (*Daily Mail* 23 April 1958). Many of these reviews avoided confronting the implication of these innuendoes: McEwan was playing an eroticized Olivia whose infatuation with Cesario was not lessened by the revelation of her identity (Myers 2010: 60). Writing about the production's revival two years later, J.C. Trewin called Olivia 'a poseuse who seemed to have escaped from a columbarium for slightly cracked doves'. Trewin remarked that McEwan 'filled her "O" in "O say so, and so be!" with sexual anticipation and found more in that "O" than Shakespeare ever guessed at or actresses have ever found' (*Birmingham Post* 20 December 1960). Tutin was similarly 'mischievous and vivacious' (Fay 1995: 93), a 'mere' child (*Telegraph* 23 April 1958) dressed like Gainsborough's painting *The Blue Boy* (*Daily Mail* 23 April 1958). Tutin's performance was not recorded, but Tutin played the part again for the Marlowe Dramatic Society on a 1961 recording directed by George Rylands. Tutin did not have a sexually infatuated Olivia to play against, but she brought a similar thigh-slapping pantomime boy-like energy to the part, exaggerating chivalric deference to a giggling Olivia when first meeting her.

By contrast, the male characters tended to be either grotesques or melancholics. Richard Johnson played a tearful Sir Andrew Aguecheek. Photographs show him gazing forlornly at the flies in a parody of melancholy. John Wain called him a 'paranoid manic-depressive' who called to mind Lucky in

Waiting for Godot, a perceptive observation as Johnson's wig of long blonde hair, which made him look more feminine than Tutin's boyish Viola, sat under a cap in much the same way as the original Lucky in Hall's 1955 production (*Observer* 27 April 1958). Patrick Wymark played a spry, stylish Sir Toby Belch (Brown 1961: 78) but he was still a caricature (*Guardian* 23 April 1958). Hall put Feste at the centre of the production as a measure of age and change to set into relief the coming of age theme he brought out of the play. Played by Cyril Luckham as 'the gravest and oldest Feste' that Cecil Watson could recall seeing (*Daily Mail* 23 April 1958), Feste bookended the production. He was the focus of the opening scene when, according to Roy Walker, the spotlights focused on a 'silvery aureoled figure in clown's costume', painted onto one of De Nobili's gauzes, 'descending into a dark world in which the faces of other characters seen in shadow were touched with the radiance'. As the lights came up, the gauze became translucent to reveal the silhouette of a still tableau of gentlemen and a small number of musicians who played in the production's first lines (Walker 1986: 84–85). The production ended with a dance which included everyone (bar Malvolio and Feste), 'dancing together in a golden distance behind a gauze curtain in love's now triumphant harmony'. Feste sat at the front of the stage as the daylight waned into evening, lit only by the light of the dancers in an ironic reversal of the opening, 'sadly remembering how the world began' (Walker 1986: 86). For his final song, Feste broke down in tears (*Observer* 27 April 1958).

Reviews were cautiously positive although Hall was exaggerating in his memoirs when he remembered the production as 'extremely controversial' and 'provoking outrage' (Hall 1993: 146). John Wain in *The Observer* gave the most cutting review, challenging both the cast and its director's youth by calling the production 'a perfect example of how a Shakespeare play can be ripped apart by the twin steel claws of naturalism and gimmickry' (27 April 1958). Some reviewers were unconvinced by Hall's innovations: Cecil Watson, for example, thought Hall had achieved no more than Michael Benthall's *Twelfth Night* which had premiered three weeks earlier at the Old Vic with a similarly young cast, including an Olivia (played by Jane Downs) who was younger than McEwan. W.A. Darlington also noticed the similarity between the productions but gave Hall credit for embracing the thematic importance of youth, using his cast's age to create an interpretation that went beyond Benthall's work: 'the dominant note is an eager zest for the happy things in life with no more than a recognition of its underlying sadness' (*Telegraph* 23 April 1958).

With *Twelfth Night*, Hall had finally created a work to rival that of Brook's *Love's Labour's Lost*: astonishingly beautiful to look at (as surviving pictures confirm), the production set out to immerse 1950s audiences in an overtly sensuous theatre world which could be at turns exhilaratingly fast-paced and melancholic. The theatre world was a form of escape, but in foregrounding such a robust nostalgic theme, even if tempered with sadness, Hall positioned Shakespeare, and classical theatre, as a way of simultaneously harnessing youth and resisting the threat of a political situation which seemed redundant and dangerous.

The cast was mainly young, and many of them stayed with Hall for subsequent productions, forming the first iteration of the RSC. In many respects, the *Twelfth Night* ensemble was the forerunner of the RSC, and during the run, Hall began to plan a revolution. He had already been sounded out as the next director and news of his appointment leaked to the press, forcing the SMT into making an early announcement in November 1958, just before Hall went on his first international tour. He took *Twelfth Night* to Russia, where he spent three snow-bound weeks in December, dogged by KGB agents and playing to rapturous houses. His conversations with directors there shaped his thinking about how he could reinvent the SMT. During one long night in a dusty, Edwardian hotel suite, with sheets thrown over the furniture to cover up the opulence of past ages with Soviet austerity, Hall spoke to Fordham Flower, the Chair of the Board of Governors, and persuaded him, step by step, to back a radical new vision for the SMT. To achieve it, Hall not only needed Flower's support but access to the considerable reserves that the SMT had built up. By the time the sun rose, Hall had convinced Flower to back him.

A Midsummer Night's Dream and *Coriolanus* 1959

In 1959, Hall, now unveiled as the SMT's 'director designate', Prince Hal to Shaw's Henry IV, directed Laurence Olivier and Edith Evans in *Coriolanus* and Charles Laughton, playing Bottom, in *A Midsummer Night's Dream*. These have since become iconic productions and, in many respects, are the foundation stones of Hall's reputation as a director. As significant as Hall's productions have become in subsequent theatrical memory, at the time they were just two of several major productions as Shaw put everything he had into his final season, which he billed as the SMT's centenary. The last was an invented anniversary: as Stanley Wells points out, the SMT had opened in 1879, not 1859, but as it had sometimes run more than one season per year, someone in the theatre worked out that 1959 would be its 100th season (Wells 1976: 5). This was a subtlety that many of the speeches, exhibitions and events celebrating the centenary elided. For Shaw, it was a good enough hook on which to hang a spectacular season. Theatrical legends on and offstage were all over Stratford that season. Edith Evans was cast in *Coriolanus* and *All's Well That Ends Well*: one of the true stars of the theatre at the time, Evans had not played in Stratford since her seminal performance as Cressida in 1913 (Wells 1976: 5). Laughton had been the leading star of the British theatre in the 1930s before Olivier, but he had not been on a British stage since moving to Hollywood. Now he played the title role in Shaw's *King Lear* alongside Hall's *A Midsummer Night's Dream*. Paul Robeson reprised his famous Broadway performance as

Othello with Sam Wanamaker as Iago, directed by Tony Richardson. Tyrone Guthrie returned from Canada to direct *All's Well That Ends Well*, bringing with him the theatre designer Tanya Moiseiwitsch. The SMT had never had such a strong season of significant plays fronted by star actors, and arguably, Stratford has yet to match it for sheer pizzazz and star power. No wonder that Wells remembers the sense of excitement he felt about the year (Wells 1976: 6). The abiding memory of that season for many was that of Olivier, playing Coriolanus, suspended upside down over a platform about to be killed. A theatrical age was passing and Hall was not afraid to upend figures of authority as he prepared plans to transform the SMT beyond recognition.

The year was a turning point for Hall as a director and set him on course for the strongly contemporary style for which he would become famous. Hall may have been, as Barton put it, the most 'romantic director in Britain' (*Guardian* 2 March 2002) but he was already beginning to chafe against his reputation. The plays offered stark contrasts between the nostalgia-tinged world of *A Midsummer Night's Dream* and the brutal political slaughterhouse of *Coriolanus*. Both were soaked with contemporary concerns as Britain continued to struggle with its post-imperial identity. As is often the case with Hall's work, the local blended with the national, which was how he elevated regional performances of a 400-year-old playwright into artistic statements that seemed apposite for a proto-National Theatre.

The productions spoke to broader political concerns. Critics noted that *Coriolanus* was 'surprisingly contemporary' in Hall's hands (*Evening Standard* 8 July 1959). For Bernard Levin, *Coriolanus*' contemporary relevance was obvious as an attack on democracy and pride (*Daily Express* 8 July 1959). Other critics seized on the play's resonance with present-day politics, seeing implicit echoes in the 'hungry mob' and the 'impetuous leader' (*Stratford-upon-Avon Herald* 10 July 1959). The lingering political aftermath of the 1956 Suez Crisis led to a general election later in 1959. As Hall worked on his productions, political leaders from the major countries (still including Britain) met in Geneva for talks about Berlin and the division of Germany: reports and speculation about these talks dominated newspaper headlines all through these weeks. It was not difficult for critics to see, in *Coriolanus*' presentation of a world destroying itself with political ambition, parallels with the present. *A Midsummer Night's Dream*'s political significance was less obvious, but here the sense of nostalgia for an idealized England was laid bare as a theatrical show for wealthy aristocrats. The 'forest' was plainly not real, its foliage wrapped around the staircases and columns of a stately home. Different ideas of the nation were presented then, both showing a new sense of cynicism and distrust in authority and its capacity to deliver change.

A Midsummer Night's Dream was in some respects a culmination of the style Hall had been developing since 1956, but the production also saw Hall move away from sentimentalizing an ideal past. At the cast's first meeting, he told them that he wanted to break with the tradition of playing the play in a 'Gothic-romantic' style: there would be no 'balletic fairies', he insisted, no 'elaborate scenic effects' and above all, 'no Mendelssohn' (*Daily Telegraph* 1 June 1959). Hall was referring to the ingrained tradition of scoring the play with Mendelssohn's incidental music, which rooted a particularly Victorian-flavoured concept of the play in the public mind. Max Reinhardt's 1935 Hollywood film was the peak of this tradition. Hall not only got rid of Mendelssohn – an innovation striking enough to be remarked on by more than one reviewer – he kept the music to an absolute minimum, with only a slight score from Raymond Leppard. (Ironically, in 1992 Hall directed an abridged version of the play for an audio recording of Mendelssohn directed by Sir Jeffrey Tate with Geraldine James heading the cast.) Hall was clear – he wanted to return the play to its Elizabethan setting, so his cast wore Elizabethan costumes.

Hall was taken by the idea that Shakespeare may have written the play for an Elizabethan wedding, a popular if unfounded piece of speculation that would mean that, in their final scenes, the wedding party watching Bottom and his company perform were themselves watched by a real wedding party of Elizabethan aristocrats. Hall could not reproduce such a unique metatheatrical experience for modern audiences, but he worked with De Nobili to create a stage set that placed all the action in an Elizabethan-timbered stately home. The floor was covered in straw creating a 'golden brown glow' which Cecil Wilson thought 'more autumnal than midsummery' (*Daily Mail* 3 June 1959). Two staircases framed the action, lightly disguised to become bridges in the forest. Lovers and fairies chased each other up and down them: as W.A. Darlington put it, 'mischief is this production's keynote' (*Telegraph* 3 June 1959). Between the staircases was a curtained bower, where Titania, played by Mary Ure, embraced Bottom, petals raining down on them, her long blonde hair wantonly dishevelled, suggesting that she was enjoying a post-coital cuddle. As she cooed 'Sleep thou', Bottom dozed with his head buried in her breasts. De Nobili dressed the mortal characters in Elizabethan costumes, a marked departure from conventional Victoriana. Warren points out that the fairies wore slightly altered versions of the same costumes, with a recognizable Elizabethan shape but made from a green and grey material which 'suggested the cobwebs, dew, and gossamer of the fairies' natural environment' (Warren 2013: 147). Oberon and Puck's legs were bare from the knees down, an earthy irreverence which contrasted with Titania's elegant, regal costume.

Towards the end of the run, the American broadcasting company NBC commissioned a film of the production (in the event, they decided not to broadcast it). The film gives a misleading impression of Laughton's performance: he dominates the film, which cut the text to 90 minutes, deliberately emphasizing those scenes with Laughton in (the surviving print runs to about 75 minutes). He was the main draw: to underline the point, the film begins with Laughton walking about Stratford, reflecting on Shakespeare, visiting his birthplace and his statue, and at one point gazing at a television aerial on a Tudor house, making the point that Shakespeare would have written for television if alive in the 1950s. Although born British, Laughton spoke about 'us Americans', firmly locating himself as the conduit for Americans into English culture. NBC shot the film in the Memorial Theatre on De Nobili's set, and so represents a good record of what the production looked like. However, although Hall appeared at the start to introduce the theatre and its set, and introduced the main characters as they appeared at the start of the play, the film was directed by the American Fletcher Markle, who sat with television equipment up in the dress circle giving orders by microphone to the actors and crew on the stage. The filming was achingly slow. The *Guardian* journalist who observed it may have been exaggerating when he wrote that the most the actors managed to achieve in one go were five consecutive lines, but it took a whole day to record 15 minutes, with the cast mostly sat around the theatre bored: 'it's a weary, weary business', said one actress (*Guardian* 1 December 1959). Laughton, a seasoned movie actor, was in his element but Hall's tight, fast-paced direction could not survive this process.

Although the film is very much about Laughton and his boisterous, humane performance as Bottom, in the theatre, most reviewers found Laughton to be surprisingly restrained and low-key: Cecil Wilson went so far as to call his performance a 'monument of restraint' (*Daily Mail* 3 June 1959). Philip Hope-Wallace described his Bottom as a 'leering buffoon' (*Guardian* 3 June 1959) and the anonymous reviewer for *The Times* missed the character's 'wonder and pathos' (3 June 1959). Laughton promised much in his first scene, when he 'waddled on bulging with comic promise, a sleepy, shapeless, ginger-bearded, head-scratching, eye-twitching Bottom rallying his fellow rustics in vaguely countrified Cockney' (*Daily Mail* 3 June 1959) and for his death scene as Pyramus, contrived to die six times before finally expiring, but in between his performance was subdued. Hall was reluctant to hide his star's face, so Laughton did not wear an ass's head: his transformation was signified only by a pair of donkey's ears and Laughton's own 'beady-eyed pout' (*Daily Mail* 3 June 1959).

Laughton had just entered his sixties. Hall thought him an unhealthy man, large and corpulent. He was, Hall recalled, obsessed by Olivier, who had forged a Hollywood career without sacrificing his pre-eminence on the British stage. Laughton was nearly a decade older than Olivier and was arguably the leading actor of his generation on the British stage when Olivier started his acting career. By 1959, this was all a distant memory: Laughton had left British theatre for Hollywood and had hardly acted on stage since. Hall thought he had been away too long (Hall 1993: 139), but Laughton was determined to 'return to his rightful place at the head of the English classical theatre' (Hall 1993: 138). Laughton's death scene as Pyramus seemed to be a parody of Olivier's *Richard III*. Although Hall enjoyed rehearsing with Laughton, he put the production's focus on the lovers' story, downplaying Bottom's role and the importance of the mechanicals.

Hall wanted to put the emphasis more on the lovers than on the rustics. In doing so, he also set out his stall as the SMT's Director Designate (his official title), shifting the focus of the production away from his Hollywood star actor to the young, mostly unknown actors playing the lovers. The Royal Shakespeare Company was not yet named, nor had Hall persuaded the governors to let him establish an ensemble company in Stratford, but his plans were in place. *A Midsummer Night's Dream* was Hall's first Shakespeare production after the long night he spent in Russia with Flower sketching out his dreams for his tenure. The production's cast was the RSC in embryo: it included Vanessa Redgrave as a galumphing Helena, Ian Holm as a memorably impish Puck, and Diana Rigg in an unnamed part. The cast also included Albert Finney as Lysander and Michael Blakemore as Snout: neither stayed on for the formation of the RSC, but both were to become significant figures in Hall's career at the National in the 1970s. Much of the lovers' performance was played on the raked forestage, 'on which the players deliberately and comically slip and slither' (*Guardian* 3 June 1959). Hope-Wallace complained that Finney was 'allowed to gabble' and

Redgrave spoke with a 'funny upper-class schoolgirl's voice' (*Guardian* 3 June 1959). Another reviewer described Redgrave as 'a tall maypole of a girl spouting tears and wrapped about with tear-bedewed timidities' (*Times* 3 June 1959). Priscilla Morgan played a 'comically shrewish Hermia' who burst into tears when Lysander called her a dwarf (*Times* 3 June 1959). Edward de Souza was an athletic Demetrius, at one point leaping over one of the staircases to escape Helena. Holm, as Puck, manipulated the somnambulant lovers with invisible strings and covered them with branches when they slept.

That same season, Hall discovered his harder edge, and for the first time started to engage with Shakespeare as a contemporary writer who could say as much as Beckett or Brecht about the modern world. His 1959 *Coriolanus* laid a foundation for Hall's political turn. The tone was different from the outset, as the production began with the sounds of a 'screaming mob' offstage which then broke down the doors and filled the stage (*Glasgow Herald* 8 July 1959). Here was a Shakespeare for the 'angry young man' generation: aggressive, uncompromising and vocal. Olivier was in his prime: imposing, athletic, piercingly enigmatic. When he entered as Coriolanus on a raised platform, he dominated the stage – both as an actor and a character. Olivier exerted his presence over the theatre, easily upstaging Hall as the main attraction. As a character, Coriolanus' entrance was political. Hall broke apart the romanticism of his previous work with this one brutal image.

Hall set the play in a brutal, bloody world very different from the romantic glades of *A Midsummer Night's Dream*. The production was visually imposing. This time Hall collaborated with a different designer, the Russian artist Boris Aronson because he admired Aronson's ability to make 'haunted landscapes of New York, so that I looked at the city with new eyes' (Hall 1993: 128). Aronson designed a single-set with red and gold shadows which seemed to some to be more permanent than the stage itself (*Stratford-upon-Avon Herald* 10 July 1959). The main part of it was a large 'craggy, rock-like structure' (as Wells describes it) with 'steps, gates, and a number of perches and platforms' built on to it and a 'central projection' which could be used to create an inner-stage (Wells 1976: 10). Aronson created a rigid, unyielding world that could be covered in bloodstains, but would never change: Alan Brien compared it to a theatre 'which has been recently attacked by incendiary bombs' (*Spectator* 17 July 1959). Much of the set was to the front of the stage, which Wells sees as Hall's attempt to subvert the pictorial bias of the SMT's proscenium arch theatre (Wells 1976: 11).

Hall also made sure that the production sounded modern and discordant. He appointed Roberto Gerhard, a pupil of Schoenberg, whose score captured the noise and the weirdness of war. One reviewer noted his 'eerie use of kettle drum glissandi' (*Leamington Spa Courier* 10 July 1959). The actors' voices also sounded very different. There was a long tradition at the SMT of actors adopting a Midlands accent when playing ordinary characters as if they had been drawn directly from the Stratford streets. Hall did not want to badge the SMT as a regional theatre; he wanted it to become a national one, so he created a vocal palette that reflected different regions. The plebeians spoke with Lancashire and Yorkshire accents, while the Volscians spoke with Welsh accents (Wells 1976: 14). Hall was deliberately looking beyond SMT's traditions and the SMT's traditional audiences towards a theatre that was young and represented the whole nation, which had something to say about the present and was alive to experimentalism.

Olivier's performance dominated the critical response. Wells, who saw the production several times, describes his appearance with memorable precision: 'He wore a black wig and was beetle-browed, heavier looking than usual. The bridge of his nose was built up, and his mouth arrogantly snarled, his knit eyebrows scornfully lifted. His walk and stance emphasized the warrior' (Wells 1976: 18). He rampaged 'full-bloodedly' (*Daily Mail*, 8 July 1959); he was 'proud and fiery' (*Wolverhampton Express and Star* 8 July 1959). He showed his range, turning from a ferocious soldier in one scene to an adult schoolboy in the next, sagging his mouth and shuffling his feet. However, once forced to face the mob, he looked sourly at them and then 'let them have it like a bull enraged by a request to tread carefully in a china shop'. (*Daily Mail* 8 July 1959). He could convincingly switch from the 'heroic to the homely', and he could 'summon the crescendo of rage' (*Financial Times* 8 July 1959), although one reviewer thought there was a 'curious hesitancy about him', a weakness in his character that made him, from the outset, a fatally flawed leader (*Stratford-upon-Avon Herald* 10 July 1959). Hall and Olivier brought out Coriolanus' deep insecurities. He was not simply proud – he was keenly aware that his pomposity before the commons was 'rather comic'. When Coriolanus said his bitter farewell to Rome, he again stood high on the stage, like a monument himself. His line, 'You common cry of curs,' dropped 'from his lips in bloody icicles, each phrase a jagged spear of frozen fury' before his final line, spoken over his shoulder, 'crumbles and melts in his mouth' (*Spectator* 14 July 1959).

Olivier played against Edith Evans as Volumnia, who resisted playing the part as 'a bloodthirsty old harridan' and instead styled her performance to emphasize Volumnia's obsessive love for her son. Evans explained her approach to the part in a lecture as part of the Annual Shakespeare Summer School, which was reported by *The Times* (22 August 1959 – all quotes from Evans are from this article and are paraphrases rather than direct quotes) and was also attended by Wells (1976: 15–17). Where, she asked, was 'the woman' to be found? In her first scene, she was knitting, and she stayed knitting through the scene as a way of indicating that she did not have a conception of the realities of war. She 'did not love war for its own sake,' Evans explained, 'but for his'. Meeting Coriolanus after his triumph, she is 'almost too excited to be coherent'. Wells is critical of Evans' performance, which goes against the character. The 'mannerisms in her wonderful voice, her capacity to colour a phrase, to suggest infinite nuances of expression, were not obviously suited to the more strident aspects of Volumnia's character' (Wells 1976: 17). Tynan thought that her voice was 'fussy' with a 'warbling vibrato' that overwhelmed 'the meaning of the lines' (quoted by Wells 1976: 17). She wore black for her final scenes, signifying mourning, and spoke in a monotone, empty of hope and love, to show that since Coriolanus's exile she had been 'wasting away' (*Times* 22 August 1959). In the end, Evans asked rhetorically, 'doesn't she realize that, instead of getting him back, she has lost him for a second time, almost certainly for good?' That, Evans said, was why she was silent when the Romans welcome her: she had nothing left to say.

Hall directed a death scene for Coriolanus so memorable that it has passed into theatrical legend. Coriolanus was stabbed with spears as he tried to flee the Volscians. He fell at the same ledge he entered on, and then hung upside down by his pursuers who drove their knives into his body. He was then lowered to the stage and trampled on. The mob execution of Mussolini inspired the staging. Hall said he wanted 'something really nasty' (*Birmingham Mail and Evening Dispatch* 8 July 1959) to shock audiences. His death was a public spectacle, but it was also meant to be a humiliating end for a character for whom physical self-possession had been such an important part of his authority. It was a savage scene that brought out the play's anti-authoritarian undertow and concluded a bloodstained production. Coriolanus' slaughter was, in a sense, a way of slaughtering Olivier as well. Olivier would never perform at Stratford again: as he hung limp and silent from the stage in the last scene of his last Stratford performance, a whole era of the SMT faced a similar execution.

Coriolanus and *A Midsummer Night's Dream* staked out Hall's claim to be the new Director of the SMT. They were bold, authoritative productions that between them laid the ground for the work Hall was to do at the RSC and the National. He showed a deft ability to revere theatrical legends and upend them at the same time, venerating the past even as he was busy making theatrical futures. His romantic period, full of nostalgia for pre-war England, reached its high point with *A Midsummer Night's Dream*, but this was also where his version of the pastoral revealed its artifice, a manufactured, theatricalized vision of the forest made for wealthy aristocrats. *Coriolanus* aligned contemporary Britain with ancient Rome, foreshadowing the political 'state of the nation' productions of the RSC and the National.

Two Gentlemen of Verona and *Troilus and Cressida* 1960

Hall's first season as festival director in 1960 built on *Coriolanus*' move towards a more intellectually grounded and contemporary approach to Shakespeare. On the day he took up his post he made a series of announcements that generated headlines across the media. He was going to rebuild the stage, create an ensemble company and find a permanent home in London. Hall wanted his tenure to be a rebirth for the company. The accent would be on 'youth' with young directors working with young actors to present young plays (*Coventry Evening Telegraph* 14 January 1960). This rebirth was to go beyond hiring young actors and directors: Hall had a grander vision. He announced plans to expand into London with a residency at the Aldwych Theatre. He also planned to recruit actors with unprecedentedly long, three-year contracts as a way of securing an ensemble identity. The press was positive about Hall's plans. The three-year contract was a 'dream come true' for *The Stage* who saw in the plan an opportunity to establish a British equivalent to the Berliner Ensemble, the Moscow Art Theatre and the Comédie-Française (*The Stage* 27 October 1960).

The new Festival director also unveiled a new approach to the Festival by announcing a themed season of six comedies that would trace the development of Shakespeare's art from one of his earliest plays, *The Two Gentlemen of Verona*, through to *The Winter's Tale*, including the dark satire *Troilus and Cressida*. The SMT had staged themed seasons before, but never with this level of intellectual coherence. Hall had been planning it since at least 1958 when he approached Paul Scofield to lead the company. At this point, he already knew which plays he wanted to do, as he offered Scofield parts in *The Taming of the Shrew, Troilus and Cressida* and *The Merchant of Venice*. Scofield hesitated and quibbled before accepting, and then resigned weeks before the season's launch (Fay 1995: 114–115). Hall was to spend a lot of the next two decades chasing, wooing and being let down by Scofield at both the RSC and the National. On this occasion, Hall made a virtue out of the crisis, as he took a risk on Peter O'Toole, whose 'animal magnetism' had impressed him in a 'rough and crude' *Hamlet* in Bristol which he found 'unendurably exciting' (Hall 1993: 165). O'Toole took all of Scofield's roles, and his success, particularly as Shylock, made his name. Hall had discovered his first star. Ashcroft co-led the company, but otherwise, the SMT was missing its stars. Instead, the ensemble was the star. Hall also revived his *Twelfth Night* with much the same cast and creative team, although Barbara Barnett played Olivia in what unfortunately was interpreted by one critic as an imitation of McEwan's earlier performance (*Times* 18 May 1960) – McEwan returned to the role when the production transferred to London later in the year.

The project was artistically thrilling and looked back to Barton's view that Shakespeare performance needed to start again with the comedies. Hall argued that Shakespeare brought a unique 'awareness of humanity' to comedy. *The Two Gentlemen of Verona* was 'the dramatic laboratory for the rest of the plays'. A study of the comedies, he insisted, could lead to a 'fuller understanding of the great tragedies and certainly to a better understanding of Shakespeare as a man' (*Stratford-upon-Avon Herald* 2 September 1960). He observed that the comedies were full of darkness, showing 'the tragic sense of life shadowing the comic' (*Tablet* 26 September 1960) culminating in the near-tragic darkness of *The Winter's Tale* before breaking into the 'almost divine comedy' of that play's final act. The season was full of risk. It began, audaciously, with the little known and little liked *The Two Gentleman of*

Verona and it included *Troilus and Cressida*, which ends with death and dishonour.

Audiences were being invited to be part of the project; their participation was crucial to the season's success. Hall was not just building an ensemble company, he was also making an audience, and both would be crucial to the RSC's success later in the decade. The post-war generation was growing up: the teenagers of 1960 could not remember the Second World War, nor did they have to face national service. Hall was not himself a baby boomer but was in an excellent position to bring the theatre into this new cultural slipstream with a comedy about youth and young love. Archive footage of the SMT's 1960 season shows Hall was reaching a young, hip audience who were content to queue around the theatre building, some slumped patiently against the wall, standing or sitting quietly reading as they waited for the box office to open (Huntley Film Archive 1960). As a gesture to this new audience, Hall had the stage extended by 15 feet into the auditorium with a rounded apron: he wanted his actors to engage with the audience in a much more direct, personal way than the traditional proscenium arch of the SMT usually allowed.

Hall was already acting as if he were director of a heavily subsidized, quasi-national theatre and, to prove it, he presented a *Two Gentlemen of Verona* whose aesthetic owed more to opera than to theatre, with big notes rather than dramatic subtlety. Characters were simplified and exaggerated almost to absurd levels, the lush romanticism of his 1950s comedies reformulated as a quasi-baroque, operatic excess of style and form. The setting was impressive and beautiful, although Alan Pryce-Jones thought the production was 'all set and clothes with Shakespeare a long way behind' (*Observer* 10 April 1960) and decried it as 'a producer's nightmare – with the revolve whizzing around so urgently that the cast had to cling to scraps of olde Verona as they flew by'. The revolve was one of the stage innovations that *The Two Gentlemen of Verona* was designed to show off, but Hall got carried away with the possibilities it presented to liberate the SMT from static pictorial-style theatre. Hall used the revolve for scene changes, but the stage also revolved during scenes, with actors walking or running across it and speaking lines as the stage turned. A fascinating silent film clip of the production, available from the Huntley Film Archive, shows the actors in full performance on the revolve in motion which, even in this archive clip, has an unfortunate sea-sick quality about it, an over-fussiness born out of an eagerness to impress rather than a hard-won theatrical effect. It was a gimmick and done with such speed that one reviewer complained that it was a 'berserk music-box' (*Evening Standard* 6 April 1960). The whole production was fast: *The Times* complained about the 'frequent scampering exits' which 'reduce any atmosphere of chivalry to a minimum' (*Times* 6 April 1960).

De Nobili's costumes were an odd mixture of the sixteenth-century French miniaturist Jean Clouet and the nineteenth-century English humourist John Tenniel, famous for his sketches in *Punch* and *Alice in Wonderland*. Pryce-Jones complained when Denholm Elliot, playing Valentine, 'was forced to grovel about in skirts and a shoulder-length blond wig, looking for all the world like Alice after she had eaten the wrong mushroom' (*Observer* 10 April 1960). The set was designed by Renzo Mongiardino, who specialized in creating beautiful sets in which the past mingled freely with the present, realism with startling illusions. He was an intriguing choice for Hall's first Shakespeare play set in Italy and signalled Hall's ambitions were not just about the institution but theatre as well and the possibility to transform it through art. Between them, De Nobili and Mongiardino conjured a world of golds, russet, faded blues and green ivy. Absurdly dressed youngsters rushed madly around Italianate ruins overrun with forest foliage. An arched backdrop showed the moon partially covered by clouds against a dark sky, creating a romantic mood for the lovers' comedic dashes across the revolving stage. Buildings mingled with the trees, branches snaking around the bottom of a castle door or creeping up the sides of the doors to a Romanesque villa. Costumes seemed to flow into the set as if the actors too were set pieces, or the set was a kind of costume.

In his autobiography, Hall barely mentions the production, except to note that it was judged 'a rather dim affair' (Hall 1993: 166). Robert Speaight, who saw *The Two Gentlemen of Verona* several months into its run, was rather more charitable. He agreed that the production was less successful than others in the season, but he argued that it was 'part of the business of the Memorial Theatre to show us Shakespeare's art in its laboratory stage'. Speaight went so far as to claim that the season had been 'an illumination in Shakespeare's book of life that we will not so easily forget' (*Stratford-upon-Avon Herald* 21 October 1960). If the production itself was a failure, seen within the context of the season it made perfect sense. Eric Gillet, who reviewed the season for the BBC Home Service in October 1960, admired the liveliness of the production which was 'perpetually in motion'. Gillet thought Hall was trying too hard to overcome the weakness of the play but, by seeing the plays in order, he could appreciate what Hall had been trying to do. Looking back over the season in October, Edmund Gardner stressed that the production should be enjoyed 'within its setting as the first play in a definite sequence', as an *hors-d'oeuvre* for the rest of the season. He defended the use of the revolve, which was justified by the changing locations in the play, and he reported that the acting had tightened considerably over the past few months. 'The overall impression', he wrote, 'is a maturing of stagecraft and production' and the sets were 'still the most beautiful of the whole season' (*Stratford-upon-Avon Herald* 29 September 1960).

If *The Two Gentlemen of Verona*, along with a revival of *Twelfth Night*, could be said to represent the final expression of Hall's dark, romantic comedies at the SMT, then his next production, *Troilus and Cressida*, was the prototype for his more political work with the RSC. Where *The Two Gentlemen of Verona* was excessive, *Troilus and Cressida* was austere, the madcap Italianate comedy giving way to a modern sense of political irony. Hall himself credits the production as a turning point which led directly to *The Wars of the Roses* and his first production of *Hamlet* (Hall 1993: 166). He had already dabbled with politics in *Coriolanus*, and as a student, he had directed John Barton's political play *Winterlude*, but otherwise, Hall's work up to this point had been more focused on aesthetics than politics, form rather than expression. With *Troilus and Cressida*, the dark edges of his romantic comedies, their ability to move from nostalgia to melancholy and despair, now bled fully onto the stage.

Troilus and Cressida was the first time Hall collaborated professionally with his friend and mentor Barton, whom he persuaded to leave Cambridge to join him as a director, voice coach, and deputy. It was Barton's favourite play (Greenwald 1985: 30). He had directed the fight scenes for the Marlowe production in 1956 and prepared the text. Hall no doubt had this production in mind when he proposed incorporating the play into his debut season, with Barton once again focusing on the text and the fights. Barton's first year at the SMT was not a happy one. He argued with his lead actors, O'Toole and Ashcroft, on his first production, *The Taming of the Shrew*, and after a cast revolt Hall was forced to remove him from the production altogether, stepping in himself to oversee the final stages of rehearsals. *Troilus and Cressida*, though, grew out of a shared vision of the play, which Hall and Barton had discussed frequently during rehearsals (Greenwald 1985: 64).

In *Troilus and Cressida*, Hall stripped nostalgia of all sentimentality, without any pretence to heroic virtue. Absurdism, which had been an abstract sense of the grotesque in Beckett's *Waiting for Godot* and Pinter's *The Birthday Party*, was now explicitly linked to politics. The *Times* reviewer found the performance 'disturbingly topical' and compared Thersites (played by O'Toole) to a 'Pinter eccentric' (27 July 1960). The politics of the Cold War were becoming increasingly absurd as America and the Soviet Union stepped up their propaganda. On the same day as the press performance, President Eisenhower issued a remarkable challenge to the Soviet Union to sign up to a worldwide election, under the auspices of the United Nations, to ask, 'Do you want to live under a Communist regime or under a free system such as found in the United States?' It was in effect a very twentieth-century way of challenging the enemy to single combat:

in such a context, *Troilus and Cressida* was indeed surprisingly topical. Hall was no longer looking back to an idealized past: he was confronting the ridiculousness of the present.

Audiences used to the opulence of Hall's previous productions were confronted with a stark world of black space and a blood-red backcloth enveloping a pit with ankle-deep sand mounted on a raised octagonal platform. The set was designed by Leslie Hurry, who was a late ultra-surrealist artist who had worked as a designer mainly in ballet and opera, although his theatre work included Brook's *Venice Preserv'd* (Lyric Theatre, London 1953). He and Hall arrived at the idea of using real sand together, and Hall was quick to exploit the theatrical possibilities of having such an unruly substance onstage. Actors kicked up sand through the performance, creating clouds in the auditorium. As Tony Church recalls, Cressida whiled away the time running sand through her fingers and playing with her feet as if at a beach, Ajax sulkily built sand piles as if in a child's sandpit, but in the closing scenes, the pit became a savage bullring. It was, Church remembered, 'the most powerful design image I've ever seen' (Greenwald 1985: 65). Hall liked the way that the sand 'slowed down movement, represented heat and intensified sexuality' (Hall 1993: 166). For Alan Brien, the simplicity of the sandpit revealed the stark realities of the 'barrenness and shiftiness' of war (*Spectator* 29 July 1960). The backcloth was a striking collage of deep reds and varied textures: to judge by photographs, the image had a primal feel about it, of stone and blood, suggesting fire shadows on the wall of a cave painting perhaps, or a world enveloped in fire and blood. The *Times* reviewer thought it suggested 'restless conflict' (27 July 1960). The contrast between the white sand and the red backcloth set the tone for a simple but effective staging with simple colours for costumes and minimal use of chairs, flags and spears to suggest the place. Lloyd Evans thought that the contrast between the costumes and the set 'hotly blazen this sharp flux between real and unreal bizarre and practical' (*Guardian* 27 July 1960).

This design was a milestone in Hall's development as a director, moving him away from the romantic excess of his work with De Nobili and setting him on a path to the austere, text-focused productions that would later be his hallmark. The raised arena allowed Hall to be flexible with the stage and this seems to have proved more effective, and given him more theatrical opportunities, than continually spinning the revolve as he had done with *The Two Gentlemen of Verona*. He could play intimate scenes here, as if in a small in-the-round theatre, focusing with cool clarity on the central characters; but the wider stage beyond, the dark, never-ending background, the Brechtian presence of the theatre's brick walls, allowed Hall to contrast these scenes with epic battles swirled in mist which, to judge by some reviews, sometimes engulfed the audience too. He returned to the same basic idea of an arena in the middle of the stage again and again, and he used the sandpit again in many of his subsequent Roman plays.

The production reflected a modern sense of disillusionment with the idea of a heroic war. Hall revelled in Shakespeare's dark, sardonic representation of the Trojan War and with Barton represented it as a descent into savagery. The production was combative from the start when Paul Hardwick, dressed in black armour, delivered a savage reading of the prologue. This ferocity carried through into the production itself, with history and politics buried in a dark, bitter comedy. Gardner called it a 'comedy of disillusionment' (*Stratford-upon-Avon Herald* 29 September 1960). Few made the leap to the world beyond the theatre, but Brien's review for *The Spectator* led on the production's implicit resonance with the Suez crisis of 1956. 'The Trojan War might be Eden's war,' he wrote, 'born in vanity and buried in irresolution.' The modern parallels 'strike home keenly'. Another reviewer, in the *Western Independent*, argued that modern audiences were more ready to sympathize with a depiction of war for 'we know that victory is inclined to fade' (*Western Independent* 31 July 1960). The world seemed to disappear in smoke and black steel. Smoke swirled about Hector as he died, the heroic values he represented vanishing into the darkness. As Greenwald recalls, he wore only a white tunic, defenceless as the black-armoured Myrmidons slowly surrounded him and stabbed him with 'concentrated thrusts' before withdrawing to let Achilles finish the job. 'Hector', writes Greenwald, 'fell at his feet.' Achilles then turned the body over carefully. The body was dragged from the arena, 'leaving blood stains on the white sand' (Greenwald 1985: 66). Pandarus, disillusioned, limped into the dark (*Stratford-upon-Avon Herald* 27 July 1960). The effect was epic, cinematic and unlike anything that had been staged at the SMT before.

Hall and Barton's interpretation of the text was unforgiving. Troilus, played by Denholm Elliott, was an unlucky dupe, a refugee from a romantic comedy unwittingly caught up in the play's madness. Cressida was a much more sexual and sensual character from the start, her 'hip wiggling appearance' (*Spectator* 29 July 1960) bringing out some of the more unpleasant prejudices of the era in the critics, several of whom called her a 'slut' whose eventual betrayal of Troilus was predictable from the start. W.A. Darlington thought her a 'lewd minx' (*Telegraph* 27 July 1960) and later reflected that Tutin was a 'daughter of the game' throughout (*Telegraph* 5 September 1960). One reviewer even called her 'evil' (*Leamington Spa Courier* 27 July 1960). Gareth Lloyd Evans was nearer the mark when he described her 'voluptuous nervousness' (*Guardian* 27 July 1960) as she balanced sexual discovery with the cruelty of war. O'Toole's understated 'world-weary and nerve-shattered' (*Leamington Spa Courier* 27 July 1960) Thersites was a sardonic chorus who spat out his lines 'with a fine, penetrating relish' (*Birmingham Mail* 27 July 1960). The world he observed, sometimes with his head resting lazily on the theatre's brick wall, was decadent, lost and irredeemable. As Lloyd Evans put it, the production was a 'cynical kick on humanity's bared guts' (*Guardian* 27 July 1960).

Hall was always at his best when dealing with epic themes; with *Coriolanus* and *Troilus and Cressida* he was finding his voice, recognizing the potential for an ensemble company to explore the present through Shakespeare's works. With *Troilus and Cressida*'s contemporary satire, *The Two Gentlemen of Verona*'s youthful energy and *Coriolanus*' exploration of politics, Hall laid the foundation for a company that would have something to say about national culture, that could engage with big questions about Britain in the post-war, post-imperial period. His early, pre-RSC work stole a march on the National Theatre (still a year from being launched) by summoning a contemporary spirit caught between political disillusion and hope. The austere, brutal world of *Coriolanus* and the minimalist, vanishing world of *Troilus and Cressida* explored the eclipse of heroic values and authoritarianism; yet the extravagantly decorated world of *The Two Gentlemen of Verona* and the cast's frenetic energy pointed the way to a remaking of national culture based on youth, experimentalism and an eagerness to embrace modernity. Hall's ideas and innovations, not to mention the huge audiences, meant that he and the company suddenly became (in Hall's own words) 'hot and fashionable' (Hall 1993: 168).

Hall introduced several innovations in his first year, but his most radical and far-reaching change was when he lobbied Buckingham Palace for permission to change the Memorial Theatre's name to the Royal Shakespeare Company. Hall disliked the old title because it 'sounded like a gravestone' (Hall 1993: 148). Hall changed the organization from a kind of museum to a modern company. Thirty years later, Hall would be utterly candid about the cultural capital wielded by such a name: 'They will give money to something called the National Theatre or the Royal Shakespeare Theatre if you scream hard enough' (Miles 1995: 204). No less significant was the introduction of the change from 'Theatre' to 'Company' in the organization's title. The SMT was a theatre that ran a festival. The RSC was a company of actors, hired for three-year terms, who would together develop an ensemble vision. The change was vital to Hall's vision of creating a European-style artistic ensemble in Stratford which would have the artistic drive to transform Shakespearean theatre into a place of discovery and reinvention.

2

Nation, Culture and Authority at the Royal Shakespeare Company

With hindsight, the most remarkable thing about Hall's success in building the Royal Shakespeare Company in the 1960s was the way he engaged a young audience, many of whom would camp overnight to secure tickets and were 'turned on' by the RSC's radical reinventions of Shakespeare. Within the world of classical theatre, Hall was a George Martin figure, an establishment enabler of iconic, era-defining performances. Some of that generation grew up to be academics, and inspired by that formative experience to look again at Shakespeare's political function, ended up reassessing Hall's achievement (for more on Hall's tenure at the RSC, see Addenbrooke 1974 and Beauman 1982). One of those was the cultural materialist Alan Sinfield, whose contribution to his highly influential co-edited collection *Political Shakespeare* was an essay that, with a crisp forensic clarity that echoed Hall's steely approach to Shakespeare, took apart Hall's achievement, exposing its ideological underpinnings and questioning Shakespeare's continued status in British cultural life. For Sinfield, the 'radicalism' of the RSC was a thin mask for a 'classically conservative' view of the world (Sinfield 1994: 184). Writing with the sting of disenchantment, Sinfield argued that the 'radical RSC identity is so well known that it may be taken for granted, but it is composed, surely, of paradoxes and surprises which suggest a more complicated and confused relationship between innovation and establishment' (Sinfield 1994: 183).

Hall's own Shakespeare productions were full of such paradoxes and surprises. He directed nine Shakespeare plays, as well as reviving two of his SMT productions and directing a Shakespeare film, while also building the RSC, virtually from nothing, in a decade transforming a self-funding provincial festival into a serious rival to the National Theatre. Ironically, Hall failed when he self-consciously chased his new audience: he aimed *Romeo and Juliet* (1961) at teenagers and *Macbeth* (1967) at counter-culture psychedelia. His successes, his history play cycle (1963–1965) and *Hamlet* (1965), were wildly popular with the new generation, even though they all presented a bleak vision of where that generation might be heading. The nostalgia which had saturated his SMT work disappeared entirely in the RSC era. Hall replaced his sense of a decline from an idealized past with an equally compelling sense of the absence of a future. In interviews, Hall worried about the threat of nuclear armageddon, with the prospect of sudden extinction as Russia, America and Britain rapidly built up stockpiles of nuclear weapons a constant theme. For the SMT, he had produced comedies in lavish, excessive settings. His RSC productions, by contrast, were all histories and tragedies, most set in stark and unforgiving worlds, steel walls and empty black spaces replacing the romantic backdrops of his previous work. Trees were now made of steel, love scenes were bitter and aggressive, the young were destined to repeat and amplify the mistakes of the previous generation, or they were too apathetic to do anything at all. For Sinfield, Hall's insistent refrain that humans are vicious animals doomed to failure was a 'powerfully conservative' political vision which ultimately affirmed the importance of establishment institutions as a bulwark against chaos (Sinfield 1994: 186).

The paradox of Hall's RSC work was that it cultivated an audience with an ingrained sense of anti-authoritarianism, hungry for cultural works which overturned the past and created something new with an immediate sense of the modern, even as Hall himself was busy building the RSC as a new institution of cultural authority. With the Beatles recording a famous cover of Chuck Berry's 'Roll Over, Beethoven' in 1963, icons of classical culture were being challenged. Shakespeare was a legitimate target for this new cultural moment as a prime symbol of the establishment, yet his works are complex and nuanced explorations of the nature of power and authority which made his work available for appropriation and reinvention. Hall wanted to stage Shakespeare with the same psychological and political edge he found in Harold Pinter, David Rudkin and Edward Bond, to rescue Shakespeare from the traditions of performance with which he had grown up. In his stagings of modern plays, Hall was in the vanguard of efforts to subvert (and eventually remove) theatrical censorship. Before this happened, Shakespeare offered an alternative route for those wanting to push the boundaries of what theatre could do, since Shakespeare's plays did not need the permission of the Lord Chamberlain to be staged. Hall's 1960s productions pushed against tradition with increasing vigour: they were blood-soaked, sexually charged and daring. Hall's political radicalism was over-stated at the time; hence Sinfield's corrective analysis, which overcompensates with a strident view of Hall's 'conservatism'. Yet Hall was without question an establishment figure: in pushing against the old establishment, Hall was at the forefront of creating a new one.

Romeo and Juliet 1961, *Troilus and Cressida* 1962 and *A Midsummer Night's Dream* 1962

Peter Hall's first Shakespeare production for the Royal Shakespeare Company, *Romeo and Juliet*, was bold in its pitch for the new generation of theatregoers, the affluent and numerous 'baby-boomers' who were setting the pace of British cultural life. The play was suddenly modish: Franco Zeffirelli's youthful, passionate production for the Old Vic was the most important Shakespeare production of 1960 and the following year, the movie *West Side Story* (based on *Romeo and Juliet*) was a hit at cinemas. Zeffirelli's *Romeo and Juliet* was an early indication of the influence that teenagers would have on 1960s popular culture. Inevitably, reviewers compared the two productions, though they did not agree whether Hall's was the 'anti-Zeffirelli' (Speaight 1961: 436) show or 'self-consciously assembled from Zeffirelli's Old Vic blueprint of the play' (*Guardian* 30 November 1961). Either way, not one critic thought Hall's production the better of the two. Hall started with bold ideas, recruiting a firebrand to design the set, a Pakistani actor to play Romeo (in what would have been a pioneering piece of colour-blind casting) and, in a gesture to cultural history, a theatrical legend to reprise one of her most famous roles. In intent, the production was a perfect demonstration of how the RSC could venerate the past at the same time as dismantling it to create something new. In practice, the production failed to capture the same spirit of youthful liberation that Zeffirelli's had done.

Hall hired Sean Kenny, a young Irish designer with radical ideas about set design who sought to 'redefine' rather than simply 'redecorate' stage space (Jackson 2002: 6). He had established a reputation as something of a firebrand noted for his realism and his commitment to creating 'environments to act in' (Jackson 2002: 37). Kenny was a revolutionary upstart in the theatre world who thought that theatre had become too detached from life, a 'mediocre, minority closed-group activity,' he wrote, which 'has nothing to do with people having bread or finding things that are exciting'. He agitated for a 'new voice: a new theatre' and dismissed the established theatre as simply 'rubbish' (Kenny 1993: 98–99). Hall was clearly after some of Kenny's radical spirit as he sought a new style more appropriate for a new theatre, but the set proved to be one of the production's problems. Kenny designed a collection of 'stairs, alcoves and columns' which 'swung to and fro on the revolving stage' (*Telegraph* 16 August 1961). The set was busier than the actors: 'constantly revolving', complained the reviewer for *The Times* (16 August 1961), and Speaight confessed that he 'got very tired of watching it go round and round' (Speaight 1961: 436). For Hope-Wallace, the set was a cumbrous distraction, 'intrusive ... without evoking any atmosphere' (*Guardian* 16 August 1961). Tynan described the set as a 'formidable obstacle course' (*Guardian* 20 August 1961). Kenny and Hall contrived some striking set pieces. The opening street brawl conveyed a sense of anarchy when feathers flung up from a servant's basket and settled across the stage (Jackson 2002: 37). Mercutio and Tybalt's duel was also a highlight: reviewers praised the 'the athleticism of the swirling swordplay' (Jackson 2002: 37) and even Tynan thought the fight 'a model of timing and inventiveness' (*Guardian* 20 August 1961). The final act showed a 'great filing-cabinet of tombs' in which Juliet woke surrounded by rotting corpses visible behind metal grilles (*Guardian* 20 August 1961). In one of the production's most vivid images, Romeo saw Juliet for the first time 'dancing in the lamplight under an arch' (*Times* 16 August 1961) but in other respects the Capulet ball highlighted the set's failings, as the guests were 'immobilized' in groups behind and around the main set (Jackson 2002: 64). Hall had not yet found a modern style. Photographs from the production look fussily old-fashioned, more like a Hollywood medieval world than the excessive lyricism of his comedies or *Coriolanus'* hard-edged austerity. Speaight was right to complain that Romeo seemed to be dressed as Robin Hood (Speaight 1961: 438).

Hall's other innovation was to cast Zia Mohyeddin as Romeo. Hall had seen Mohyeddin play Dr Aziz in a popular stage adaptation of *A Passage to India* in 1960. The casting was inspired: Mohyeddin would have been the first Pakistani actor to play a leading role on the Stratford stage, and if it had gone ahead it would undoubtedly have been regarded as a historic, mould-breaking example of colour-blind casting, years ahead of its time in a British context. Rehearsals were demanding, and a week before opening night, Mohyeddin left the production. The RSC put out a press release announcing that Mohyeddin was ill with a virus, a thin story which critics openly mocked in their reviews. Brian Murray was hastily given the part and his performance, prepared at such short notice, was noticeably shallow and one of the reasons that the production suffered in the press (see Farber 2014 for more insights into Mohyeddin's departure). Fortunately, Dorothy Tutin, as Juliet, had played the role before and carried the production. A brief clip of Tutin's previous Juliet (directed by Glen Byam Shaw) exists on a British Pathé news film: she spoke the part then with breathless naivety, clasping Romeo's hands with childish passion in a way that managed to look submissive but was clearly very dominating. Reviews suggest her performance was much the same in 1961: Tynan dismissed her as 'an intense little elf' (*Guardian* 20 August 1961) but Hope-Wallace thought her 'touching in her childish eagerness and distress' and 'vulnerable not tragic'. Tutin again spoke in a way that suggested 'the breathlessness of thought newly formed' (*Guardian* 16 August 1961) and she moved 'like a bird' (Speaight 1961: 436). She started as a surprisingly convincing child, with just 'hints of maturity of spirit' (*Telegraph* 16 August 1961) which flourished in the final act. The *Times* reviewer thought Tutin was very believable as a 'young girl, impetuous, romantic, humorous' (16 August 1961). Even Lloyd Evans wrote that Tutin 'shone with aristocratic splendour' (Evans 1967: 134). For Speaight, Tutin was the best Juliet he had yet seen: 'Her variations of ecstasy in the Balcony Scene and of terror before she swallows the potion were breathtaking in their beauty, subtlety and insight' (Speaight 1961: 438). Darlington agreed, calling Tutin 'the most completely satisfying Juliet that we have had since Peggy Ashcroft [in 1935]' (16 August 1961).

Ashcroft had played her Juliet with Edith Evans as the Nurse and, in a nod to theatrical history, Evans returned to

Stratford to play the part again, in what would prove to be her final performance in one of her signature roles, which she had played many times in both Britain and on Broadway. (Ashcroft was also in town, playing Emilia to Tutin's Desdemona.) For many reviewers, Evans was the draw, her performance widely celebrated as 'definitive' (Jackson 2002: 63). Lloyd Evans thought her performance was 'superb in its mumbling pathos' (*Guardian* 30 November 1961) and Hope-Wallace called her 'the Nurse as Shakespeare might have dreamed of seeing it played'. According to Jackson, her performance had 'softened', and she spoke with a Welsh accent (Jackson 2002: 63). (Evans recorded the part for the Shakespeare Recording Society several years before with a faintly Scottish accent.) Now in her seventies, Evans' face had aged to match her performance. Hope-Wallace described a 'rounded, apple-cheeked portrait ... that Vermeer would not have been ashamed to sign' (*Guardian* 20 August 1961) and she did indeed look as if she had escaped from a Vermeer painting, dressed unfussily in the garments of a mature seventeenth-century working woman.

With a reprised Juliet and a theatrical legend playing the Nurse, the production seemed to be looking backward rather than forwards, the last gasp of the SMT rather than the brave new world of the RSC. Yet the production deserved more than its subsequent reputation. Overshadowed first by Zeffirelli's generation-defining *Romeo and Juliet,* and then by Hall's successes with *The Wars of the Roses* two years later, the production's many qualities were overlooked: even the production's most pointed critics admired Evans as the Nurse. Tutin's powerful charisma, her vulnerability and her strength are evident in production photos, where she is a striking, forceful Juliet playing against Murray's forgettable Romeo. Tynan skewered Hall and the RSC in his review of *Romeo and Juliet*: he mockingly praised the company for its exemplary demonstration of 'the art of acting on staircases' and for never presuming to 'shock us by engaging our deeper emotions'. They were, he wrote, 'as nice a bunch of young people ... as ever jived at a tennis-club social to the music of Mr. Acker

Bilk' (*Guardian* 20 August 1961). Tynan's remarks anticipated Sinfield's more level-headed critique of Hall's politics: Hall may have been looking for a new approach to Shakespeare that better reflected the growing anti-authoritarian mood of the new generation, but the production was still mostly rooted in a very conservative version of the play which lacked the sense of dangerous eroticism that Hall would explore in his later productions of tragedies.

Although Hall's plan to recreate the SMT as the Royal Shakespeare Company progressed – the Queen's assent to the company's new name was announced on 20 March 1961 – the spectre of the Memorial Theatre still haunted the programme as Hall returned to his SMT successes in 1962 with revivals of *Troilus and Cressida* and *A Midsummer Night's Dream*. He revived *Troilus and Cressida* with many of the original actors reprising their roles, including Tutin as Cressida and Derek Godfrey as Hector. Ian Holm took over the role of Troilus, injecting the part with a sense of innocence and bewilderment which made him seem very juvenile against Tutin's 'raw and sensuous pertness' (*Guardian* 27 September 1962). The production started with a tour of the North, using hard-won Arts Council money which was, in effect, a foot in the door for future subsidy. It started at the Edinburgh Festival, a first for the RSC, and ended in its new London home at the Aldwych. Hall was the sole director this time, Barton's credit ignominiously downgraded to 'fight arranger', although the production stuck closely to the ideas that he and Hall had developed two years previously. The *Times* reviewer thought that Hall's direction improved the production, moving it on from Barton's 'donnish' work, with Tutin now 'close to greatness' (16 October 1962). However, Hall had done little more than polish an already well-received work. His second revival that year, of his *A Midsummer Night's Dream*, was a more far-reaching remounting which was one of the most critically well-received works from this period. Even Tynan was impressed, commenting that the 'revival is better than the original' with a lighter touch, better pacing and less slapstick. He did not miss

Laughton, who was too ill to reprise Bottom (Laughton died later that year) and praised his replacement, Paul Hardwick, as a 'pleasantly bashful' Bottom. Tynan, characteristically, could not resist a few digs at Hall – his review was titled 'Good News for Tinkerbell' (*Observer* 22 April 1962). Hall retained De Nobili's sets, and he kept doggedly to his interpretation of the play, but the production was almost wholly recast, with only Ian Holm reprising his performance as Puck. Most significantly, Hall cast Judi Dench as Titania, a role he would direct her in for his 1969 film and at the Rose Theatre in Kingston in 2010.

Three years into his tenure, Hall had thoroughly reinvented the Memorial Theatre, but he had yet to prove that this theatre was better able to speak to new audiences than its predecessor. As *Romeo and Juliet* showed, he risked being trapped by the past: his attempt to engage a young audience misfired with a production that was better at paying homage to the past than it was at forging new ideas for the future.

The Wars of the Roses 1963

The Wars of the Roses was the most important production of Hall's career. It established him as a political director, even though, as Sinfield argues, much of this was at root a conservative view of politics and order that bore the influence of critics such as E.M.W. Tillyard, whose books on Shakespeare's history plays and their relationship to the so-called Elizabethan World Picture were cutting-edge works when Hall was an undergraduate. More importantly, the production set the tone for the RSC and finally brought together a company identity and a recognizable house style. Having spent much of his Shakespeare career to date saturating the comedies with romantic nostalgia and melancholic longing, Hall treated Shakespeare's version of the past without sentiment. Hall and his generation had lived through the war and began their adult lives with conscription and food rationing still in place, and many cities still in ruins. The past, it turned out, was a brutal place, where ambition and folly went together, and where good men like Henry VI were unable to be good kings. By combing eight of Shakespeare's English history plays, Hall made a statement about the RSC and its ambition. He was telling the national story, to a nation that was still scarred by the memory of recent war, to a new generation that had no loyalty to the past or the notion of a ruling British Empire.

A full history play cycle was a pet project of Hall's, which he had been discussing with Barton since his Cambridge days (Greenwald 1985: 39). The SMT had staged the second tetralogy in 1951 as a way of celebrating the Festival of Britain, and that cycle made a significant impression on Hall, who also saw the Birmingham Rep's *Henry VI* plays staged across several years in the early 1950s, directed by Douglas Seale. Having launched his tenure at the SMT with a series of comedies, a set of history plays was the next natural step. Hall was also mindful that the upcoming quatercentenary of Shakespeare's birth in 1564 would give the new company an excellent opportunity to raise its profile and beat the new National Theatre at its own game by making a big statement about Shakespeare and the nation. Government funding was proving to be more difficult to secure than Hall had anticipated and with the SMT's reserves depleted because of its investments in the theatre, the company and the London base, Hall urgently needed a watershed production to secure the RSC's place at the funding table. He was quickly overwhelmed by the task he had set himself, directing one of the most ambitious productions of Shakespeare on the one hand and fighting a long trench war for public funding on the other, without which the RSC was doomed to bankruptcy. In the background, his marriage was collapsing. Hall had two breakdowns, one of which delayed the opening of the first productions. His assistants, John Barton and Frank Evans, stepped in to keep rehearsals going, and Hall acknowledged their contribution by naming them as co-directors (Hall 1993: 183).

The RSC asserted its authority by adapting the plays; something Hall later called the 'ultimate literary heresy'

(Barton and Hall 1970: vii), a heresy in keeping with the anti-authoritarian mood of the day. The company was experimenting with much more radical treatments of the text such as Charles Marowitz's thirty-minute *Hamlet* (1964), but the changes to the *Henry VI* plays were more visible. *The Wars of the Roses* was not a fringe production, it was at the heart of the company's 1963 schedule and would remain in repertory for two years. Hall did not set out to be seen as a young director subjugating Shakespeare to modern theatre. Hall originally wanted to stage the *Henry VI* plays as three plays, but this would have been a risky endeavour and staging the first tetralogy at all was risky enough. When Peter Brook passed on the plays, Hall hired Barton to adapt the plays into two, eventually giving them the titles *Henry VI* and *Edward IV*, to which they added *Richard III*. The trilogy was named *The Wars of the Roses* and was in effect a single production with three parts. Barton worked on the adaptation through the autumn of 1962, meeting Hall every day to discuss progress on the work and talk through issues to do with narrative and characterization (Greenwald 1985: 42). As well as cutting and reshaping the material, Barton added linking passages of his own, imitating Elizabethan blank verse. The adaptation attracted a great deal of publicity and Hall seemed to enjoy defending Barton's right to change Shakespeare in the interests of reviving the *Henry VI* plays for modern audiences and was never short of anecdotes about a cast member or reviewer defending a passage only to discover it was one of Barton's. Hall was later apologetic and called the adaptation 'reprehensible' in his memoirs, decrying his folly in daring to alter Shakespeare (Hall 1993: 183). Even at the time, Hall found himself reining Barton in, with many of the new additions cut in the rehearsal room (Pearson 1990: 15–16). For the RSC's new audiences, the RSC's daring in changing Shakespeare's text had a potentially powerful anti-authoritarian appeal. Roll over, Shakespeare.

Pearson reproduces some of the memos that Hall and Barton exchanged during the adaptation, which reveal some of the creative tensions between them. Barton, who did not regard himself as a political director or writer, was preoccupied with character development and giving the characters a narrative line that explains their behaviour. Hall, by contrast, was reluctant to impose new meanings on the text, but at the same time wanted to articulate the broader political context. Barton made real people out of the plays' sometimes two-dimensional characters, and Hall added a sense of the epic, of the role of these characters in a grander view of power and humanity. For example, Barton worried that the 'lack of depth, development or interplay of character among the principals is particularly worrying as far as the character of the King himself is concerned' and went on to suggest a character arc for Henry who would 'become more interesting if we gave him a definite line of development throughout the play'. The death of Winchester became a key turning point that goads Henry into 'positive, concrete, morally-motivated action' (Suffolk's banishment). Hall's response was telling: 'We certainly need Winchester's death-bed confession making the moral point that self-seeking and wickedness breed guilt in the doer and rejection by other people,' he wrote, ignoring the idea of a character arc, but 'My basic feeling is that we need to pare down the inessentials, clarify the plot line and have fewer scenes.' Hall went on to say that the main theme of the play is order: 'You said to me that you thought we should cut down on the amount of railing Gloucester does; I believe this to be wrong. The turbulent, self-destructive temper that this very virtuous man has is a perfect theme for the play. He is nearly ordered, but not quite' (Pearson 1990: 13–14).

Barton's most important interpolations were a series of scenes set around a council table, realized as a steel lozenge shaped desk across which generations of barons argued. Hall and Barton wanted to get away from the 'thrashing of barons' that for Hall had marred Seale's productions (Pearson 1990: 14–15). The table was for Barton a device with which he could shape disputes and offer audiences a visual representation of the divisions unfurling in the kingdom. From Hall's point of view, the table had the added advantage of anchoring the actors and the text to a physical prop. It focused the action and discouraged grandstanding rhetoric in empty spaces: the *Times* reviewer praised the actors' 'total indifference to rhetoric and hand-to-mouth effects' (18 July 1963). The passage of history was also marked by the table, which, along with the throne, was a constant across all three productions, marking time as the faces around the table slowly changed as each of its members fell victim to the vicissitudes of history. The table brought a modern gloss to medieval power politics: it could just as easily have been Prime Minister Harold Macmillan's cabinet table, around which his ministers were fighting for the succession even as he tried to hold on to power through 1962 and 1963. Connecting past and present, the table helped Barton create clear narrative lines, allowing for a quick but clean progression through the narrative, and signified Hall's interest in history as a destructive, implacable force. As the *Times* reviewer put it, the 'characters seem all to be in the grip of the spell which hurries them on helplessly from one disaster to the next' (18 July 1963).

The RSC previewed *Henry VI* and *Edward IV* on the same day, 17 July, with press making an unusually early start to see the plays together. Curiously, Barton's adaptation made the *Henry VI* plays homogeneous so that *Edward IV* felt like a continuation of *Henry VI*. *Richard III*, which opened a month later, was more of a standalone play, although some of the characterization, particularly that of Margaret, gained extra depth and tension from the play's combination with the adapted *Henry VI*s. Rehearsals were exhausting and manic. The cast worked until the early hours of the morning, often combining performance and rehearsal. Doctors were summoned to give actors vitamin shots to keep them going. Hall collapsed more than once, and according to theatrical legend was either carried to or from the rehearsal room on one of the biers used for the performance (like many theatrical legends, the story changes depending on who tells it). On some days, following Hall and Barton's original ambition, all three plays were performed together, with *Henry VI* opening at 10.30 am. The Stratford run ended in December and the London run began in early January 1964, leaving the cast little time for rest.

Hall's vision for the production was audacious: he wanted it to speak directly to the contemporary experience of politics, stating that 'We live among war, race riots, revolutions, assassinations ... and the imminent threat of extinction. The theatre is, therefore, examining fundamentals' (Goodwin 1964: 47). An editorial in *The Times* begged to differ, reflecting that the cycle is 'splendid costume drama' but 'offers little insight into the current mechanics of western diplomacy'. Charitably, the writer conceded that 'it may have such an application ... in some parts of Asian and African politics' (24 August 1963). That the production should attract the attention of a *Times* editorial at all marks the very different status theatre had then than it does today, but this reaction against Hall's work was patently naïve. The year 1963 was a turbulent one for Western politics, with Harold Macmillan barely hanging on to power as his cabinet and backbenchers schemed like medieval barons. For Hall, the nuclear threat was uppermost in his mind and echoed Jan Kott's argument in his book *Shakespeare our Contemporary*, which looked for echoes of the present in Shakespeare's work. Forced to get a train to Stratford for the first rehearsals, when his car broke down, Hall spent the journey reading a manuscript of Kott's book, which he had been sent in advance of its publication. Their thinking coincided. Hall later told Stephen Aris (during rehearsals for the second tetralogy in early 1964) that it is

> not enough to let Shakespeare speak for himself ... He must be interpreted so that what is coming across is both meaningful and needful to contemporary audiences. What we are trying to do is to build a bridgehead between the times we live in and the text. Recently we have been very preoccupied with the subject of violence and its consequences; an eminently contemporary theme when you realize that the world could be blown to bits at any

moment at the touch of a button. And it seems that society is becoming more and more violent (*New Society London* 12 March 1964: 12)

Kott's chapter on the history plays was particularly pertinent, as Kott argued that Shakespeare pitched his characters into the merciless and destructive cycle of power politics. Hall already had a speech prepared for his cast which made much the same argument. Over two days, he and the other directors outlined a vision of the plays which was firmly rooted in a strong sense of the contemporary relevance of Shakespeare's anatomy of power politics. He told them that the 'stuff of these plays is our lives today' and discussed Suez, the Cold War, and the Soviet Presidium before concluding that the plays were, in total, 'a study of power, the need for power, and the abuse of power' (Fay 1995: 156). Recent modern drama influenced Hall's vision. Plays such as *Afore Night Come* by David Rudkin and *The Empire Builders* by Boris Vian, which the RSC performed in 1962, uncovered the primal ritual violence underlying the contemporary world. Hall recognized similar patterns in the first tetralogy, which he believed was structured by a 'heavily ritualistic pattern' (Hall 1964: 46). Hall's contribution to the production's souvenir programme was titled (after *Macbeth*) 'Blood will have blood' and in it, he describes York's death as a 'pagan ritual'.

The pressure of history was felt through the months that the company performed the cycle. As *The Wars of the Roses* opened in July with a special press run of the first two plays on the same day (*Richard III* was added the following month), Britain, America and Russia were meeting in Moscow to discuss a nuclear test ban treaty. Hopes for a denuclearized world were dashed when President Kennedy was assassinated on 22 November in an episode of acute historical force that resembled several scenes in the early histories. The news was announced to theatregoers across London that evening before the curtain went up: in the RSC's case, the news broke during a performance of *Richard III*. Some actors heard it on the radio in their dressing rooms and passed it on to the rest of the cast while waiting in the wings. The impact was palpable: Susan Engel, who played Queen Elizabeth, remembers when announcing the death of Edward IV, looking at the audience and thinking, 'They don't know that Kennedy is dead'. News spread around the audience during the interval and gave the cycle's concluding act a powerful context. Hall, who was in the audience that night, recalls that the 'artificial sense of evil on the stage seemed now to correspond with a sense of evil in our own lives. I never remember a blacker atmosphere in a theatre. The second half of Shakespeare's chronicle of blood and violence seemed unbearably true to human behaviour' (Pearson 1990: 63). The cycle's Stratford run was extended into December and then transferred to London, gaining as it did so some darker hues as cast and audience grappled with the enormity of recent political events. Tellingly, the father–son scene in *3 Henry VI* (Act 2, Scene 5), which had fallen flat in Stratford, took on a new force, an added echo to the voices distancing 'the scene most beautifully' (*Guardian* 13 January 1964). Coincidentally, President Kennedy had read a very similar speech from *King John* to a group of civil rights activists only a few months before, using Shakespeare's language to style himself as a leader caught in the middle of a pitched battle. Newspaper coverage of Kennedy's murder (*New York Times* 23 November 1963) recalled the episode as an example of his leadership. Hall did not have to look far then for contemporary resonance as discussions about leadership and the fragility of power were rife. If anything, the cycle proved to be prophetic, the resignation of Macmillan in October 1963 and Kennedy's assassination confirming Hall's bleak vision of history as a cycle of fortune that crushes lives and cheats ambition. Although conceived too early to directly reference Kennedy's murder, in a sense the production was always about that event, about the 'pagan ritual' of killing the king and the bloodletting which follows.

Hall's vision for the plays started with the image of the sword – 'cold, keen, death-dealing' with 'cutting edges' – and from that, he developed the idea of a metal world entrapping its human protagonists. Hall recalled, 'we started with a texture ... a style of speaking, a style of presentation, a style of looking, which was all one' (Pearson 1990: 26). To realize this vision, Hall poached the designer John Bury from Joan Littlewood's Theatre Workshop, where Bury had started as a van driver and graduated to become the designer for many of Littlewood's iconic productions, including, most pertinently, her satirical, quasi-Brechtian anti-war musical *Oh! What a Lovely War*, which was one of the hits of 1963 and undoubtedly influenced *The Wars of the Roses*. Bury was one of the most significant creative collaborators of Hall's career, and they worked together for the next twenty years.

Bury's work was crucial in marking the difference between the RSC and the SMT: the world onstage may have been a medieval past, but its grim realism made it a very modern take on the past, one that broke decisively with the romantic tradition of staging history familiar to audiences at the time. Bury's set, a giant steel cage, materialized history as an oppressive trap for its participants. History was both the centre of the production, its 'main protagonist' (Hodgdon 1972: 175) and its surface. The stage was largely bare, creating a brutal fighting arena faced by two large metallic walls, which could swing open in a manner which the *Times* reviewer compared to that of a battleship (13 August 1963). In *The Spectator* (26 July 1963), David Pryce-Jones observed that the doors were 'shifting and swinging within certain gaunt patterns to match the stylized manoeuvres onstage'. The movement of the doors in relation to the actors denoted an essential symbiosis between the actors' bodies and the world that they inhabited. The human subject was immersed in these great historical forces, unable to determine them, but determined by them. Bury covered the stage floor and walls in steel plates (Greenwald 1985: 53) so that heavy broadswords scraped metal on metal across the floor. In *Richard III*, soldiers wore metal soles on their feet so that, as Hall himself remembered, 'the inhuman tramp of authority was heard throughout the theatre' (Hall 1993:

185). Tables were made from steel and the staircases out of axe-heads; even the trees were iron. The combined effect was, as Worsley put it, 'menacing and claustrophobic' (*New York Times* 18 July 1963). On either side of the stage stood large periaktoi 'that could be turned to suggest different locales and to modify the playing area' (Greenwald 1985: 53). Costumes, black and gold over distressed leather, rusted over the course of the cycle, becoming more 'disheveled and blood-spattered' as history plunged the world into chaos (Greenwald 1985: 53–54). As Bury put it, colour 'drains and drains from the stage until, among the drying patches of scarlet blood, the black night of England settles in the leather costumes of Richard's thugs' (Barton and Hall 1970: 237). There was no curtain to bring up, flying in the face of entrenched traditions of performance: instead, guards stood solemn watch over Henry V's coffin as audience members took their seats. Today's audiences will be familiar with such devices, but at the time the trick was novel enough to warrant mention in some reviews. The production was gory (something which the television version tones down considerably), full of blood-spurting severed limbs, decapitated heads played like footballs and then impaled on the iron walls. Offstage murders such as Clarence's in *Richard III* were brought onstage: Bernard Levin remembered hearing his body splashing as it was tipped into the malmsey-butt (*Daily Mail* 21 August 1963). Murderers were 'strapped to a medieval torture wheel' (Greenwald 1985: 54) and most horrifically, for Greenwald, Margaret ran a sword through York's chest (54). The cycle was, as Hope-Wallace put it, a 'pageant of carnage' (*Guardian* 18 July 1963). Hall wanted the plays to be unforgettable in their brutality, unsparing in their dark vision of history as an oppressive force.

Appealing to a young audience, Hall made a daring piece of casting with Henry VI, who was played by David Warner, then in his early twenties with virtually no experience of Shakespeare. The actor was an immediate hit: Bernard Levin called him the 'find of the decade' (*Daily Mail* 18 July 1963). Dressed in peasants' clothes as if religiously repulsed by court finery, Henry was 'awkwardly, sweetly boyish, a tow-haired fringe falling across his forehead' (Hampton-Reeves and Rutter 2006: 71). Warner was imprinted with the cool, analytical style of acting that Hall aimed at for his ensemble, a style that was 'sparse, highly selective, antiromantic, yet robust and lifelike' (Greenwald 1985: 54). His gently spoken speech on kingship was, according to Hope-Wallace, 'an oasis of Shakespearean feeling into what is much too often a desert of rage and vengeance' (*Guardian* 18 July 1963). The *Times* reviewer thought Warner 'extraordinarily touching', at times pitiably reliant on Gloucester but when arguments broke out across the council table, he could calm things with a sweep of his 'sweet nervous smile' (18 July 1963). Yet his pacifist look masked an inner steeliness unexpected for the character. In one of the production's most remarkable scenes, the last before the end of *Edward IV* (Scene 52, based on Act 5, Scene 6 of *3 Henry VI*), Henry embraced Gloucester and gave him a tender forgiving kiss which Greenwald describes as 'a loving embrace of forgiveness' (Greenwald 1983: 55). The *Times* reviewer thought this 'an inexplicably moving invention'. By the time the production reached the Aldwych in 1964, Warner had 'practically invented a new Shakespeare hero' who transfigured 'spineless ineffectuality into the attributes of a Dostoyevskian saint' (*Times* 13 January 1964).

Warner soon became a cult figure for younger playgoers, but the production also honoured the theatrical past by casting Peggy Ashcroft as Margaret. She would be the first English actress in living memory to play Margaret over all four plays (the Birmingham Rep cycle stopped at *3 Henry VI*). Ashcroft was in her mid-fifties and had the challenge of playing the coy teenager with whom Warner's Henry was besotted and then, over ten hours, had to progress into the old, bitter Margaret of *Richard III*. Reviewing the London transfer, Hope-Wallace admired the way she

> skipped on to the stage, a light-footed, ginger, sub-deb sub-bitch at about 11.35am and was last seen, a bedraggled

crone with glittering eye, rambling and cussing with undiminished fury, 11 hours later, having grown before our eyes into a vexed and contumacious queen, a battle-axe and a maniac monster of rage and cruelty who daubs the pinioned Duke of York's face with the blood of young Rutland, taunting him the while so horribly that even the stoniest gaze was momentarily lowered from this gorgon (*Guardian* 13 January 1964)

Ashcroft played the part with a French accent, emphasizing Margaret's outsider, foreigner status, which she never quite lost. Ashcroft insisted on speaking the part this way, exasperating Hall, who had directed Janet Suzman to play the equally French Joan of Arc with an English accent (Billington 1988: 200). Ashcroft brought experience and energy to the part, as Hope-Wallace noted, 'things fairly buzz every time she came on' as if 'everyone on stage took a charge of electricity' (*Guardian* 25 July 1963). She was a steely Margaret who, as war and political ambition tore away at Henry's court, found within her an animal-like ferocity that manifested itself in her unearthly shrieks when her son was murdered at the end of *Edward IV*. Even Donald Sinden (playing York) was shocked at the 'genuine hate' in Ashcroft's eyes as she spread blood across his face. Ashcroft was influenced by Hall's observation that York is the real power in the scene, Margaret was 'the weak one' and knowledge of this drove her to extreme violence 'out of hysteria, hatred and violence' (Billington 1988: 201–202).

Where the *Henry VI* adaptation had been bold and provocative, discovering new vitality and relevance in a set of relatively unknown plays, *Richard III* remained mostly faithful to the source texts. *Richard III* opened in August, several weeks after *Henry VI* and *Edward IV*, and was received at the time with a faint sense of disappointment from critics, who initially felt that the production was an anticlimax. *The Times* thought it a 'disappointing finale' which missed the 'sense of accumulating history' and criticized Ian Holm's 'juvenile, open-faced and friendly' Richard Gloucester. The reviewer thought Holm a 'high-spirited minor' who exhausted his 'lung-power' and ended on Bosworth Field 'loaded down with an armory of medieval weapons, crooning to himself like a baby inside his vizor' (21 August 1963). Not all reviewers agreed: covering the London run, Hope-Wallace described Holm as 'hideous with the ferocity of a poisonous reptile', reeling about Bosworth, 'blindly swinging ball and mace' (*Guardian* 13 January 1964). The *Times* improved its opinion of Holm in January, seeing him as a 'manifestation of the disease from which the country suffers'. The reviewer found Holm 'incisive and intelligent' admitting that 'if he attempts few of the big things ... his performance is full of clever and effective detail' (*Times* 13 January 1964). Holm avoided Olivier's exaggerations and instead presented a more subdued, introspective Richard, in some ways a mirror to Warner's gently spoken Henry. Bernard Levin, writing for the *Daily Mail*, thought Holm's naturalism made Richard's villainy 'credible without being psychopathic', springing from 'the savage times in which it is set' (21 August 1963). 'At the end,' wrote Levin, 'Richard, broken, mad and exhausted, a Hitler with only his visor for a bunker, summons up his last strength for the duel with Richmond. It is savage, primitive and horrible.'

Hall's bleak vision of the chaos that follows when institutions collapse was manifest at this moment, the full brutality of history laid bare by Richard's tyranny. Eric Shorter understood Hall's point that Richard was 'a product of his violent age: an epitome of medieval cruelty' (*Telegraph* 21 August 1963). *The Wars of the Roses* may have spoken forcefully to a new audience hungry for art that upset traditions and dared to impose modern meanings, and new words, on Shakespeare, but they missed the point that Hall was aiming at in his exploration of the paradoxes of political order. In his early twenties when the productions were staged, Sinfield, in his later essay, reflected the disenchantment of a generation when he scrutinized Hall's politics and found that, far from being a radical mischief-maker, Hall was looking to redefine the establishment, to make a case for social and cultural institutions (such as the RSC) as a bulwark against human society's tendency to violence. It is a stretch to call this conservative, as Sinfield does, given that Hall was essentially making Shakespeare the prophet of the British Welfare State and arguing for the public subsidy of the arts, but nor was Hall a radical activist. *The Wars of the Roses* set a course that the RSC would follow for at least the next decade. To an extent, it is still following it, as the achievement of that production in creating a new audience for Shakespeare, and a new urgency in the staging of Shakespeare, remains one of the critical milestones in the modern history of British Shakespeare production.

Richard II, *Henry IV* and *Henry V* 1964

In 1964, the year of Shakespeare's 400th birthday, Hall completed the history cycle with *Richard II*, the two parts of *Henry IV* and *Henry V*, all of which he co-directed with John Barton, Clifford Williams and Peter Wood. This time, the plays were presented without adaptation or significant alteration. The productions spoke directly to the experience of the young audience that Hall had cultivated: they were plays about the handover of power and authority from one generation to the next, which in Hall's hands became brooding reflections on the suffocating, corrosive presence of history. The lead casting mirrored *The Wars of the Roses*. Warner, who had become something of a cult figure for the RSC's young audience, was cast as Richard II, another weak young king slaughtered in the game of power politics. Ian Holm played Henry V, inverting his *Richard III* performance, representing a new generation contemplating the burden of the past and the future.

Under pressure from the workload of running the company, as well as a host of personal and health issues which dogged him through the year, Hall created a delegated model of directing. He did not attend initial rehearsals: the heavy lifting was done by Wood, who worked on the interpretation of lines, with Barton focusing on fight sequences and Williams on stage blocking. Occasionally Hall visited the company to watch several scenes right through and then retired to discuss them with his co-directors. Rehearsals were chaotic. The company was playing *The Wars of the Roses* at the Aldwych in the evening and rehearsing the second tetralogy during the day in London. The RSC had nowhere in London large enough to act as a central rehearsal space: instead, it split rehearsals across different locations, including the Donmar, a YMCA, and a room just off Covent Garden large enough to enable the company to mark out a map of the Stratford stage with gaffer tape and batons. Actors were constantly moving between them clutching ragged copies of their scripts, often losing track of which play they were rehearsing.

A radio documentary for the BBC Third Programme, *An Anointed King* (broadcast in October 1964) chronicled the rehearsals for *Richard II* and offered a fascinating glimpse of Hall's methods. Having watched the opening scene, Hall got straight to the point: the company had not solved the problem of why Mowbray throws down his gauntlet. By the finished performance, this had become the scene's pivotal moment, exploding the formality of the staging with a sudden burst of anger. As rehearsals progressed, the co-directors focused their attention on different actors so that, for example, Barton worked closely with Roy Dotrice on his parts (Gaunt, Hotspur, and Shallow), but even so, the actors found the process messy and bewildering. The company worked better together when rehearsals moved back to Stratford. Hall's conception of the plays was full of his usual insight and conviction. He summoned the heads of all the backstage departments and acted out all the plays before a model of the set. As the opening night drew closer, Hall took charge of the rehearsals. He sat at a desk in the middle of the stalls, scribbling notes on his script as actors ran through scenes on set but not in costume, without their scripts, assistants reading out the musical cues and prompting missed lines. After the opening scene, Hall addressed the company in his slow, thoughtful, gentle voice: 'I think what is wrong', he said, 'is that everyone is a little too square in showing who they hate and who they like.' The gravity of the scene was missing; the entrance lacked speed and urgency: 'I don't think you're quite going with the situation of a challenge to the king from your various points of view.' Hall was also happy to let scenes pass with little interference: after Act 1, Scene 3, he gave his approval – 'it's very, very good this ... very good rhythm' – but said little else. By this point, the company were doing little else but rehearse and perform: rehearsals started at 10 am and continued after the evening's performances until 2 am.

Warner struggled with the part of Richard. Henry VI is a passive character, Hall observed, whereas Richard is active: the play does not happen to him, Hall explained to Warner in a moment captured by *An Anointed King*, Richard *is* the play. Warner's performance was remarkable, and the contrast between his rehearsals (captured on the radio) and his actual performance shows what Hall brought to the production: he lifted an average performance into a great one. In the surviving audio recording, Warner dominates and controls the stage: his voluntary renunciation of kingship is the performance's signature moment. His voice, powerful yet strained, allowed for many pauses, space for other characters to speak, but they did not, leaving Richard in control as he claimed to let go of his authority. Photographs of this scene show Bolingbroke standing impotently, confused, as Richard reclines on gnarled branches as if being absorbed by a forest, looking pained, his eyes shut, his face looking Christ-like to the sky. As he took his crown off, 'this heavy weight from off my head' he spoke as if every word were a weight: 'and ... ', he paused, 'this', he paused again, history blowing through the silences, 'unwieldy sceptre ... ' Then his voice became soft, slow, gentle at first but getting firmer, as if realizing a sense of potency in his self-abdication as he said, 'with my breath .... All pomp and majesty I forswear'. His voice sunk to a dark rasp as he realized the end would be 'an earthy pit', and said 'what more remains' with an exhausted, terrifying finality. Even on a recording more than fifty years later, Warner's performance is powerful, moving and vivid.

He did not impress all reviewers. Bamber Gascoigne thought he was 'not a full enough character to pull the play together' who spoke in a voice that 'tips and slides like the drifting flight of a seagull, beautiful but repetitive'. Gascoigne admired Richard's death scene, when Richard was 'hooked by a chain about his waist and slowly drawn, like a fish on a line, to the point of a ready dagger' (*Observer* 19 April 1964). Alan Brien described him as a 'suffering Christ-figure' later transformed into a 'kind of Mithraic Pope', in the Flint Castle scene dressed in golden robes, and later, for his deposition, in 'dazzling' white, a true 'king of snow' (*Sunday Telegraph* 19 April 1964). Photographs corroborate the almost unreal brightness of Richard's robes, an effect achieved by a combination of costume and lighting.

The *Henry IV* plays were better received. They were Hall's favourite plays (Hall 1993: 412): he had vivid memories of seeing Olivier as Hotspur (Hall 1993: 113) and Antony Quayle's 1951 productions for the Birmingham Rep, with Richard Burton as Hal, seemed to the young Hall to be a clarion call for a new generation (Hall 1993: 89). His influence on these productions was more deeply felt: while Barton worked with Dotrice on his parts (including Hotspur) and Williams took charge of directing Eric Porter as Bolingbroke/Henry IV, Hall worked intensively with Hugh Griffith as Falstaff (Addenbrooke 1974: 205). Griffith was one of the few actors in the company who only played one part: moreover, he was recruited to the RSC specifically to play the fat knight. The experience was not a happy one: Fay, who had access to Peter Hall's letters, records the increasingly fraught relationship between the actor and his director, which ended with Griffith leaving the production after a year, his place taken by Paul Rogers (Fay 1995: 168–169). Griffith played a complex Falstaff, who could be crafty and unexpectedly tender and by the end of *Part Two* had shrugged off his clowning to embrace a reflective melancholy 'heavy with the sense of mortality', as the unsigned *Times* review put it (17 April 1964). Gascoigne thought Griffith was 'magnificent' and remembered him sitting on a 'vast old leather armchair in the middle of the floor, a gross throne that only he could aspire to fill' (*Observer* 19 April 1964). In an audio recording of the production's first performance, Griffith speaks with a soft Welsh burr and acts almost as if parodying the now-dated Shakespearean heroes of the 1950s. Ian Holm, as Hal, was more attached to Falstaff than to the world of the Eastcheap Tavern, evoked by smoke-blackened beams as a distressed, decayed world at the heart of England's decline. Playing the King to Falstaff's Hal, he teased the knight as a 'villainous abominable misleader of youth', a line resonant for the new generation who camped outside the RST for the new season's tickets, but his tone darkened when he said, slowly and with 'cool tenderness' (*Sunday Telegraph* 19 April 1964) 'that old white-bearded Satan'. When, in his early twenties, Hall had seen Burton play Hal, he thought Burton's performance marked the difference between his generation and the one before it (Hall 1993: 89–90); now, through this scene, Hall seemed to be trying to recreate that sense of a modern world rejecting the past. Threatening to banish the old knight, Hal said assertively, 'I do', then there was a long pause before he said softly, almost inaudibly, and perhaps only to himself and the audience, 'I will'.

Holm developed a markedly unromantic interpretation of Hal and then Henry V. He had already faced off Hotspur, played by Dotrice as a flame-haired, kilted, over-the-top warrior that Gascoigne called a 'mad, music-hall MacDuff', and in doing so faced down the heroic bravado of Olivier's famous film portrayal of Henry V (*Observer* 19 April 1964). The opening of Henry V opened up his world with a 'vast golden relief map' of France suspended over the stage (*Times* 4 June 1964). For Hall, Henry was a man of contradictions, someone who was, he wrote, a 'devious politician' and yet sincere, 'a hypocrite and an idealist' (*Henry V* Programme). He wrote this for an article entitled 'The Empirical Empire' in the souvenir programme: the designer had, perhaps mischievously, placed the article under four portraits of Hall in various poses, some authoritative and some ridiculous. Hall was inadvertently describing not just Henry but himself as many others saw him, for even his most loyal actors regarded him as something of a 'benign dictator' who might claim to be open to everyone's idea, but 'always had the answers' (Holm 2004: 75). Holm avoided bombast and flourish: his reading of Henry's great battle speeches was low-key and conversational, delivered to a small band onstage rather than to the vast army of the audience. After Agincourt, he and his soldiers were silent and exhausted, rather than triumphant cheers there were only 'the sounds of dying men and screaming metal' breaking the 'smoke-filled stage' (*Times* 4 June 1964). Reviewers found little in *Henry V* to talk about, no doubt themselves drained by Hall's relentless theatrical enterprise, and several unfortunately made unkind jibes about Holm's height (his subsequent CV includes two hobbit parts): he was Henry V 'scaled down', according to *The Times*; he did not 'quite measure up', wrote W.A. Darlington, who thought he lacked the 'inches' to play a romantic hero (*The Daily Telegraph* 4 June 1964). Holm's performance had developed into a darker reading by the production's 1965 transfer to the Aldwych: under Barton's direction, Henry became a 'tough, weary' King, rescuing the play from Olivier and recreating it for a modern audience more sceptical about authority (Loehlin 1997: 49).

Hamlet 1965

Hall concluded his most significant three years of Shakespeare directing with a landmark production of *Hamlet* with David Warner as a 'scruffy undergraduate' Prince (Dawson 1997: 134). The text was cut, with nearly a fifth of the play edited out, but this time Hall avoided the kind of controversy he and Barton had attracted with *The Wars of the Roses*. He was more interested in confronting the present, literally so, as he began the production with a cannon aimed squarely at the audience, many of whom were as young as Warner. Hall had the present generation in his sights. Hall wrote in a programme note, 'For our decade I think the play will be about the disillusionment which produces an apathy of the will so deep that commitment to politics, to religion or to life is impossible.' The cultural world of 1965 was very different from 1956 when Hall first started directing Shakespeare, and *Hamlet* registered and engaged with this change. The year had started with the funeral of Winston Churchill, an event which seemed to underline the emergence of the country from the long shadow of the Second World War. The year also saw the first major battles in the Vietnam War and significant civil rights demonstrations in America. The new generation was affluent, permissive, politicized and anti-authoritarian. By this point, Hall was in his mid-thirties, still young to be running a public theatre but not young enough to be anything more than an interested spectator to the cultural revolution of the 1960s. *Hamlet* was an ideal vehicle for Hall to explore his response to this generation.

The production struck a chord with young people, with many of them queuing for two days to get tickets for the opening (Dawson 1997: 136). It helped that some of the newspaper critics were less than enthusiastic about the production, particularly Warner's anti-heroic depiction of Hamlet. By breaking with the Hamlets of Olivier and Gielgud, Warner and Hall asserted a new kind of hero that the new generation could more readily identify with. The reviews served to enhance the production's anti-establishment credentials since it seemed that the establishment was rejecting it. The production's success increased through its run (Dawson 1997: 136). Hall continued to view his young audience critically; although they embraced Hamlet, Hall himself was concerned about their political apathy. *Hamlet* was meant to be his way of stimulating the new generation into political action, but it had the opposite effect of creating a heroic ideal out of apathetic inaction. Dawson concluded that *Hamlet* was, in the end, ambivalent in that it criticized the values of the young people that Hall wanted to attract into the theatre: 'As a critique of apathy,' Dawson writes, 'the production in some way paradoxically espoused it, though it also succeeded in defining brilliantly the nature of the enemy' (Dawson 1997: 138).

Bury's set was dark and claustrophobic, with a fake black proscenium and walls which slanted inwards towards two 'massive' doors, echoing the doors in *The Wars of the Roses* (Wells 1977: 27). Panels in the wall opened at times to reveal bookshelves for Polonius' study and frescoes such as blue sky or a 'broken funeral column' (Wells 1977: 28) so that even the outside was enclosed in the suffocating interior of Denmark's corrupt court. The stage was a black marble floor flecked with silver that mirrored the actors' bodies. Dim lighting created a sense of 'entrapment' and 'impenetrability' (Dawson 1997: 135). For Dawson, the set played a crucial role in 'carrying the production's anti-establishment' message (Dawson 1997: 135). Hamlet's ghost was achieved with smoke and machinery, the ghost (played by the already imposing Brewster Mason, who also played Claudius, standing on a platform that made him look twelve feet high) gliding through the fog towards the younger Hamlet. L.C. Knights, who reviewed the Aldwych transfer, was impressed by the 'extraordinary image of Hamlet reaching up towards the Ghost, which enfolds him in its arms' (*Observer* 19 December 1965).

Hall wanted to highlight Hamlet's dissonant presence within a world which he did not belong to, which he could change, but which would eventually oppress him. Dawson describes this as Hall's most important idea: Elsinore was an 'oppressive social milieu', an 'efficient and dominating court' which left little room for Hamlet to manoeuvre (Dawson 1997: 134). Claudius' court was mechanically efficient and busy in a way which highlighted Hamlet's apathy. Hamlet was introduced as part of this world, seated at the table with the rest of the court, a prisoner rather than a malcontent: 'That table was the cage of circumstance in which he was caught up, and only through his own death and the death of others would he be able to escape from it' (Speaight 1965: 320).

The production's Ophelia was one of its most radical innovations, and the critical backlash against its bold interpretation led to an unusually rapid recasting as first Glenda Jackson and then Janet Suzman left the role during the run, with Estelle Kohler ending the production with a more toned-down performance. As Maher recalls, Jackson was the 'harshest' of the three and received 'the roughest treatment' (Maher 2003: 258). Jackson's Ophelia spoke with a 'harsh voice' and had an 'abrasive personality' so that, to Wells, she seemed 'most unlikely to be dominated by her father, or anyone else' (Wells 1977: 31). The *Times* bristled at Jackson's 'eccentric' performance and criticized her for barking her lines (20 August 1965). Jackson played an Ophelia with keen intelligence, full of anger and bitterness. Alan Brien called her a 'quacking deb of an Ophelia' who was 'shrill in her aggression, dangerous in her anger', a modern-day 'Chelsea-set beatnik who could swop obscenities any night' (*Sunday Telegraph* 22 August 1965).

In one of the best assessments of Jackson's performance, Penelope Gilliatt praised her as 'exceptional and electric, with an intelligence that harasses the court and a scornful authority full of Hamlet's own self-distaste'. She shouted her lines 'as though she could do murder, drumming a heel on the floor and lifting her upper lip in a rictus of contempt'. When alone after Hamlet ordered her to a nunnery, Jackson delivered a speech which was 'jagged with pain': the line 'blasted with ecstasy' was 'hideously screeched, not bleated', the mood 'spiked with suicidal sarcasm' (*Observer* 22 August 1965). Jackson began Ophelia's final scene singing an angry, discordant song with a lute on which she beat savage chords, almost as if parodying the 1960s generation's faith in rock music. Harold Hobson panned Jackson's 'harsh, bitter, setting teeth-on-edge' performance (*Sunday Times* 22 August 1965). Suzman replaced Jackson, but her performance was just as complex and difficult. For Charles Marowitz, Suzman's Ophelia was 'all neurotic repression' whose final madness was 'the last stage of the malady we have spied from the first' (Marowitz 1973: 110).

Hall cast David Warner as Hamlet, a move which proved Hall's foresight as Warner's performance became iconic.

Although Warner had played the lead in three of Hall's recent productions, he was still a risky and unexpected choice. Warner was young, he was not a classical actor and as Wells puts it, although very tall, he was 'unheroic in build ... not conventionally handsome' and hence 'no princely, romantic embodiment of the role'. In short, as Wells observed, Warner's casting 'was itself a major interpretative decision' (Wells 1977: 33) which presented an awkward, scruffy, vulnerable Hamlet, more a modern student than a medieval Prince. Hall had seen Warner as a future Hamlet since his first audition for the RSC in 1962 (Hall 1993: 195). Although the costumes evoked the past, Warner's outfit hinted at the present. He wore a 'crumpled college gown' and an impossibly long red scarf which, despite becoming bound with the production in theatrical memory as one of its defining images, was dispensed with later in the run to help improve the pace of Warner's performance (Wells 1977: 37). Warner was, wrote Gilliatt, a 'red-brick undergraduate' who was 'more touching than tragic' and often 'whey-faced' (*Observer* 22 August 1965). Hall himself called Warner 'the very embodiment of the Sixties student' (Hall 1993: 196). Warner was, in fact, struggling: rehearsals sometimes lasted until 6 am (Wells 1977: 34), and the actor started to suffer from insomnia. 'I feel very blue and weak on a Hamlet day,' he told one interviewer: 'I wake up feeling tired, under a great black cloud. I save energy: all day I move slowly ... I eat daintily' (*Observer* 17 April 1966). By the time the production reached London, he was dogged by stage fright (*Observer* 19 December 1965).

Rather than reflect inwards, Warner's Hamlet spoke quickly, his mind continually shifting: as Speaight wrote, 'His thoughts tumble over one another with the same rapidity as his emotions' (Speaight 1965: 321). Warner's soliloquies were directed at the audience, which broke a tradition of Hamlet speaking contemplatively to himself. Sometimes they spoke back: one night, when he asked them, 'Am I a coward?' (2.2.506), one person shouted back, 'Yes!' (Thompson and Taylor 2006: 24). He was, as one reviewer put it, full of 'vitality and humanity' who displayed 'zest and joy' when plotting with the players and in his scenes with Polonius (*Montreal Gazette* 5 February 1966). Yet he could be unexpectedly violent: when he kissed Ophelia before *The Mousetrap*, it was 'brutal' (Speaight 1966: 396). Bryden saw him as a 'cloud of immature and unfocused emotions in search of means to express them' (Bryden 1969: 63). For *The Times*, Warner was channelling the immaturity and neediness of Henry VI, hugging his father's ghost and nuzzling a pillow as if 'looking for the comforts of the nursery' (20 August 1965).

Like the marble, mirrored surface of the stage, this Hamlet was in part a reflection of the audience, but it was a reflection mediated by Hall's ambivalence towards them. Hamlet died laughing, the irony of his life and his failure to overcome his apathy defining his tragedy (*Guardian* 28 September 1967). For many in the audience, for whom Warner was the Hamlet of their generation, such gestures were not taken as critiques but as a positive affirmation of a new spirit of cultural politics: Sinfield argues that they 'saw Warner's Hamlet not as a figure of apathy but as one of rebellion or, at least, refusal' (Sinfield 1994: 193). Although initially received coolly by critics, *Hamlet* quickly gained a cult following among the under-25 generation that was quickly dominating cultural life. By the time it reached London, the hype around the production was extraordinary. Hall's *Hamlet*, along with his landmark debut of Harold Pinter's *The Homecoming* in the same season, became iconic, making Shakespeare as relevant to the cultural moment as the most cutting edge modern drama.

Macbeth 1967

Hall's last theatrical Shakespeare production for the RSC in the 1960s was *Macbeth* in 1967, with Paul Scofield in the title role, Vivien Merchant as Lady Macbeth and Ian Richardson as Malcolm. In his memoirs, Hall recalls the experience as 'one of my most disastrous productions' (Hall 1993: 215). Hall initially wanted to explore the play's Christian themes, in particular, the nature of evil. Scofield was incapable of playing an irredeemable Macbeth, and as they worked together in rehearsal, Hall moved away from his original ideas to create with Scofield an unusual, introspective and edgy Macbeth. By the time it reached the stage (delayed when Hall fell ill with shingles and nearly lost sight in one eye), the production was a mish-mash of ideas and experiments that failed to cohere into a compelling interpretation of the play. Yet the production was nothing if not bold. Staged during the 'Summer of Love', *Macbeth* was a psychedelic horror show, a blood-soaked tragedy that gestured to the escalating war in Vietnam.

Scofield's performance as Macbeth mystified some critics and frustrated the actor, but it was a remarkable, original creation, arguably ahead of its time. Hall found Scofield incapable of delivering the idea he initially had of a Macbeth who was inescapably evil: Scofield was just not able to perform without bringing out Macbeth's humanity and with it the futility of his tragedy. Scofield shook off centuries of dusty tradition with a thoughtful, brooding, unpredictable and quietly unsettling performance. He experimented with Macbeth's speech patterns, putting in extra punctuation and emphasis as if each line was not something scripted, but a thought that he had just experienced. Scofield created a sense of immediacy, haunted by the possibility of redemption – maybe this time, for once, Macbeth would not be fooled by the witches, but of course, he always was. Lloyd Evans called him a 'speculating actor'. Scofield started a speech and 'we overhear him in his agonized task of discovering all of its meaning'. The agony is, Lloyd Evans continues, both intellectual and emotional, but rarely physical, leaving the audience time 'to ponder on every nuance and pause' (Lloyd Evans 1968: 120). However, when Macbeth gained power, he became manic, 'his thoughts and speech hyperactive, accelerating wildly' (Rosenberg 1997: 238). J.C. Trewin admired Scofield's 'explorer's technique', his idiosyncratic way of speaking giving the impression that the actor was thinking on the spot (*Illustrated London News* 26 August 1967).

Bryden, writing for the *Observer*, wrote about Scofield's journey from a noble Macbeth to the 'savage exhaustion of a gambler damned' (7 January 1968). When Macbeth wished that Duncan would live again, Scofield delivered the line in a heartfelt way rather than with irony. However, the care with which Scofield constructed his performance also frustrated Bryden, who felt he went too far, was too literal, in depicting the 'deliberately clogged' steps of a man whose tragedy is marked by 'conscience-stricken self-knowledge'. Hope-Wallace was less patient with Scofield's 'strange' way of speaking, his 'staccato, barking, rhythmless splitting up of the lines and misemphasis' (*Guardian* 17 August 1967). Wardle wrote that Scofield clung to language 'as tenaciously as a man on a rock face'; Wardle found the performance 'thrilling', fully accepting the 'unexpectedly disjointed phrasing and the displaced climaxes' (*Times* 16 August 1967). Darlington complained that Scofield seemed to be 'grinding' his speeches 'word by word' but felt that his unexpected pauses had 'undeniable effectiveness'. Darlington's interpretation of Scofield's performance was as close as it was possible to get between Hall and Scofield's contrasting view of Macbeth, whom Darlington saw as 'a very wicked man with enough imagination to know how much better off he would have been as a good one' (*Telegraph* 17 August 1967). Scofield made his hands a focus of his performance. Macbeth was constantly looking at them, trying to puzzle them out. After he murdered Duncan, they were red with blood, and he held them up, horrified and fascinated at the same time. When Lady Macbeth (Vivien Merchant) returned the daggers, her hands also bloody, she took Macbeth's hands with, in Brien's words, a 'ghastly, orgiastic unction' (*Sunday Telegraph* 7 January 1968).

Bury had based his ideas on Hall's original vision of a profoundly religious play with a pervading sense of evil but, in rehearsal, Hall had moved away from this as he worked with Scofield's interpretation of the part. Tonally, everything was red or white, including the set's floor and walls, which were covered in red carpet over white plastic. At times, strips of the carpet were pulled back to reveal the shiny white plastic underneath. Photographs show how vivid the contrast was, the set seemed unreal, almost (and topically) psychedelic, and connected both the idea of a world soaked in blood and the colours of the Catholic Church. Macbeth, having stolen the throne, dressed in a long white robe that covered his hands and feet with flared sleeves, adorned with a ridiculous, heavy medallion. With his court also dressed in white, against the red background, they looked bleached, sketched in outline, like smears in blood. Bury's other keynote was the crucifix: one appeared at the beginning, held upside down by one of the witches, who poured blood down it into the mouth of another witch, prostrate on the floor and squealing orgiastically; and the production closed with Malcolm kneeling to another crucifix, the original blasphemy redeemed. The stage was steeply raked, adding to the psychedelic feel, like one of those 1960s films shot at weird angles. The opening was so spectacular that nearly all the press reviews wrote about it. Bury put a white gauze as a 'curtain' over the stage, with the witches' silhouettes briefly visible before the gauze was flown off to reveal the set. Most of the cast were hidden below the carpets, some on the stage floor, others on the wall, and they moved rhythmically as the witches performed their ritual with the cross, so that it seemed as if the stage world was pulsating, alive, in physical as well as spiritual crisis. It was by all accounts an extraordinary opening, praised even by some of the production's most unkind critics. The mixture of inverted religious imagery and the suggestion of a world soaked in blood beyond redemption captured what Hall wanted to get out of the play. The production aesthetic was more 'Purple Haze' than 'Lucy in the Sky with Diamonds', a proto-*Apocalypse Now* overshadowed by Vietnam and its moral implications. The atmosphere was heavy, imposing, suffocating: Darlington complained that the set was 'dreary' and 'murky': actors dressed in long overcoats and they 'come and go in darkness' (*Telegraph* 17 August 1967). Speaight called the set 'daringly original' (Speaight 1967: 393).

The modern, psychedelic tone of the production was enhanced by Guy Wolfenden's score, which blended earthy, paganesque music for the mortal world and discordant, experimental sounds for the supernatural scenes. Wolfenden crafted unique acoustic instruments for the musicians to play: they came onstage, with instruments fashioned out of what appeared to be animal horns, playing in 'weird keys'. He worked with the BBC Radiophonic Workshop to create strange, deep bass electronic sounds, barely describable as music in the conventional sense, for the witches. Some were such a low frequency that they could hardly be heard so that the effect was to create a subliminal sense of unease (*Sunday Times* 13 August 1967).

Hall, Bury and Scofield were drawing on the experimental mood of the times. They were influenced by some of the fringe work the RSC had been doing during the 1960s, particularly Peter Brook's experimental 'Theatre of Cruelty' season. In 1966, Brook staged *U.S.*, a docudrama about the Vietnam War – this was the RSC's most stridently political work of the decade. *Macbeth* was a mainstream, big-ticket production but Hall was influenced by these fringe works, building into his *Macbeth* a physical sensuality, an obsession with blood, and an unforced gesture to the futility of the war in Vietnam. *Macbeth* was a natural sequel to his histories and *Hamlet*. In those productions, Hall had put the weight of history on the post-war generation who were queuing overnight for tickets to his productions and then, in *Hamlet*, he had pointed a cannon directly at them, challenging their apathy. *Macbeth* combined history and tragedy, taking this critique to its furthest extreme and underlying how problematic the RSC's reputation for political Shakespeare was.

A Midsummer Night's Dream 1968

Hall's last project for the RSC before standing down as its Managing Director was a film of *A Midsummer Night's Dream*. The film was a coda to his time at the SMT and RSC rather than a climax, yet it served as a summation of some of the key themes of his tenure. The film looked back to his SMT comedies and Hall was not shy of recycling ideas from his earlier productions of the play. The increasingly dark and bloody tragedies that characterized his RSC works left their mark, as did the general atmosphere of experimentation typical of the time. Hence the film was full of strange camera angles, nightmarish visions and Carnaby Street-style outfits that made it very much 'of its time', a Shakespeare for the flower-power generation. The cast was, as Hall himself put it, a roll-call of his twelve years in Stratford (Hall 1993: 370). Ian Holm again played Puck. Judi Dench and Ian Richardson reprised their roles as Titania and Oberon from the 1962 revival. Diana Rigg, who had played a bit part in the 1959 version, had been promoted to Helena in 1962 and now retook the role. Other actors may not have been in Hall's earlier productions of the play but had become RSC mainstays, including Paul Rogers as Bottom, Derek Godfrey as Theseus, David Warner as Lysander, and Clive Swift as Snug. Here was Hall's long-imagined RSC ensemble captured on film, along with gestures to the company's past and future. Barbara Jefford, who played Hippolyta, had been a Stratford regular through the 1950s but left before Hall's arrival. Helen Mirren, playing a doe-eyed Hermia, had only just joined the company but would become one of its stars in the 1970s.

Hall brought his cast to the stately home at Compton Verney. The interior superficially resembled De Nobili's staircase stage, while the grounds afforded plenty of opportunities for Hall to crawl through mud and brambles to film a naked Judi Dench (wearing only green paint) cavorting with Bottom. Hall intended to expand on his original idea that Shakespeare had written the play for a wedding in a stately home: however, without a framing device to make this clear, the conceit did not work. He insisted on a nearly full text and used a hand-held camera to emulate the realist techniques of documentary cinema (Mullin 1975: 532–533). Given that Hall's work with Bury had created a highly detailed realism onstage, it is surprising that so much of the film feels unreal. As Bury himself discovered when he substituted real branches for props in *Macbeth*, sometimes the real is not very realistic. Hall's theatrical skills looked absurd on film. The actors wore stage make-up, their hair fixed in a way that may have worked onstage, but looked plastic on-screen. Theseus and his court looked like they belonged in an early 1950s Errol Flynn movie, while the women wore mini-skirts except for Hippolyta, who wore a kinky leather mini-dress. Bottom and his fellows were better presented, although tended towards stereotypes of 'onion-chomping English workmen, clad in tweeds, moleskins, and leather' (Mullin 1975: 532). Worse still, Hall had no way of recording audio on location, so the whole film had to be dubbed (Hall 1993: 370) with a recorded performance that lacked the acoustic dimensions that would suggest lines spoken in an airy, marbled hall or a thick forest. As Richard Roud pointed out in his review, the clumsy syncing destroyed the sense of realism Hall was trying to achieve (*Guardian* 31 January 1969).

Hall deliberately waited until the autumn to film so he could capture the 'damp' look of the bad summer Titania describes, although circumstances forced the shoot back to the winter of 1967–1968 (Hall 1993: 370). The sound of heavy rain dominates the opening shots tracking across summer landscapes. Hall tried some modish (but not dated) shots, so that Helena first appears in the background of a close-up of Demetrius, lingering out of focus; often he took his hand-held camera up a ladder to film head-shots from above, with Mirren staring up at the camera with wide-open eyes. Although Hall kept to a mostly uncut text, he played with locations so that scenes were not always continuous: Helena and Hermia's first scene together switched suddenly to a boat, Hermia now wearing a different costume, then just as suddenly Hermia has made it to the shore. In one speech, Hermia cuddles Helena, and then the film cuts to Helena on her own with no break in her speech.

These disorientating film devices came into their own when the action moved to the fairy world in the forest, where the film became something of an 'erotic nightmare', as Mullin memorably puts it (Mullin 1975: 532). Hall's cuts became even more sudden as Puck and Oberon seem to change location with supernatural speed: strange noises and bright lights turned the gardens of Compton Verney into a green-washed psychedelic fantasy world. Dench, seen first from below, was bare-breasted and covered in patterned, green paint. Her Titania was earthy, erotic and powerful. Rogers played a down-to-earth Bottom, lacking Laughton's bombastic presence entirely.

The lovers arrive into the forest crawling through the undergrowth: one of Hall's more effective ideas was to show the lovers becoming increasingly mud-smeared, their fashionable 1960s clothes soon wet and dirty, as if the flower-power generation was being overwhelmed by the forest's ancient power. When the camera finds the lovers the next morning, all mended, they look like children asleep, Helena sucking her thumb. After the play, a bell tolls, and the mortals go up to bed. The film switches to a close-up of Puck's face, pulling back to reveal him on the staircase. As he slides down the banister, mischievously subverting the space's decorum, fairies appear from behind chairs and start running through the house, singing songs as Titania and Oberon ascend the stairs carrying candles, making their way towards the lovers' bedrooms. Puck's epilogue, delivered very quickly, is set against the sunrise: it is no longer raining, the only background sound as 'The End' flashes up is birdsong. Despite some very fine verse-speaking, the film is something of a curiosity today. It was a film of its time, but its time did not like it much. As Mullin recalls in a brave if a not entirely successful defence of the film, reviewers were scathing: it was 'shockingly inept' according to the *Observer*, 'just damn silly' in *The Guardian* and *The Times* dismissed it as 'frankly terrible' (Mullin 1975: 529).

A Midsummer Night's Dream brought to an end twelve years of directing Shakespeare, during which Hall had directed most of the histories and a selection of key comedies and tragedies. Over that period, he had moved from nostalgia for a vanished past to anxiety about the future, the blood-soaked *Macbeth*, in particular, a startling contrast to his romantic, melancholic *Twelfth Night*. Both productions created theatrical force out of excess: his stages were overflowing with scenery and spectacle, just as the works themselves overflowed with ideas, drawing on contemporary politics and avant-garde techniques to recreate Shakespeare as a modern playwright, capable of speaking to the present. Hall's relationship with the counter-culture of the new, anti-authoritarian generation which filled his theatres was complex. He was busy building a new cultural institution with the RSC, but as part of that he wanted the theatre to have a radical side, and he brought some of that into his mainstream Shakespeare productions, which became increasingly edgy. He had helped forge a new theatrical language for Shakespeare and established a new audience with an appetite for innovation, but his final works, *Macbeth* and *A Midsummer Night's Dream*, struggled to build on that legacy in a way that either his audiences or Hall himself valued. Hall had undoubtedly reinvented Shakespeare for the 1960s, his critical productions as important to the theatre as Warhol was to art or the Beatles were to popular music, yet his legacy was mixed, and Hall was incapable of keeping up with the radical tendencies of some of his audience. The turn towards 'political Shakespeare' in academic studies in the 1980s and 1990s was in part inspired by Hall's work: *The Wars of the Roses* and *Hamlet* were defining theatrical moments for many of the people who drove that work. Hall's work did not stand up to political scrutiny, as Sinfield's critique, tinged with disenchantment, shows. Hall was never a radical himself, although he was open to experimentation and valued innovation over tradition. By transforming the Shakespeare Memorial Theatre into the Royal Shakespeare Company, he elevated Shakespeare from being a locus of memory and tradition, a memorial writer, to a writer who made statements about the modern world, whose insights into power politics and the psychological impact of authority had genuine resonance with the themes dominating national culture through the period.

3

Authority in Crisis at the National Theatre

Peter Hall became the Director of the National Theatre in 1973, taking over from Laurence Olivier. Since stepping down as the Managing Director of the RSC, Hall had not directed any Shakespeare. The six-year gap between *Macbeth* and his inaugural National Theatre production, *The Tempest*, was to be the most extended interregnum of his Shakespeare career. He continued to direct modern plays for the RSC and had a brief spell running the Royal Opera House. When he returned to Shakespeare, it was with some reluctance: *Hamlet*, his last significant success, was nearly a decade behind him, and the cultural moment which had helped to make that seem so important had also dissipated. Hall at the RSC had always been on the back foot, an upstart provincial theatre man pushing his way on to the national stage; at the National, Hall felt the pressure to produce epic, era-defining work more keenly. Yet he directed only nine Shakespeare plays in his fifteen years at the National, with long gaps of several years between some of them, and four of which he directed in his last two years when he had effectively stopped running the organization. I have divided his National work into two chapters, this chapter covering his first six years, when he directed a baroque *Tempest* (1974) with John Gielgud, an edgy *Hamlet* (1975) and an austere *Macbeth* (1978), both starring Albert Finney, and finally a sedate *Othello* (1980), with Paul Scofield in the title role. The following chapter moves forward to 1984, when Hall directed a political *Coriolanus* with Ian McKellen after a long break from Shakespeare, and continues to his final productions, the epic *Antony and Cleopatra* (1986) with Judi Dench and Anthony Hopkins, and a reflective 'Late Plays' Trilogy (1988).

Hall's years at the National Theatre were difficult: he was consumed by building projects, strikes, discontented directors, bitter in-fighting and culture wars that spilled out into the press. When he started, the company was still based at its original home at the Old Vic in London: the major challenge of the first part of his tenure was to oversee the construction of the National Theatre building on London's South Bank. This proved to be a complex undertaking, immersing Hall in a nightmare of construction problems, strikes and delays. He also had to face the expectations of the theatre world and the scepticism of those who saw the National Theatre project as a waste of money at a time of economic hardship. In his mind, Hall was still a rebel, still fighting for arts funding, but to many, he was a problematic figure, a Nixon-like operator for whom power was more important than art. At a meeting of the Associate Directors in March 1976, Michael Blakemore read out a prepared statement critiquing Hall's management style in Hall's presence. The statement has since been published in full by Blakemore in his riveting memoir of his work at the National and Hall himself makes much of the evening in his *Diaries* (see Hall 1983: 221–222 for Hall's account of the meeting and Blakemore 2013: 275–286 for the full text of his paper). The various tussles at the National, which have been well-documented and studied, were as tortuous and mundane as any management regime change (for more on the history of the National see Lewis 1990, Callow 1997, and Rosenthal 2013). That the press became involved elevated these bitter corridor spats into big questions about what a national theatre should be, including its responsibilities and sense of accountability as a handler of public money.

The crisis of authority at the National mirrored a wider crisis of authority in Britain and beyond. In the United States, President Nixon was forced to resign over the 'Watergate' scandal in 1974, an episode which quickly came to exemplify the corrupting nature of authority. The ongoing war in Vietnam, which finally came to an end in 1975, fuelled generational discontent and soured the sense of optimism which briefly ignited culture in the 1960s. Industrial action and a fuel crisis dominated British public life, leading to a crisis in the public services and a period known as 'the three-day week' when the government rationed energy in a way which harkened back to the austerity of the war years. The British economy was in a mess, gripped by stagflation which hit incomes; in Northern Ireland, violent reaction to British authority led by the IRA spilled over to mainland Britain. Hall later called his experience of the 1970s 'the story of a dramatic struggle', a phrase which he used as the subtitle of his published diaries. Struggle and crisis overshadowed many of his Shakespeare productions, through which Hall articulated an increasingly problematic and complex interpretation of power and authority, his vision of the nation often overlapping and interweaving with his frustrations running the National Theatre.

The Tempest 1974 and *Hamlet* 1975

The general air of disillusion with political figures dominated Hall's production of *The Tempest*, which starred John Gielgud as a disenchanted autocratic Prospero. For Hall, Prospero was 'a tired old man who did not want the kingdom back at all', as Gielgud himself recalled (Lewis 1990: 103). The magus went through the play with 'a kind of contained hatred', bringing out the character's 'cruelty and selfishness' (*Financial Times* 6 March 1974). The spectre of Nixon hung over the production, in which power and abuse went together; the British political crisis was more present, as lights in the Old Vic were dimmed to save power. Hall directed Gielgud to play the role without any sentimentality: Prospero was to be a harsh figure, not easily moved. He looked like a wiry John Dee holding a long white staff, his cloak lined with runic symbols: Harold Hobson called him a 'haggard Don Quixote' (*Sunday Times* 16 March 1974). The archived recording of his performance captures the dead weight of his sonorous voice, implacable and unapologetic as he manipulated those about him.

Recalling the play's roots as a reaction to the masque form, Hall legitimized his interpretation of Prospero as a bitter, sinister man, a compromised figure of power rather than the benign magician of theatrical tradition. He called *The Tempest* a 'series of masques' (Frost 1983: 464), locating the play firmly in the aesthetic of power. This may have been 'national' theatre, but the production was soaked in the baroque imagery of Jacobean theatre, bringing together 1970s austerity with seventeenth-century opulence. Hall also drew inspiration from baroque opera, particularly Monteverdi's *Il Ritorno d'Ulissein Patria* and Cavalli's *La Calisto*, which he had recently directed (Frost 1983: 463). An exhibition at the Banqueting House in Whitehall about Inigo Jones and the theatre of the Stuart Court inspired Hall, who was struck by the similarities between Jones' work and the play. He commissioned the curator Roy Strong, who also edited a two-volume book from the exhibition with Stephen Orgel, to write a programme note arguing that Inigo Jones' designs for Jacobean masques inspired *The Tempest*. This idea gave Hall a palette to work with: under his direction, *The Tempest* was a political spectacle, simultaneously an overly anxious demonstration of what the National Theatre could do with Shakespeare and a harsh, somewhat cynical reflection on the relationship between theatrical illusion and power. The production was indulgently spectacular: 'flamboyant', as Frost puts it (Frost 1983: 484). Hall brought out the special effects for the opening scene, raising part of the stage to represent the front of a boat, which remained oddly still while a mast behind it swayed in the storm. *The Tempest* was one of the most technically challenging Shakespeare productions Hall had directed and as a result was dogged by mechanical failures (Shaughnessy 2018: 162–164). One critic was unconvinced: 'the storm creaked, rather than raged', wrote John Elsom in *The Listener*. Prospero's banquet was laid by 'bulbous, faceless heads and babies growing through their buttocks' (14 March 1974). The Juno and Ceres masque became a keynote scene in the production where Hall's exploration of the masque form as a way of understanding the play was made explicit. Frost described the scene as 'sumptuous' and 'operatic' (Frost 1983: 483) with the entire text of the masque sung rather than spoken, turning it into a mini-opera (Frost 1983: 463). It was certainly extravagant, scored with operatic singing that led some reviewers to worry that the whole production was slipping into opera (*Sunday Telegraph* 16 March 1974). There were touches of modernity too, connecting the Jacobean masque with medieval rock music. Hall hired the progressive rock band Gryphon (billed as a '12th century Slade') to write a score for *The Tempest*, which they pre-recorded and later released under the title 'Midnight Mushrumps'. The band performed the score at a special concert at the Old Vic after *The Tempest*'s final performance (Gryphon's score is discussed in more detail in Shaughnessy 2018: 143–144). *The Tempest* managed to be both operatic and, as Gielgud sniffed, 'trendy' (*Evening Post* 10 June 1975). Hall instructed Bury in a note to make Iris and Juno 'Rubenesque' with 'glorious false breasts' (Frost 1983: 463), which both fascinated and horrified Hobson (*Sunday Times* 16 March 1974). For Frost, Hall was using the scene to portray the nature of Prospero's magic, demonstrating the extent of his power to give extra tension to his eventual renunciation at the play's conclusion (Frost 1983: 484).

To underline Prospero's controlling presence, Gielgud was on stage for most of the performance, silently observing when not participating in a scene. The set was in some respects a very traditional proscenium arch affair with three layers of sliding flat scenery. There was also a semi-circular rostrum in the centre, a gesture perhaps to the amphitheatre-like design of the Olivier, the National's new main house which was still under construction. Bury decorated the stage with rocks, trees and foliage, mixed with reflective metal bars, with Prospero's hut a driftwood shack at the side of the stage. Prospero was aloof with Ariel (Michael Feast), stern with Caliban (Denis Quilley). Ariel, small, curly haired and hobbit-like, flew in on trapezes, wearing a body stocking that made him look half-naked. Quilley played Caliban as a 'savage from the New World' (Blakemore 2013: 208), a 'fish-scaled humanoid with redskin hair' (*Punch* 20 March 1974). A bandaged leg hobbled him, which he dragged across the stage, and he showed his ignorance by struggling with words like 'utensils' (3.3.96) (Frost 1983: 488). Prospero was cold with Miranda (Jenny Agutter), vengeful with the courtiers and his brother. In the final scene, Prospero drew a 'circle of light' around him with a staff, as if casting a spell to transform himself from a bitter exile to 'a gentle and dignified old man' (*Financial Times* 6 March 1974). However, there was no easy resolution of the conflict at the play's heart: in their final moments, Prospero and Antonio stared at each other in an unresolved, Pinteresque silence. Hall refused to dignify power with a peaceful end.

However, he added a twist. In a gesture to the tradition that Prospero is a cipher for Shakespeare himself, abandoning his art, Gielgud stepped forward to give the epilogue and removed his cap, revealing his Prospero to be, unmistakably, Shakespeare in disguise. He spoke his lines with a note of 'pained eloquence' (*Plays and Players* April 1974) missing from the rest of his performance: Shakespeare's voice, rather than Prospero's, closed the production, offering up a vision of Shakespeare as an artist for whom the exploration of authority, its necessity and its corruption, was ultimately exhausting, imprisoned by an audience that wanted spectacle rather than truth. When Gielgud said his final line, begging the audience to 'set me free', it was not Prospero, nor Gielgud, but Shakespeare himself who cried out for freedom. Shakespeare, it seemed, was being presented as the 'author' of the National's take on the national crisis, yet by fielding him in this way, Hall signalled his discomfort as he moved into a position where he was both rebel and courtier. The tension between the two would dominate his time at the National.

Hall was also keenly aware of his neo-realist, political style, which he felt was dated: his Shakespeare did not just want to be free of the burden of authority, he wanted to be free of the modern way of staging Shakespeare which he had played a significant role in defining. This final reveal was not only just about political authority but also about cultural authority. His 1960s Shakespeare, starting with *The Wars of the Roses*, exemplified the triumph of modernity over tradition. Hall was turning back to a reverence for the text which preceded interpretation. This textual turn was not untypical of Hall: he was always a reluctant adaptor and editor of Shakespeare, and he frequently spoke through the 1960s about the primacy of the text. However, he was increasingly convinced that the work of the director was to develop interpretation through rehearsal with actors. Hall's confidence in his cultural authority was waning. In short, he was proposing to free Shakespeare from a prison he had created. The conceit was a direct reference to a book that influenced Hall's future work (although it was in turn inspired by Hall's work). *Free Shakespeare* by John Russell Brown was published in 1974. Brown helped to shape Hall's thinking about Shakespeare; he was impressed enough with Brown to hire him as Associate Director (Scripts), a role Brown held until Hall stepped down in 1988 when all the Associate Directors were asked to tender their resignations. Many critics regard *Free Shakespeare* as a rejection of directorial theatre and a clarion call for productions free of interpretation. 'Directors are not only organisers and interpreters,' Brown complained, 'they are also manufacturers and salesmen' (Brown 1974: 11). However, Brown did not reject interpretation – on the contrary, he revelled in it. It is possible, he reflected, that 'our Shakespeare may not be modern enough' (Brown 1974: 8). For Brown, productions frequently lost the creative energy found in the rehearsal room, which was an experience with which Hall could identify. Brown imagined a theatre where the creative exploration of the actors does not end in the rehearsal room but continues into performances, with audiences joining in the process of creating and recreating the play: this would be, Brown imagined, 'a theatre of ... endless originality' (Brown 1974: 111). He did not reject interpretation then but resisted the idea that interpretation ends when the curtain rises on the first performance.

Hall's ideas were moving in the same direction, shaped by his difficulties with *The Tempest*, with which he had ultimately been unsatisfied. He had lunch with Brown during this time and talked openly about his struggles. Hall concluded that he had been 'too didactic, not freely creative enough' (Hall 1983: 81). *Free Shakespeare* gave Hall an academic justification for moving into a more austere, text-focused style. The operatic excesses of *The Tempest* had gone too far. Hall's next Shakespeare, *Hamlet*, stripped the stage back to its most essential elements, mixing Brown and Pinter to create a strikingly different theatrical aesthetic that was perhaps more in keeping with 1970s austerity than the flamboyant spectacle of *The Tempest*. Hall's views on theatre and text were changing: with *Hamlet*, he began a path towards textual fundamentalism which would shape his future work and appal many who saw its early fruits. This time, he wanted to play a 'full' text. Hall worked with Brown to prepare a script based on a combination of the Folio and Quarto editions, with much of the punctuation edited out. In his diaries and autobiography, Hall gives the impression that he more or less woke up one morning seized with the sudden ambition to direct *Hamlet* again, but minutes of the Associate Directors meetings show that plans for a new production of the play were frequently discussed. At one point, Blakemore was set to direct, but Hall was taken by an unambitious and probably unworkable plan put forward by Brown for a more workshop approach in which *Hamlet* would be a never-ending production with a succession of directors and actors. This would have exemplified Brown's vision of a production which captured the creative energy of rehearsal. Although the plan was never enacted, *Hamlet* is the first production of Hall's which shows Brown's influence – and, as Hall's diaries show, rehearsals do seem to have been more rewarding for Hall than the production itself.

Brown had been particularly critical of what he called 'too assertive décor', and as an illustration of such overly determined design work, he had used Bury's set for the 1967 *Macbeth* (Brown 1974: 82). *The Tempest*'s elaborate spectacle may have had a political point, but its ostentatiousness was out of step with audiences enduring inflation and austerity. Although the 'three-day week' had ended, the political and economic crisis continued through 1975. Hall responded to Brown and to the times with a *Hamlet* that was bare to the point of severity. Bury's set was a largely unadorned stage, its black austerity offset only by a circle in the middle which became a focus for action. In some respects, this was a typical Hall-Bury stage set, with the circle recalling the sandpit from his *Troilus and Cressida* and the revolve from *The Two Gentlemen of Verona*. The circle stripped these ideas back to their basic form, but the principle remained the same, giving Hall the flexibility to move between enclosed and vast spaces. It captured the claustrophobia of Elsinore castle with a sense of the dark, strange world beyond, the void from which the ghost emerges and to which Hamlet addressed his metaphysical questions in frantic tones. Perspective lines crossed the stage, radiating from the back to carve the circle up, suggesting both a renaissance vanishing point and a sense of entrapment, like prison bars drawn on the floor. The only call back to Hall and Bury's political theatre of the 1960s was an imposing grey wall, apparently made of slate, with a large, arched door which only opened when the action moved outside the castle. The wall was also the backdrop for *The Mousetrap*, which was played on a rostrum tilted towards the audience, the court facing the back of the stage and fanned out in symmetry with the onstage lines.

Hall's first production of *Hamlet* had engaged with a young generation: this, by contrast, was a *Hamlet* of old men 'generally standing about in attitudes of shock' (*Spectator* 20 December 1975). Horatio was played as an ageing academic by

Philip Locke, grey-haired and bespectacled, more likely to be Hamlet's tutor than a fellow student. Albert Finney, as Hamlet, was nearly forty and even Susan Fleetwood, playing Ophelia, was in her thirties: *The Spectator* described her as a 'robustly hefty girl' (20 December 1975), an unkind review which nevertheless pointed to the fact that Hall was not reaching for a stereotypical, pre-Raphaelite Ophelia. She was, as the *New York Times* put it, 'a tough, straightforward woman': when she lost her mind, she cut off her hair and sang her mad, wild song barefoot and wearing only 'a dirty chemise' (24 December 1975). Nothing about the production suggested youth: this was a middle-aged man's *Hamlet*, confronting mortality and decay not with the reflective melancholy of an undergraduate, but with the frustrated rage of a theatrical mid-life crisis. Mortality intruded in different ways. In rehearsal, the cast spent a day with a real skull as Yorick. Angela Lansbury (Gertrude) lost her mother, causing her to break down during rehearsals and then, just before the first preview, Finney learnt that his father had passed away. He struggled with grief through his first performances (Hall 1983: 196); Hall later urged Finney to 'go the whole way in the first part in rawness and pain' (Hall 1983: 198).

Finney's intense, psychological scarred and edgy Hamlet was a vivid contrast to Warner's quiet student rebel. The political context shaped this interpretation. Finney's Hamlet was a caustic critic of political corruption, and when Marcellus mused that there was 'something rotten' in the state, the production summoned the spectre of Watergate. In 1965, Hall had positioned *Hamlet* as a play about generational apathy; Finney, by contrast, was a radical activist constantly on the edge of violence. Denis Quilley brought a 'Nixonian delight' to the part of Claudius (*Guardian* 11 December 1975). Hall raced his actors through the lines, scenes overlapping each other at 'headlong speed' (*Telegraph* 11 December 1975) so that, even though the production was using an uncut text, the running time was shorter than Hall's 1965 *Hamlet*. Finney approached the part with tremendous energy, giving a vigorous performance which surprised (and appalled) many critics more used to reflective princes. After meeting the Ghost, Hamlet hit his head repeatedly with the back of his hand as if trying to beat the doubts out of his mind. For 'to be or not to be', Finney charged through the quiet, sombre ghosts of Olivier and Gielgud by sprinting onto the stage wearing a Samurai headband and wielding a dagger through a frantic delivery of the speech as if Hamlet was about to kill himself. In another soliloquy, he closed his fists and boxed the air angrily (*New York Times* 28 December 1975). Finney held Yorick's skull as high as he could and stared at it 'fiercely' (*Telegraph* 11 December 1975). He spoke with his own Lancashire accent: *The Spectator* sniffed at his 'aggressive, regional rasp', thinking it unprincely and mistaking it for a Scottish accent (20 September 1975). Some reviewers commented on Finney's lack of royal bearing: the *New York Times* described him as 'mature, tousled and forcefully unpoetic' (24 December 1975). His hair was unruly, and he grew a short beard to give Hamlet the look of a wildman. His costume was black, save for a dirty white shirt. Later he wore simple hessian robes 'like an out-of-work farm labourer' (*Telegraph* 11 December 1975). Finney's performance energized Hall, and his account of the rehearsals in his *Diaries* is his most detailed and compelling record of directing a Shakespeare play. Hall and Finney created a performance which was 'undecorated and uncomfortable' (Fay 1995: 248). For Billington, the work was a success: 'I have never seen such a totally satisfying blend of actor and concept,' he wrote in *The Guardian*, adding that the production restored 'Finney to the front-rank of heroic performers' (11 December 1975). Robert Cushman thought Finney was 'exhilarating' (*Observer* 8 February 1976).

The press night performance was rough around the edges, with many of the actors missing lines and ad-libbing their own words throughout the performance (*Times* 2 January 1975): reviewers expecting a masterwork had to work hard to talk Hall up, while those looking for him to fail saw their opportunity (for more on the production and its reception, see David 1978 and Shaughnessy 2018). The frantic pace of rehearsals and the impact of the deaths of Finney's and Lansbury's parents took its toll, Hall noting 'signs of revolt' two days before the opening night, when his cast protested, 'are we not to get any time off?' (Hall 1983: 198). Hall himself was proud of the work: '[t]his is the closest I have reached to the heart of a Shakespeare play in my own estimation,' he said after the first preview: 'it is the production which over the last fifteen years has the least gap between my hopes and the facts on the stage' (Hall 1983: 199). However, this enthusiasm dampened as the production moved in to one of the new auditoriums in the South Bank complex, the mid-sized proscenium arch theatre the Lyttelton (named after Oliver Lyttelton, an early campaigner for a national theatre) because the main theatre, the Olivier, was not yet ready. Although Hall finally had a production of his own on the South Bank, the transfer was beset by difficulties and trailed bad reviews. 'I have a sense of morbid disappointment,' he told his diary three months later; '*Hamlet* will never be seen as I meant it' (Hall 1983: 218). Bernard Levin made a fair judgement when he called Finney's performance 'a sketch for a portrait, not a finished performance' (*Times* 2 January 1975). Reflecting on the experience, Hall echoed Brown's critique when he complained that 'what the critics have grown used to in this country ... is a simplistic theory grafted on each production' (Hall 1983: 239).

Macbeth 1978 and *Othello* 1980

The political landscape internally and externally continued to be tumultuous through the rest of the decade. Hall's diaries give a sense of the broader political landscape, which was tilting away from the world in which Hall had made his career. The rise of Margaret Thatcher as leader of the opposition party and then as prime minister in 1979 was a decisive moment in British political history, which led to the widespread privatization of public services. Hall voted for her in 1979, something he would later regret but, as his diary entries from this month show, he was conflicted and still unsure how he would vote on the eve of the election (Hall 1983: 434). He voted, he wrote, for change. Strikes across the public services had reached a high point in 1978, which the press named (in Shakespearean fashion) the 'winter of discontent'. Hall had his own problems as National Theatre workers also took to the picket lines: strike action dogged his tenure at the National. The times were as ripe as they ever had been for the brand of political Shakespeare which Hall had pioneered in the 1960s, but the two productions Hall directed in these years, *Macbeth* and *Othello*, are among his least distinguished works. *Macbeth* received (as Hall himself recalls) some of the worst notices of his career (Hall 1983: 356) and *Othello* is the only one of his National productions of Shakespeare that Hall ignores in his autobiography. Hall distanced himself from the plays even as he was directing them. Neither were plays that he had chosen or wanted to do, yet they could hardly be more apt at a time of simmering revolution, festering relations between the public and its leaders, and the emergence of virulent individualism triumphing over decaying political structures.

Macbeth exemplified Brown's vision of performance as a continuous process of discovery, an actor's Shakespeare rather than a director's. Hall was so invested in *Free Shakespeare* that he even gave Brown a co-directing credit, although Brown later described himself as the assistant director (Brown 1982a: 1). They spent 'hard, sweating' days in rehearsal (Hall 1983: 351), disciplining actors to focus on interpreting the text, which was once again virtually uncut. Hall told his cast that he was now 'militantly classic' (Hall 1983: 356), his belief in the text absolute. Authority was displaced onto the text: all meaning, all discoveries, had to be rooted in an exploration of Shakespeare's words. Geoffrey Wheatcroft saw Brown as the main force behind the production and decried the 'dead hand of theory' which he brought to the play (*Spectator* 17 June 1978); Nicholas de Jongh called Brown Hall's 'eminence grise' or, rather unkindly, his 'Fourth witch' (*Guardian* 7 August 1978). In a sense, Hall's crisis of authority at the National, which was a microcosm of the wider political and social crisis gripping the country, was deflected by this insistent, unapologetic turn towards textual reverence. Yet this *Macbeth* was significantly different from his 1967 production: there was no sense of spiritual crisis governing the production, none of 1967's religious imagery that Brown cited as an example of contemporary Shakespearean excess (Brown 1974: 35). This *Macbeth* was about political crisis, not religious doubt, with Finney playing an isolated Macbeth, more apart from the events of the play-world than Scofield had been.

Hall juxtaposed Macbeth's story, played in a small circle in the middle of the vast Olivier stage, with epic spectacle, giving a sense of the way in which the claustrophobic chamber drama was part of a bigger national story. The Olivier stage was bare, a black void with spaces divided by a black curtain and a brick wall at the rear. Spectacle was created instead by arrangements of the actors into pictorial 'pageants' of crowds and armies which reminded de Jongh more of Verdi's *Macbeth* than Shakespeare's (*Guardian* 7 June 1978). Hall and Bury could be extravagantly literal – when Duncan entered Macbeth's castle, plates of 'steaming meats' were carried across the stage by a bustling crowd of servants (*Times* 7 June 1978). The banquet scene was 'lavish', Banquo's ghost appeared with a 'clot of blood' on his head to terrify the already frantic Macbeth (*Times* 7 June 1978). Most remarkably, in the witches' final scene, a massive, hissing cauldron emerged in the middle of the stage out of which arose the various ghosts summoned by the witches, including the eight kings who passed 'like some royal parade' (*Guardian* 7 June 1978) to a 'vast army' of extras (*Times* 7 June 1978). What could have been a highly topical tension between the personal and the political, between the individual and society, between self-determinism and historical destiny, simply confused critics, who were unsure of what to make of the production's odd blend of austere staging and rich spectacle. De Jongh even managed to criticize the production for being too 'bare' and too 'pictorial' in the same review (*Guardian* 7 June 1978).

Macbeth was an impotent figure of authority: each of his attempts to dominate the world around him only isolated him further. Finney's Macbeth was a 'troubled and trapped figure' who seemed as impressionable and vulnerable as a scared child who fell into the 'warm embrace' of Lady Macbeth (Dorothy Tutin) like a 'little boy' (*Country Life* 13 July 1978). He wore a red doublet with puffed up sleeves and a huge, open collar that exaggerated his bulk and had the odd effect of making Finney's head look small, the collar obliterating his neck. He looked like a man trapped in his outfit, hiding from himself. The red of his costume matched the colour of the blood on his hands after murdering Duncan, as if Macbeth was covered in blood. His soliloquies were all addressed directly to the audience, as if Macbeth could step outside the play-world like an Iago or Gloucester, so detaching him from the main action for speeches marked by 'slow, bewildered introspection' (*Guardian* 7 June 1978). In other scenes, he rolled his eyes and roamed about the stage 'fretfully' like a man already on the brink of madness before meeting the witches (*Telegraph* 7 June 1978). By his last soliloquy, Finney's voice was hoarse, as if Macbeth were exhausted and lost, his face convulsed by 'a mass of nervous twitches' (*Times* 7 June 1978). Tutin, by contrast, was 'cool and calculating'; she dominated the banquet scene with 'magnificent authority', quivering with 'sensuous excitement' (*Country Life* 13 July 1978). Her maternal authority over Macbeth was mixed with a sense of 'erotic domination' (*Guardian* 7 June 1978). However, her sense of power, both erotic and political, also broke into sudden anguish, in her final scene, she wrung her hands 'frenetically' (*Times* 7 June 1978).

If *Macbeth* became a play about the impotence of power, Hall's next production, *Othello* (1980) was more directly and literally about impotence, this time that sense of crisis transferring from the body politic to the sensual body. Hall had been planning an *Othello* since at least 1974, as he records discussing it with Paul Scofield in his diaries (Hall 1983:

110) and the play is listed as a planned work in the regular updates supplied to the Associate Directors for their meetings throughout the 1970s. The rationale was a simple one: Hall desperately wanted Scofield at the National Theatre and to entice him, Hall and Brown devised a list of plays they thought likely to interest him. *Othello* was among them, and Scofield chose it: having recorded the part for radio (O'Connor 2002: 298), Scofield said that he 'felt ready for *Othello*' (O'Connor 2002: 294). If Scofield and Hall had produced it in 1975, it might have been better remembered: by 1980, the idea of a white man blacking up to play Othello was already looking dated, and Scofield was one of the last white actors to play the part on a major British stage. In *The Guardian* that year, Polly Toynbee castigated the National and the theatre establishment for its lack of black representation: writing about Scofield's Othello, she thought there was 'something perverse, and offensive about a blacked-up white, rolling his eyeballs, beating his breast and pretending to a grand black passion' (*Guardian* 3 November 1980). The souvenir programme reflected the National's lack of sensitivity to race issues, as its brief account of the play's performance history described Paul Robeson as 'the Negro actor' (a term that had been problematic for at least a decade). Scofield had once said that Othello's colour 'was not important' (*Guardian* 26 August 1972) and he downplayed it in his performance, giving an unusually tender reading of the character before raging with savage jealousy. His colour seemed to vary, as one review remarked that he had only a 'light dusky tan' (*Times* 24 March 1980), but the production photographs show him properly blacked up with, as Arthur Holmberg puts it, 'a ludicrously grimy visage set off by equally ludicrous red lips' (Holmberg 1981: 259).

The production had other problems: it was slow and stately, where audiences were used to over-wrought, highly charged *Othello*s, and Othello and Iago lacked the right chemistry for the production to succeed. Michael Bryant played an older, white-haired Iago: he was 'drab, dour, realistic' and, worst of all, 'too honest' (O'Connor 2002: 299). O'Connor blames Hall for not being committed to the production, which followed *Amadeus*, one of the biggest hits of Hall's career. At the National, Scofield had played Salieri, a lead part written with more than a hint of Iago, but chose to play Othello rather than take the performance to Broadway. American union rules prevented Hall from taking most of his cast with him, so he had to spend a lot of the year in New York auditioning new actors and rehearsing the production from scratch (Fay 1995: 275). Hall was, O'Connor argues, too distracted by *Amadeus* to give Scofield's performance his full attention: the production lacked the 'hunger for success' which it needed (O'Connor 2002: 298).

Scofield played a subdued, impotent Othello in a theatre defanged by Hall's militant commitment to the stripped-down aesthetic of 'free Shakespeare' so that the National itself seemed to be exemplifying its sense of powerlessness in a political environment increasingly hostile to publicly funded arts. Hall dispensed with spectacle entirely, rendering impotent the vast, epic space of the Olivier. Gone were the pageants of actors and supernumeraries who had created a sense of a social world in *Hamlet* and *Macbeth*; there was no sense of context, of 'life-going-on-in-the-background' without which, Billington complained, Othello's raw emotion looked 'fairly ludicrous' (*Guardian* 21 March 1980). Bury's set was virtually bare save for a central archway representing a 'Jacobean porch' (*New York Times* 13 April 1980) and bits and pieces of furniture. Hall and Bury's signature large doorway stood in the middle before a rectangular playing area. There was a balcony above the doors and to suggest other locations, over-sized silhouettes were projected onto a back screen, sometimes the shadows of battlements or windows, other times just dark clouds swirling in lights. The world beyond the action of the stage was vague, diffuse, far away, with the playing space itself both empty and enclosed.

The bare stage reflected barrenness in the relationship between Othello and Desdemona (played by Felicity Kendal), which outwardly expressed itself as tender and chaste, Othello's inner anger severely repressed and only erupting into violence in the last part of the performance. He wore a short goatee beard, his upper lip shaved, and grey hair flecked his temples and fringe, his maturity visibly contrasting with Kendal's demure Desdemona. In military dress, he wore a ribbed black doublet and a black cape with a deep red inner lining. When relaxing, he wore a black jacket casually open – but the costumes were always black, tinged with blood red. In his early scenes, he strode about the stage confidently, 'irredeemably sane and gentlemanly' (Hankey 1987: 119–120), but perhaps too sane, too confident: there was 'already something ingenuous about him,' mused Benedict Nightingale, 'and perhaps a little complacent' (*New York Times* 13 April 1980). He had the 'right indigo voice', thought Billington (*Guardian* 21 March 1980), a 'deep, dark voice' that turned 'somersaults of disgust', as Nightingale put it: 'a gulp becomes a sickened grunt becomes half a cough, half a sneeze' (*New York Times* 13 April 1980). Holmberg thought Scofield strained too hard to 'keep his tones low'. In Act 4, decrying Cyprus' 'goats and monkeys', his body jerked, and he staggered off the stage (*New York Times* 13 April 1980). However, there were 'no fires, no torment' as Robert Cushman put it (*Observer* 23 March 1980). Scofield was, according to Cushman, 'sonorously somnolent', not so much angry as driven by a 'quiet pride' that looked inwardly with 'self-approbation', his movements and gestures after his fall into jealousy seemed 'studied' (*Observer* 23 March 1980).

Scofield and Kendal had already explored the territory of sexual abuse and power in *Amadeus* when Kendal played Constanza, Mozart's wife. In one of the pivotal scenes in *Amadeus*, Salieri pressurizes Constanza to sleep with him in return for using his influence to support her husband's flagging career. Now, as Othello and Desdemona, they played a different, more extended game. Kendal read Desdemona as a 'spirited, defiant, upper-class girl' who teased Othello (O'Connor 2002: 300). She wore green throughout, including a green gown with pearl cuffs and matching green gloves, and later a green heavy hooded robe, a gesture perhaps to the colour of jealousy. One scene also called for her to wear a black domino mask, the search for which particularly irritated Hall, who complained in a memo to Bury that the masks he had seen so far failed to highlight Kendal's mysterious eyes. Hall wanted to bring out something deeply exotic and sensual from Desdemona. By contrast, Othello treated Desdemona like a child, radiating a 'touching pride and delight in her', dealing with her gingerly as if she were a fragile possession. His reading of 'perdition catch my soul' was unusually tender: he was 'innocent', 'vulnerable' (*New York Times* 13 April 1980) and when he recounted his stories about his adventures, which had enchanted both Desdemona and her father, he did so in a knowing way, 'with a sense of irony and awareness of its exoticism' (*Globe and Mail* 8 April 1981). It was almost as if Hall had reversed the Salieri–Constanza relationship: Desdemona was sexually more confident, Othello distant. Salieri's attempt to rape Constanza was rooted in sexual frustration. As Othello, Scofield continued to develop a sense of the violence lurking beneath Othello's solicitous treatment of his young wife, his sexual impotence eventually emerging when he murdered her. He showed 'numb, gaping horror' in his facial expressions when Iago exposed his inner jealousy. At one point, Othello mimed putting cuckold's horns on his head. He only lost control when he slapped Desdemona hard on the face and then threw himself onto their bed 'like some insensate, angry child' (*Guardian* 21 March 1980).

In their final scene together, the bed was placed centre stage, low to the floor, its canopy obscuring the large doors. The lighting tightened on the bed as if enclosing the space with darkness. A single candle holder stage right suggested the fragility of light and the imminence of darkness. Rehearsal photos show how the actors used their sizes to emphasize both the violence and tenderness of the murder scene. Scofield knelt behind Kendal, her body curled into his, Scofield's large hands around her slight neck. In another photo, her head, either sleeping or dead, is cradled in his two hands from behind, a portrait of tenderness or violence, or both. The promptbook carefully notated how the murder was to be staged. Othello entered with a taper, which he took to the candle stand, then he crossed behind the bed and drew back the curtains to reveal Desdemona sleeping. As he mused 'Should I repent me', he turned to face Desdemona and then, on 'thy light relume', he went behind the bed, stooping over her on 'must wither'. He knelt, then rose again, crossing downstage left of the bed and keeping his distance from it, as if unable to face the bed and what it meant. He advanced towards the bed, telling Desdemona to think 'on thy sins'. Desperate, she reached her arms out to him, and as he crossed behind the bed once again, she started to weep. He pushed her back on to the bed at 'down strumpet', they struggled, and then he picked up a pillow and smothered her first, then on 'so so' throttled her. Later, realizing his error, Othello took a dagger from a crucifix he wore on a chain and stabbed himself in the back of the neck, then fell onto the bed, leant over Desdemona and kissed her as he died. The blocking made the bed the centre of Othello's movements, the focus of his internal drama, something which aroused fear and disgust that went beyond jealousy. His last speeches, when the totality of his tragic error became apparent to him, were delivered 'very simply and affectingly' (*Observer* 23 March 1980).

Othello and *Macbeth* were both staged against a backdrop of economic and political crisis. Superficially, neither production engaged with this context at all, yet both explored in different ways a sense of powerlessness, of being overwhelmed by history. During *Othello*'s run, unemployment soared, reaching two million for the first time since the 1930s. Meanwhile, inflation continued to rise, the economy shrank, and the new Conservative government started its project to roll back the state with significant cuts to public spending. The Arts Council budget was cut by 10 per cent (which, as Rosenthal points out, meant a 20 per cent cut in real terms) and Hall darkly warned his directors that they must work within limited resources otherwise 'the Iron Maiden [Margaret Thatcher] may be round from Westminster' (Rosenthal 2013: 318). Hall was right: there were testing times ahead for the National and the post-war subsidized arts.

4

Protest and Politics at the National Theatre

Hall did not direct another Shakespeare for four years. He had not been engaged with Shakespeare since *Hamlet*, but the gap had more to do with two epic projects which took up much of Hall's time and energy. In 1981, he directed Aeschylus's *Oresteia*, a trilogy of ancient Greek tragedies in a new translation by the Yorkshire poet Tony Harrison. Aeschylus's plays had never been professionally staged as a trilogy in England. As the Olivier was inspired by Greek amphitheatres, it was inevitable that Hall would put on Greek tragedies there – and he also took the production to Epidaurus. The plays tell the story of the emergence of a new social order from a period of war and civil conflict. The similarities with *The Wars of the Roses* would not have escaped Hall – here was another chance to make an epic statement about Britain after the war. With Harrison's translation, the *Oresteia* also became a way of exploring the experience of the Northern working class – the cast included Barrie Rutter, who would later found the Yorkshire theatre company Northern Broadsides. The cast was all-male and wore masks, an experience which fascinated Hall and led to him rethinking the nature of theatre and 'masks' (whether real or metaphorical). The NT had been so keen to extend Hall's contract that he could negotiate favourable terms that allowed him to pursue other projects and lessened some of the pressure at South Bank. This alienated some of his colleagues, particularly Harold Pinter, who resigned from the NT citing Hall's absence as the main cause. One of these projects was Benjamin Britten's *A Midsummer Night's Dream*, which Hall directed for the Glyndebourne Festival in 1981. This was as close as Hall got to Shakespeare in these years, as the libretto is almost entirely from Shakespeare's play, albeit much cut and in places rearranged. The production proved to be definitive and has been revived many times, most recently in 2016. The production was neither austere nor overly reverent to Shakespeare and in that sense marked the different paths Hall was taking in opera and theatre. Britten cut the first act, robbing Hall of his concept of the play as an entertainment for a wedding party; it was set mostly in a misty, moonlit forest designed by John Bury. The opera was an exquisite, moving spectacle, a nostalgic escape from the economic chill of the early 1980s. In 1983, Hall was invited to direct the centenary production of Wagner's *Ring* cycle at Bayreuth. Producing four operas over one summer exhausted Hall and drove him close to another nervous breakdown, again echoing his years working on *The Wars of the Roses*. Hall was under pressure at the National. He was an increasingly absentee director, taking on large projects (such as the *Ring* Cycle) which had little to do with his day job. He also enjoyed one of his biggest successes with *Amadeus*, which transferred to Broadway. There was little time for him to run a theatre or direct Shakespeare.

Through this time of Hall's personal artistic success and activity, the National was facing its most serious crisis yet. The spending cuts brought in by the Conservative government were being keenly felt, and labour relations at the National were as fraught as ever. Faced with funding cuts, Hall was forced to announce that the Cottesloe would be closed and 100 staff sacked if the government did not restore funding. At a press conference in 1984, he stood on a coffee table and dramatically threatened a 'day of reckoning'. After years of facing industrial action at the National, Hall had decided to join the picket line (Hall 1983: 334). Hall's day of reckoning was drawing closer. After a politically charged *Coriolanus*, a production which made a radical break in both style and quality from his earlier National Shakespeare productions, Hall hit his stride with *Antony and Cleopatra* in 1986, followed by a trilogy of late plays in 1988 which marked the end of his tenure at the National and laid the foundation for his subsequent work. As he grew more and more detached from the day-to-day running of the National, Hall matured as a theatre director and his productions in these years are among the best of his career.

Coriolanus 1984

As Robert Ormsby has argued, Hall's *Coriolanus* was framed by the funding crisis at the National which Hall believed, not without some foundation, was rooted in a political agenda against the subsidized arts. By the time that *Coriolanus* made its way to the Olivier stage, the Cottesloe had been rescued by a grant from the Greater London Council (GLC), the local authority in London which at the time was led by 'Red' Ken Livingstone, whose hard-left policies were so antithetical to the politics of Margaret Thatcher's government that she produced a white paper in 1983 calling for the GLC's abolition. The dispute between Thatcher and Livingstone continued through 1984, with Livingstone and his colleagues resigning in protest and then winning landslides in their re-election later in the year. This was all ripe material for a production of *Coriolanus*, a classic clash of tribunes and political elites. Hall was not shy about pitching the National into the middle of the struggle. *Coriolanus*'s theatre programme included two large announcements, on the first and last pages, which both read: 'The NT's Cottesloe Theatre, closed due to insufficient Arts Council subsidy, re-opens in the autumn thanks to a special GLC grant'. Hall had the text printed on plain, salmon-pink paper, so that it looked like a flyer for agitprop theatre. The page was an extraordinarily bold gesture of defiance to the government from the Director of the National Theatre, which, like Hall's theatrical press conference, showed a new militancy in Hall's approach to theatre and national culture. He mocked the Arts Council and gave implicit support to one of the government's most vocal and organized opponents.

Coriolanus was a smart choice of play for Hall to explore this cultural and historical moment, as it is about the relationship between power and the people. The programme cover was garish green and purple with a black and white image of Coriolanus (scribbled over in red ink) that was meant to recall the famous image of Che Guevara. The set, the last that Bury would design for one of Hall's Shakespeare productions, was dressed with ragged, fading posters from the recent Tribune election, contrasting with parts of the set apparently propped up with scaffolding and bearing warning notices, creating 'the sense of an ancient society in the last stages of deterioration and decay' (Bedford 1992: 30). One of the posters promoted the Democrazia Proletaria, an Italian socialist party that was prominent in the 1980s (Ormsby 2014: 144). In the opening scene, citizens held placards with slogans and sprayed graffiti on the main door, 'Corn at our own price': visually at least, this was Hall's most outwardly Brechtian production, a signal that he was returning to a more politically engaged, directorial Shakespeare.

The production stressed the political nature of the play by creating space onstage for members of the audience, who were included in the action at various times during the performance. Financial pressures had forced Hall to abandon the large number of extras in his early National productions, but he was determined to have a crowd on stage, and minutes of the Associate Directors from this time record Hall asking his associates for ideas about how to do this. His solution, to use members of the audience for his crowd, was both pragmatic and inspired, but it was derided by press reviewers, who thought the whole thing was a gimmick. None of them were given onstage seats, so there are no reviews based on what it was like to be onstage, immersed in the action. They mocked the spectacle of people in ordinary clothes 'in forlorn transit' between their seats and the stage, lamely chanting 'it shall be so' when directed to banish Coriolanus (played by Ian McKellen). Benedict Nightingale compared them to 'shoppers at a bargain counter' (*New York Times* 6 January 1985). The cast did not appreciate the innovation, and McKellen wrote to Hall at one point asking for the audience to be put back where they belong. Hall accused McKellen of 'undermining everything I think about the production' (McKellen 2003: n.p.). For McKellen, the audience was an absurd distraction which rarely responded to direction and occasionally missed the point altogether: the actor remembers being interrupted at the start of one soliloquy by a woman asking for his autograph (McKellen 2003: n.p.).

Surviving audio and photographs suggest that Hall's critics were exaggerating. The audience was seated close to the action on crumbling steps that deliberately echoed the ruins of Epidaurus, the amphitheatre on which the Olivier was modelled. The extra seats narrowed the playing space considerably, so the audience was always up close and involved in the action, sometimes coming onto the stage to fill out the crowd, and in one scene selected members were sat cross-legged around the sandpit as Coriolanus spoke to them. The blurring of audience and actor was unique in Hall's career, an early experiment in immersive theatre that we now take for granted. Hall wanted the onstage audience to be part of the debate and shape their view about Coriolanus and Rome's political crisis. As Kristina Bedford (who observed the rehearsals) recalls, Hall wanted to create and populate 'an arena for public debate' (Bedford 1992: 45).

The debate was set at the beginning of the performance when a leaflet was handed out to the stage audience which read, 'CITIZENS OF ROME: Caius Martius is chief enemy of the people. We want corn at our price. We are hungry for bread. The patrician storehouses are crammed with grain. LET US REVENGE THIS WITH OUR PIKES!' Hall originally intended to include the audience in eight scenes, including both riots and triumphs and Coriolanus' assassination, but once the previews began the audience involvement was reduced (Bedford 1992: 43).

Their involvement was limited and more carefully scripted than Hall originally intended: for Volumnia's triumph, Bedford recalls, all they had to do was stand and clap (Bedford 1992: 43). Despite resistance from inside and outside the production, Hall remained dogmatically committed to keeping a tenth of the audience onstage: it was the whole point of the production that the audience was embedded in the wider national debate.

Political comment radiated from the production: Volumnia reminded Ormsby of Thatcher's martial self-fashioning during the Falklands Crisis, and the 'mob' onstage recalled the Miners' Strike (Ormsby 2014: 143). Hall's point (and this is a rare work of Hall's which had a 'message') was that Britain was in the grip of political extremists on both sides: a radical, authoritarian right-wing government, facing down the militant left. For Billington, Hall exemplified the ideal of a national theatre by turning the Olivier into 'a public forum where the issues of our own time are being debated' (*Guardian* 17 December 1984). Reflecting on the production the following year, Billington recognized it as a direct comment 'on the Britain of the Coal Board closures: two powerful forces unable to communicate, with compromise first man down' (*Guardian* 24 September 1985). Roger Warren viewed the production as a comment, he wrote, on 'the state of Britain in the winter of 1984–85, reflecting a confrontation between intransigent leaders of the political left and right' (Warren 1986: 118). Irving Wardle, one of Hall's prickliest critics, appreciated that Hall had turned the Olivier into a 'debating chamber' but turned the issue back on Hall, seeing the confrontation between 'workers' tribunes and managerial patricians' as an allegory of the NT's recent history. As Ormsby points out, in many ways Hall's take on national politics was a direct reflection of his frustrations with the Arts Council: the 'crumbling amphitheatre steps' which the onstage audience sat on were an image of the damage being done to the theatre (Ormsby 2014: 140).

This national crisis pushed Hall to produce the most contemporary and eclectic Shakespeare production of his career. The set combined ancient Rome and modern fora for debate such as the United Nations (Bedford 1992: 30), and was dominated by massive, reversible doors at the back of the stage, which were the gold-studded gates of Rome but could be transformed into the blackened gates of Antium and Corioli (Bedford 1992: 30), serving both as a symbol of imperial power and shattered authority. Remarkably (and uniquely in Hall's career as a Shakespeare director), some of the actors wore modern dress. Hall had gestured towards modern fashions in his film *A Midsummer Night's Dream* (1969), but that was still rooted in a mostly traditional approach to costume. Now Hall abandoned his life-long, Poel-like commitment to sixteenth- and seventeenth-century costume with a costume aesthetic that mixed modern suits with Roman togas. The onstage audience may have pushed Hall to think about how they would blend in with Roman senators and plebeians, turning *Coriolanus* into an explicitly contemporary play in which ancient costumes were merely relics of a vacuous power structure. In battle, costumes were lost altogether as Romans and Volscians clashed nearly naked. Coriolanus fought with a sword and shield, wearing only a loin-cloth and streaked with blood. Aufidius entered after the battle, naked beneath a modern black trench coat over his shoulders, his body 'streaming with blood, still trailing his sword' (Ripley 1998: 327). There was blood throughout the production. Four red silk banners dropped from the ceiling as emblems of Roman power, with a fifth laid across the sandpit and through the door like a long streak of blood, connecting the symbology of authority with the violence of war. McKellen demanded more blood for his entrances: one of the production memos notes that several performances in, McKellen requested extra blood in the Front of House area so that he could make an entrance literally dripping with blood (memo from Janet Mayo to Jill Trevellick, 19 December 1984: the blood was kept in one of the theatre's toilets, stashed there after the audience had gone into the theatre and cleared away before the interval).

Greg Hicks, who played Aufidius, had been one of the near-naked actors in Howard Brenton's controversial play *The Romans in Britain* at the National in 1979, for which the director Michael Bogdanov ended up in court accused of gross indecency in 1982. The overall look of *Coriolanus* recalled that production's mix of Roman uniforms and naked bodies: the homoeroticism that was overt in Bogdanov's production became an implicit part of Hall's *Coriolanus*. Coriolanus first appeared above the gates of Rome in a dapper white suit with a blue tie and shirt, a sheathed sword lazily balanced across his neck, moodily addressing the onstage audience, acting as 'the mob'. McKellen did not seek depth in Coriolanus; instead he drew out of the character his sardonic humour, his physical agility, his arrogance and, as Billington put it, his 'high-chinned condescension' (*Guardian* 17 December 1984). When making his reluctant plea for the popular vote, he stood on a stool, wearing his gown of humility and a floppy hat: later, he was found in beggar's clothes, 'a vagrant in a dirty raincoat' as Warren put it (Warren 1986: 118), still wearing the same hat. Coriolanus is always a very physical role, but McKellen pushed this as far as he could. When the Aediles attempted to arrest Martius, he grabbed two of them around the neck and used them as a battering ram to escape (*Guardian* 17 December 1984). In one of the defining images of the production, he stood on another soldier's shoulder to hear the onstage audience cry 'make you a sword of me?' (1.6.76).

This was a Coriolanus who was, as Wardle observed, 'the hero as political outsider' (*Times* 17 December 1984). He spoke with something close to his native Lancashire accent, which Nightingale described as 'stretched-out vowels' that 'melodiously throb, then soar or swoop into little cadenzas all their own' (*New York Times* 6 January 1985). At times, he was diffident, indifferent to the plebeians, or at best cuttingly sarcastic, but when he became enraged, as John Barber noted, he shouted, 'teeth vulpine, with lungs like a smithy bellows serving a voice like a battle clarion'. After being banished, he denounced Rome quietly, 'hands in pockets, with a disgust beyond all rage' (*Telegraph* 17 December 1984). He dashed off long speeches with 'arrogant ease' but he 'shook with rage' (Warren 1986: 119) when he told his mother 'I am going to the marketplace' (3.2.131).

For McKellen, Coriolanus' relationship with Aufidius was crucial to the role. McKellen had played Aufidius in 1963, directed by Tyrone Guthrie in a production which explicitly brought out the homoeroticism of their fights. Hall left it to McKellen and Hicks to work out the nature of their relationship. They did not go as far as Guthrie had done in foregrounding the sexual nature of their fight, but it was heavily implied, both being near-naked in their main encounter. McKellen described this as a ' remnant from Tyrone Guthrie' (Friedman 2015: 399). Martius strode around the sandpit as they fought, always proud and in control, relentlessly hacking at his opponent who crouched in the sandpit as the pitiless blows continued. If there was sexuality in the relationship, it was characterized by domination: Coriolanus came alive in battle, exulted in his blood-streaked torso. McKellen and Hicks worked to bring out the subtlety of their relationship in their embrace in Act 4, Scene 5, improvising different versions through rehearsals and repeatedly changing it in performance. Bedford recalls that in their first attempt to play the scene, Aufidius' response to Coriolanus' offer of his throat was 'almost sexual'. In early performances, Coriolanus knelt first, and Aufidius put his arms around his enemy from behind, helping him to his feet: by the end of the run, Aufidius strode around Coriolanus, gazing at him in 'exultation' before offering his arms in friendship (Bedford 1992: 117). The original staging was sensual and affectionate, now it was simply a comradely embrace: 'I think it's better if you simply work on Coriolanus's sense of Aufidius – and he never stops thinking about him all the way through the play,' he told Bedford, adding, 'It's at the centre of the play; you don't have to push it' (Bedford 1992: 141).

The production reached its climax with Volumnia's desperate plea to her son to hold back his invasion of Rome. Volumnia, played by Irene Worth, began by prostrating herself in the sand and then stood between Coriolanus and Aufidius, 'the two rivals staring at each other across her' (Warren 1986: 119) and made her point with an angry force that played against the text. With Coriolanus apparently unmoved, she turned as if about to walk away in anger, when Coriolanus snatched her hand and 'held her by force amid a prolonged, tense, electric silence' (Warren 1986: 119) which he held 'for an eternity' as if 'aware that he is signing his own death-warrant' (*Guardian* 17 December 1984). For McKellen, it was the sight of his son that swayed Coriolanus: 'the future of the play is in the little boy' (Bedford 1992: 144). Hall wanted Coriolanus' final moments to be swift and brutal. Olivier had been held upside down by his murderers; McKellen was instead surrounded and shot. As he said, 'Cut me to pieces' (5.6.111), Coriolanus stripped off his Volscian clothes, returning to the semi-naked 'primitive warrior' of his prime (Bedford 1992: 135). The crowd threw sand at him and pointed at him 'in a gesture of threatening accusation' (Bedford 1992: 135). He drew his sword, desperate and furious, and then ran at Aufidius. In the original staging, blocked by fight director Malcolm Ranson, he was killed with several knives, the last cutting his spine so that his head sagged forward and he fell to the stage 'like a broken puppet' (Bedford 1992: 136). Hall changed this, following a suggestion from McKellen, so that Coriolanus was gunned down before he reached Aufidius, who came down and stood on his enemy's corpse in a final gesture of triumph (Bedford 1992: 136).

Coriolanus is a unique work in Hall's career, and it was a pivotal one too. Although he had a reputation for discovering political Shakespeare in the theatre, this was one of the few times that Hall used Shakespeare to make a very specific political point. He never again indulged in audience participation for Shakespeare, keeping the audience firmly in their seats in his subsequent productions. Hall makes very little of the production in his memoirs, as if not sure what to make of this oddity, but *Coriolanus* electrified critics at the time and restored Hall's reputation as a front-rank director of Shakespeare. For Billington, the production was not just Hall's best work, but 'the best Shakespeare production to emerge from the National in its 21 years' (*Guardian* 17 December 1984);

Barber agreed that it was 'one of the National's outstanding achievements' and even Wardle, Hall's sharpest critic, praised the production's 'joyous, blood-soaked carnage' (*Times* 17 December 1984).

Antony and Cleopatra 1986

Despite this return to form, Hall stayed away from Shakespeare for another three years. He was becoming an increasingly absent director, and of the seven productions he directed in 1985 and 1986, less than half were for the National. In 1986, a scurrilous story in *The Sunday Times* questioned his financial probity, effectively accusing him of using the National to make himself rich. In this context, his next Shakespeare production, *Antony and Cleopatra* with Judi Dench and Anthony Hopkins, was fitting. Hall was becoming Antony, an absent commander facing charges of corruption overseas. The rehearsals for *Antony and Cleopatra* coincided with a suitably epoch-making event: the day after the first rehearsal, Hall's resignation from the National was formally announced (Lowen 1990: xiv). Once again, controversies and politics in the external world seemed uncannily appropriate to the dramas that the company was exploring in the rehearsal room. Hall may not have been a great soldier seduced by glamour and wealth, or a capricious queen who artfully manipulated those around her for own personal and political purposes, but aspects of Hall's public persona inescapably hung around the production as the company dug into one of Shakespeare's longest plays.

Hall had found a play with an epic vision to match the Olivier and his concept of the National Theatre. The *Los Angeles Times* hailed it as his best work since the 1960s (13 June 1987). The grandness of the production was evident at every level. The production was long – in its previews, it stretched to five hours and even on the press night it was running at four hours, with many reviewers complaining that it dragged.

Hall set the play in a sumptuous Renaissance world. He was resolute that the play was about the classical era as a Jacobean would have conceived it (Lowen 1990: xiv). His designer Alison Chitty promised that she would make sure that there was 'not a bare knee or snake headdress in sight' (Lowen 1990: xiv). The dominant tones of the production were red and burnished gold, seemingly representing passion and wealth. The programme reproduced Paolo Veronese's *Mars and Venus Bound by Cupid* (also known as *Mars and Venus United by Love*) in sepia (Lowen 1990: 48) at Hall's suggestion. Hall was inspired by a reference in Harley Granville-Barker's preface to *Antony and Cleopatra* in which he used Veronese's paintings to illustrate 'how Shakespeare saw his Roman figures habited' (Lowen 1990: 170). He may also have remembered Jonathan Miller's 1981 television version of the play for the BBC Shakespeare series, as Miller also took inspiration from Veronese. Lowen believes that this painting was the foundation for the production concept and costume designs (Lowen 1990: 170). The painting, usually dated to the 1570s, shows Mars bearded and dressed in a cream gold suit with Roman-style sleeves and a pinkish-red cloak falling from his shoulder. He is kneeling by Venus, who is naked and expressing milk from her breast. Hall and Chitty brought this mix of classicism and romanticized medievalism to the sets and costumes, taking the reds and golds out of Veronese and weaving them through the production. Dench wore gold and cream robes, whose hue echoed that of Mars' suit, and plain gold bands and necklaces; the simplicity of both was offset by her long, auburn curls which were bound in some scenes by a gold circlet. This mixture of the plain and the exotic, the controlled and the uncontainable, was a brilliant foundation for Dench's extraordinary performance. Hopkins was, like Veronese's Mars, bearded; he wore a simple red suit which took its colour from Dench's wig and Mars' cloak. The set's floor and walls were also dusty cream and gold and seemed to blur into each other. The boundary of stage and audience was repeatedly tested, with Roman soldiers marching onto the stage through the auditorium, as if the audience was itself a Roman colony, a part of Antony and Cleopatra's – and Hall's – epic world.

The stage's homogeneity allowed Hall to explore Rome and Egypt's continuities. The characters talked obsessively about their differences, but in Hall's vision, they emerged as similar places with differing dynamics. Both were intensely political – in Egypt politics was played through passion and games; in Rome, it was through families. Antony and Enobarbus' tragedy was that they saw Egypt as a refuge from politics, but Cleopatra emerged as the most political animal of them all, her life a constant positioning, or resisting being positioned, until the end. It is tempting to see echoes of Hall's institutional history in this. Hall was neither the ever-changing Cleopatra using all her wiles to stay in the game nor a great man trading off past glories as Antony was, viewing the empire he had set up from the outside with jealousy and despair – but he was, like both, a survivor capable of surpassing his critics' expectations.

Antony and Cleopatra opened with an extravagant show, with Cleopatra walking Mardian like a dog tied to a rope, and Antony carried on Mardian's shoulders (Madelaine 1998: 122). From the beginning, Hall established the inherent theatricality of the affair between the Roman general and the Egyptian queen. Their banter was all performance, perhaps a performance to each other but a performance which needed an audience. Philo and Demetrius prefaced the show with an angry, bitter reading of the play's first lines, spitting with contempt about Cleopatra as a 'tawny front'. A trumpet heralded the show, exotic drums, and pipes played as the court sauntered in. The courtiers lazily enjoyed the display, but Antony and Cleopatra were lively. On the audio recording archived in the British Library, both Hopkins and Dench quickly lose their breath, with Dench moving so quickly around the stage that her voice fades in and out. As Cleopatra pursued (and eventually caught) Antony, those in the court laughed. Antony sometimes played, sometimes became very serious, as if to demonstrate the struggle between the casual freedom of the Egyptians and the weighty seriousness of the Romans. He whooped when Cleopatra captured him, but then his voice darkened for 'Let Rome in Tiber melt' (1.1.34) before returning to a more teasing tone as he chided his 'wrangling queen' (1.1.49) Nevertheless, there remained an undertow, a hint of the big questions that the lovers' games left unanswered. They quit the stage in haste, acting like teenagers, leaving behind a court too naively in love with life to pay attention to the ominous warnings from a soothsayer clearly out of place in this frivolous court.

For Hopkins, Antony was a man looking to escape the trap of his upbringing. One reviewer commented on Hopkins's 'broody mannerisms' which 'chillingly convey a soldier caught not merely in the web of amour but of time' (*Time Out* 24 April 1987). The *Daily Mail* thought him 'boozy and besotted' (24 April 1987), another reviewer complained that he was 'so consistently boisterous that he becomes a little tedious' (*Tribune* 24 April 1987). News of Fulvia's death ended his reverie, his performance quickly sobered, and when he promised that 'these strong Egyptian fetters I must break' (1.2.120) he did so with anger – at Cleopatra, at himself. He took the news quietly, pausing for a few seconds, loftily proclaiming, 'There's a great spirit gone' but provoked titters from his onstage audience when he started, 'She's good, being gone' (1.2.131).

The scene gave Dench an early opportunity to display how infinitely varied her Cleopatra could be. As Antony backed away, she was serious, sad, angry, her temper shifting with every line. She spoke of 'ancient folly' softly with a slow, controlled passion which exploded on the word 'water' before she sobbed, angrily, 'my death received will be'. Antony was unmoved, so Cleopatra turned back to a steady, controlled fury – she could summon passion and anger in ways which could manipulate most, but not Antony. As the *Sunday Telegraph* put it, she stalked around the stage like 'a famished cat' (26

April 1987). For *Time Out*, she was 'husky and somewhat bedraggled' and 'part-bitch, part-sadist, robust, horny and utterly beloved of her handmaidens' (24 April 1987). Dench sketched a Cleopatra who is restless, manipulative, playful, artful yet insecure and needing constant reassurance. Dench demonstrated her extraordinary range, running through a series of emotional states in just a few lines. She effortlessly moved from being strident and determined to being playful and then offended.

Their final scene together was remarkable. Antony was hoisted on a hammock rigged up to a pulley, which Cleopatra and her handmaidens desperately pulled on. Chitty designed the exterior of Cleopatra's tomb as a ruined fragment. It looked like a garden folly, with an imposing column on one side and the start of an old brick wall on the other. The monument was 20 feet high, and to descend it Cleopatra dropped into the arms of several actors below. The physical daring recalled Olivier's acrobatics at the end of Hall's *Coriolanus* thirty years before. Hall told Dench that in the last act Cleopatra should go into 'overdrive'. She had to find a 'fifth gear' for the character to take her through to the last scenes. For her final scene, Cleopatra was dressed in an extravagant gold robe over a blue dress, her red curls held tight at the top by a gold crown. Long sleeves with feather-like creases buried her body, entombed her in costume as if she was already more a legend than a person. She knelt to take the asp out of a wicker box, holding it firmly above her head. The opulence was a display both of Cleopatra's power and of the NT's resources as if Hall were trying to say: this is what a National theatre can do.

The late plays trilogy 1988

Hall's swansong was a trilogy of late plays performed by the same company over consecutive nights. Hall had significantly reduced the number of Shakespearean productions at the

National when he took over with one play at most staged per year, many of them directed by himself. By returning to a high concept, themed season with an ensemble company, Hall was also returning to the ambitions he had had in the late 1950s. This was the most 'RSC'-like season Hall had ever initiated on the South Bank and seemed to look back to his first 'early comedies' season when he took over the SMT. In that sense, the Late Plays season was not just a farewell to the National but a farewell to the RSC as well. Hall was laying down his staff, abjuring his magic: he would never again run a theatre as large or as significant as either the RSC or the NT. Hall, being Hall, was well-aware of the historic significance of the occasion and made himself available for two television documentaries (it is impossible to imagine any subsequent directors of either company generating the same level of public interest on their retirement). Michael Billington made *Peter Hall – Work in Progress* for Channel 4 and cameras were invited into the rehearsal rooms for a *South Bank Show* special. He also invited academics into rehearsals, producing a monograph (Roger Warren's *Staging Shakespeare's Late Plays* (1990)) and a detailed account of *The Winter's Tale* in Judith Dunbar's contribution to the *Shakespeare in Performance* book series. Hall had time for them all for, although he was technically still Director of the National Theatre, he had in practice already started handing over most of the work to his successor, Richard Eyre and his deputy David Aukin. As Eyre recalls in his diaries, Hall told Aukin that 'he no longer wants to be bothered with the details of running the NT, he's too involved in his productions' (Eyre 2003: 31).

As a trilogy, the season was a troubled elegy to Hall's tenure. Each play presented happy endings overshadowed by the cost of achieving them. As John Peter put it, the 'ending of all three plays is heavy with the ambiguity of penitence, of resignation, and of self-knowledge and salvation bought at a huge price'. Peter may have had Hall in mind when he described the common theme running through each play, which 'turns on a misjudgment by a king who abuses his authority' (*Sunday*

Times 22 May 1988). Hall himself noted that 'their partially happy endings are all achieved with effort and ambiguity' (*Daily Telegraph* 19 January 1988).

In an article written for *The Daily Telegraph*, Hall set out his rationale for bringing the three plays together: 'We do not necessarily improve with age', he wrote, 'for better or worse, we become more like ourselves ... It may be reassuring to think of Shakespeare saying farewell to his art through a gentle, forgiving Prospero ... But the facts are quite different.' Hall was in no mood for gentle forgiveness. His Prospero was a dark figure, as were all the authority figures in the trilogy. Hall believed that Shakespeare worked on the three plays at the same time. Although Hall thought them very different plays, he saw them occupying the same 'special world' where 'betrayal, jealousy, sexual insecurity and lust for power is purged, but only in part, by integrity, fidelity, penitence, and reconciliation'. He thought *The Tempest* the 'most searching of these plays' and the most ambiguous. He rejected 'nostalgia and regret' in late works and instead argued that they should be 'questing and restless creations, posing new questions with an urgency, even a rage'. He added: 'For time is short' (*Daily Telegraph* 19 January 1988). Hall was fifty-eight when he stepped down from the National Theatre role: apart from a brief interregnum in the early 1970s, he had been running theatre companies since his mid-twenties. Time was indeed short. In *The Mail on Sunday*, Kenneth Hurren dismissed the season as 'an ego trip' (22 May 1988). In a sense it was, in that the season was as much Hall's late work as Shakespeare's; Hall's restless ambition and showmanship were fully on display, but so was his discontent with modernity, his self-doubt and his powerful sense of irresolution at the end.

The trilogy was mired in controversy while still in rehearsal. For *Cymbeline* Hall had hired Sarah Miles to play Innogen (reflecting scholarly opinion, Hall chose to call her Innogen rather than Imogen (King 2005: 72)), but during rehearsals regretted his decision and asked her to leave the production. Miles had been a risk: although a successful actress, she had no recent experience of acting Shakespeare onstage. With only a month to go, Hall recast the part, hiring Geraldine James. Miles was a popular actress and, through her marriage to the playwright Robert Bolt, part of theatre's aristocracy. The story was run across the tabloids in the following days, with Miles' interview about the matter taking up two pages of the *Daily Mail* (Fay 1995: 337). Hall also faced accusations of nepotism in hiring his daughter Jennifer Hall to play Miranda in *The Tempest*. She left the production without explanation near the end of its run, leaving Hall 'embarrassed and angry' (Fay 1995: 337).

There were financial and technical problems. The stage machinery was expensive and unreliable; delays in putting the sets together led to the cancellation of five previews, and budgets for the costumes were out of control. The stage manager's reports for the trilogy, held in the National Theatre archives, show how frustrated the technical crew, as well as the actors, were with these ongoing issues with the machinery. Particularly problematic was machinery designed to 'flip' the centre stage, so that a sandpit could be transformed quickly into a grassy lawn. The equipment either failed or stalled repeatedly. On 23 July, towards the end of the Cottesloe run, the stage manager ran out of patience, writing, in angry capital letters in their report, that there was not enough time for complicated change overs. For the final performance of *The Tempest*, the production log noted the company's relief as the lights went down. Unusually for Hall, his productions were not popular with audiences, so much so that one report, in October, optimistically noted a larger audience than usual. In the end, the trilogy was 45 per cent over budget. Fay describes the impact on the theatre's finances as 'catastrophic'; Eyre, said he felt 'sick as a parrot' when he learnt how severe the deficit was (Fay 1995: 338).

Hall worked with Chitty again to produce lavish sets for each of the productions. They were initially performed in the Cottesloe, which Hall pointed out had similar dimensions to that of the Blackfriars stage on which the plays were most likely to have first been performed (*Daily Telegraph* 19 January 1988). Chitty and Hall set out to recreate a sense of Jacobean elegance. Above the stage, Chitty mounted a golden astrological disc which tilted during Time's speech in *The Winter's Tale* and opened in the middle so that Ariel, Juno and Iris could be lowered onto the stage in *The Tempest*. At the centre of the disc was the sun, with stars and planets connected to it on a grid which one critic described as a 'celestial dartboard' (Lewis 1990: 212). Below, Chitty put an 'earthly circle' (*Sunday Times* 22 May 1988) which enclosed a rocky landscape in *Cymbeline*, a village green in *The Winter's Tale* and a sandpit in *The Tempest*.

Cymbeline was not the disaster that Hall feared it might be. Rather than revive the fairy-tale world of his 1957 production, Hall now saw in the play a much darker and troubled world, a 'complex confrontation of virtue and vice' as Billington put it (*Guardian* 23 May 1988). Francis King in *The Sunday Telegraph* admired the 'stylized scenes of warfare' (22 May 1988). Tim Piggot-Smith's Iachimo was the stand-out performance for many critics. Piggot-Smith played him as an 'Italian arriviste' whose body moved 'with the ingratiating vulgarity of a gigolo still defining his pitch' (*Observer* 22 May 1988). James played Innogen without sentiment and deliberately explored the more difficult aspects of the character as a way of resisting the traditional version of the character (Bate, Rasmussen and Sharpe 2011: 165–166). Warren remembers that Posthumus cut eye-holes into the bloodstained cloth and wrapped it around his head 'like a guerrilla's balaclava'. At the end of the play, his face was 'not only caked in grime but streaming with blood, his own and other people's' (Warren 1990: 74).

In *The Winter's Tale*, Piggot-Smith played a Lear-like Leontes who was both violent and paranoid. He wore a deep red and green robe and held a long, gold candlestick, but the opulence of his dress contrasted with the tightness of his body; he was pale, his face shrunken with anger as he looked suspiciously over his shoulder, convinced he was being watched or laughed at. Christopher Edwards noted 'the look of vigilant disgust in his narrowed eyes' (*Spectator* 28 May 1988). John Peter thought his performance was 'merciless': 'His jealousy is a kind of brainstorm: the unhinging of a mind which had never felt the need for self-control' (*Sunday Times* 22 May 1988). As Billington put it, he 'almost reasons his way into madness' (*Guardian* 20 May 1988). Many of the photographs from the production show him with a greenish pallor as if he was ill. Piggot-Smith played Leontes as if he were suffering from a heart condition. He researched the symptoms of myocarditis, in which 'the inflammation of the heart results in a racing pulse, breathlessness, and feelings of intense weakness' (Warren 1990: 105). Sometimes he would clasp his heart, struck by a sudden, maddening pain.

The two halves of the play were linked by Time, who was 'bald, pallid and staggering beneath a hefty scythe' (*Listener* 26 May 1988), the sound of 'ticking and chiming of clocks' (Sound Plot IV 1–1) marking out a cacophony of time under his speech. Billington was impressed by the way Hall found an emotional unity between the play's two halves. Hall achieved this by darkening the scenes set in Bohemia, which was not a pastoral idyll but a 'Watteauesque *fête champêtre* with a violent, pagan undertow'. To bring out the earthy sexuality of these scenes, Hall introduced a fertility ritual with a satyrs' dance which Billington described as a 'primitive sex rite' (*Guardian* 20 May 1988). They were masked, bare-chested, bare-bottomed and adorned with phalluses. Ken Stott's Autolycus was a 'ruthless con man with shifty, red-rimmed eyes and a wolfish smile' (*Sunday Times* 22 May 1988). The detour into a chaotic, primal ritual culture turned back to a 'hypnotic sense of ritual' (*Listener* 26 May 1988) in the final scene. The statue of Hermione faced away from the audience so that the audience's attention was focused more on Leontes' reaction to her movement than on the miracle itself. For Peter, this conclusion was 'a surge of life darkly qualified by a sense of past wrong-doing which cannot be forgiven, only understood' (*Sunday Times* 22 May 1988).

The Tempest was Hall's most significant, and perhaps most personal, work in the season. As he prepared to break his staff and leave in a spirit of painful reconciliation, Hall could not have chosen a more appropriate character than Prospero to stand as his epitaph. The production opened with a deceptively low-key storm. Every word of Act 1, scene 1 could be heard, creating a 'stillness at the heart of it which makes Prospero's magic, for a moment, all the more eerie' (*Spectator* 28 May 1988). Hall might as well have played Prospero himself; he even cast his daughter as Miranda. However, this was no benign Prospero. If there was an element of Hall in the performance, it was the Machiavellian Hall of the tabloids. Billington described Prospero as 'a tyrannical Satanist' (*Guardian* 31 May 1988). Peter thought Michael Bryant's performance was one of the main achievements of the trilogy: 'there is nothing saintly about the exiled magus,' he wrote, 'he's tough, choleric and irascible. To have his enemies in his power gives him huge satisfaction; and his final forgiveness is the generosity of the strong' (*Sunday Times* 22 May 1988). Hall directed Bryant to play Prospero as a man driven by the need for revenge. Hall saw Prospero as an older version of Angelo from *Measure for Measure*, a 'terribly neurotic old man' (Lewis 1990: 211). He was a restless character, who was one minute angry, the next indignant. Hall wrote that Prospero 'restages his life in an anguished attempt to get control of it': the applause he begs at the end is so that the actor can be free of Prospero's despair (*Daily Telegraph* 19 January 1988). Lois Potter called Prospero's magic 'deeply sinful' (Potter 1992: 450).

Tony Haygarth played Caliban as a 'wild animal turned into a bitter slave' (*Sunday Times* 22 May 1998). He was dirty and covered with sores which oozed blood, and wore predatory, vampire-like teeth (Lewis 1990: 212). He was virtually naked apart from a rudimentary codpiece with a lock which one reviewer described as 'wicked-looking box' (*Listener* 26 May 1988); another wrote that his genitals were 'muzzled like a dog' (*Observer* 22 May 1988), a reference to Caliban's near-rape of Miranda. He was 'fierce, sensual, ecstatic' (*Observer* 22 May

1988). He looked like an animal, but his wounds looked like he had been flayed with a whip, and the box he wore over his genitals were there to contain his sexual urges. Caliban was more than a slave: Prospero had horrifically abused him. This violent image of a suppressed desire not only gave force to Caliban as a character but also added an extra undertow to his enslavement of Ferdinand (foppishly dressed to resemble Charles I). When Prospero said, 'this thing of darkness I acknowledge mine' (5.1.290), he referred to both Caliban as a character and the suffering which he had inflicted upon him.

With the Late Plays, Hall signed off from the National with as bold an artistic statement as he could make. He had begun his tenure at the Memorial Theatre with Shakespeare's earliest comedy, *The Two Gentlemen of Verona*, he had moved through the histories, and at the National he had tackled Shakespeare's greatest tragedies, leaving only *King Lear* for his old age. The Late Plays was a natural place for him to finish, but where audiences may have expected redemption, Hall offered only dark irresolution, twisted figures of authority who found no peace in the reconciliations at the end of each play. He had steered the National through a succession of crisis, and he emerged at the end with his reputation damaged by newspaper exposés, his artistic standing compromised by the enemies he made at the National. Throughout this period, Hall was keenly aware of the political and economic transformation of the country, the severe erosion of the political consensus about funding for the arts. The programmes for the Late Plays tell their own story. The programmes for its first run at the Cottesloe, when Hall was still Director of the National Theatre, were thin and printed on cheap paper. When they transferred to the Olivier that autumn, with Richard Eyre now in post, the programmes ballooned in size and quality, with most of the extra pages taken up with adverts and sponsorship notices. Without Hall, the National was ready to engage more creatively with the new economic situation: and Hall, without the National, was free to develop his style in his own way.

5

Death and Sexuality after the National Theatre

Critical accounts of Hall's theatre work typically stop at the point he left the NT. However, his post-National period spanned over twenty years and included a period of self-imposed artistic exile in America. Leaving the National was, to begin with, liberating. Without the burden of running a theatre, Hall was free to direct what he wanted, working furiously for most of the rest of his career, typically directing seven or eight productions a year. He was peripatetic, directing plays at different theatres and in different countries. He had his own company, the Peter Hall Company, which allowed Hall considerable artistic freedom but also meant he lacked the resources he used to enjoy. Over the same period, the political landscape changed significantly. When he left the National, the country was still led by Prime Minister Margaret Thatcher, whose monetarist policies and emphasis on individualism had done much to dismantle the public funding scaffold for the arts. The subsequent years included: the reinvention of the Labour Party under Tony Blair, whose election compelled Hall to briefly leave British theatre (discussed in Chapter 6); the terrorist attack on the World Trade Center followed by wars in Iraq and Afghanistan; the rise of the internet and many other historical and cultural events which were rich material for a director who never lost his commitment to sounding Shakespeare's contemporary resonance.

Although his post-National work was in many respects a more fragmented set of productions, harder to fashion into a narrative that suits a work of theatre history, there were several recurrent themes which showed Hall moving both forward and backward in his thinking about Shakespeare and his place in modern theatre. One was modern sexuality. Hall had always been interested in sexuality, and many of his productions pushed the edge of mainstream Shakespeare by exploring the physical sensuality of actors' bodies onstage, most notably his homoerotic *Coriolanus* (1984). Freed from the need to court government for subsidy, Hall could bring his musings on modern sexuality centre stage, starting with his *Merchant of Venice* (1989), which contrasted a passionate, thinly disguised relationship between Antonio and Bassanio with Bassanio and Portia's chilly, chaste love story. The AIDS crisis informed his *Hamlet* (1994), and the political scandal surrounding President Clinton was directly referenced in his US production of *Measure for Measure* (1999). Mortality and ageing also came to the surface. Death had been a presence in his work since his melancholic *Twelfth Night* (1958), a play which he revisted in 1991, but now those themes were personal. In productions such as *Hamlet* (1994), death and sexuality mixed in disturbing ways.

The Merchant of Venice 1989, Twelfth Night 1991 and All's Well That Ends Well 1992

Hall's first three Shakespeare productions from this period were all comedies of a sort, although they were dark comedies in which the political was subsumed in sexual desire, mortality, cruelty and violence. His late comedies season at the National had completed a career which had begun with Shakespeare's early comedies, but in the interim, he had directed mainly histories and the great tragedies. Hall's play choices showed that he was not looking for easy wins. Apart from a return to *Twelfth Night*, he opted for plays he had never directed before, both of which were problematic in their own way. With *The Merchant of Venice*, he had the ideal play for the Thatcherite decade, a play about the corrupting and destructive impact of merchant capitalism on love, friendship and society. He concluded this phase of his career with a troubled *All's Well That Ends Well*, his first 'problem' play since *Troilus and Cressida*, which in his hands became a twisted mirror of the times.

In 1989, Hall cast the film star Dustin Hoffman as Shylock in *The Merchant of Venice*, which was performed at the Phoenix Theatre in London's West End and later transferred to Broadway. The New York Public Library has in its archives a video of the production which I have used as the basis for most of my performance descriptions (reviews focused on Hoffman and have little to say about the production itself). Hall chose *Merchant* to suit Hoffman's strengths, but the play also suited the times. *Merchant* was a thoroughly unsympathetic portrait of Venice's merchant culture, with human beings reduced to commodities, love turned into an economic transaction, and the poor a silent presence. As Michael Billington observed in his review, it was 'money as much as passion' which drove the plot (*Guardian* 2 June 1989). The connection between Shakespeare's Venice and 1980s materialist Britain was palpable. The UK economy was booming, and a new wave of individualism was sweeping the country. Margaret Thatcher claimed the country was experiencing an 'economic miracle' but, if it was, the benefits were not being shared equally. The government's 1988 budget introduced significant tax cuts for the top 5 per cent of wage earners but neglected social policy (Seldon and Collings 2013: 84). Hall had direct experience of the modern underclass. Cardboard City, the country's largest community of homeless people, was located on the South Bank, not far from the National Theatre. Every day that he was working at the National, he would have seen the consequences of the economic boom on the most vulnerable people in society. Audiences for the National travelling from Waterloo train station had to walk by Cardboard City to get to the theatre. At its height, over 200 people slept rough there, warming themselves on fires in steel drums at night as audiences made their journey home. Hall may have been remembering this experience when he staged *The Merchant of Venice*. The production opened with a beggar slumped against a Roman column: one merchant tossed him a coin. When Antonio (Leigh Lawson) opened the play ruminating on his melancholy, and parading his riches, he did so ignoring the real poor sleeping in the arches behind him, a grim echo of Cardboard City on the stage. The set, designed by Chris Dyer, evoked a 'quintessential Italy' with pillars representing wealth and exoticism (*Guardian* 2 June 1989). Although not performed at the National, the production was haunted by the stark contrast between middle-class self-pity and grinding poverty on the National's doorstep.

Hall's Venice was brutal, self-serving and highly masculine: Portia would need to disguise herself as a man to have an influence in this world, which was so rooted in the sense of mercantile brotherhood that relationships with women were financial transactions. The most passionate relationship in the production was between Antonio and Bassanio (Nathaniel Parker), which Hall made clear was a highly physical one. On their first meeting, they hugged and shared a long kiss, and in the trial scene, Antonio was obsessed with Bassanio. With his shirt open ready to give up his 'pound of flesh', Antonio held Bassanio's hand and then tried to hug him, but was stopped by a guard. Antonio knelt again, and Bassanio put his hand tenderly on Antonio's shoulder, where it stayed through the next few speeches. It was a homoerotic gesture, and when Shylock said, 'these be the Christian husbands' (4.1.293), he looked right at them. Although Billington thought Antonio 'less the latent homosexual' in his review of the London premiere, this was not true of the archived Broadway performance (*Guardian* 2 June 1989).

By contrast, Portia's relationship with Bassanio was empty: she did not want money (*Guardian* 20 May 1988) but someone she could dominate. Geraldine James played Portia as a strong-willed woman who swept restlessly about the stage and massaged her servant's shoulders, a role reversal which showed her to be both impatient and in charge. She was in control throughout the Belmont scenes, unimpressed by the lavish spectacle of her first suitors, who declaimed the verses they found in the caskets, the Prince shouting his over an angry drumbeat. The mood was different for Bassanio, who was about ten years younger than Portia. A mournful fiddle scored Portia's song as he considered his choice; she then sat on a bench watching Bassanio throughout his soliloquy before he chose his casket. Portia seemed in control of the scene and led Bassanio to their first shy, cold kiss.

Shylock's role in this world was ambivalent: the other merchants, who saw him as less than human, physically abused him. If he touched them, they reacted with disgust, as if Shylock had contaminated them. In Act 1, Scene 3, when Shylock has most of the lines in the first part of the scene, the merchants ignored him most of the time, turning away so that Shylock had to push into their circle to continue his point. The fact that Antonio wanted money out of him did not mean that they treated Shylock with any dignity. When he said, 'those were Jacob's' (1.3.86), the merchants reacted with contempt. Shylock reminded Antonio that 'you spet on me on Wednesday last' (124): Antonio spat at Shylock again and then slapped him. Shylock wiped the spit away with a handkerchief: he was used to this abuse. Unlike the merchants, Shylock did not display his wealth through his costume: Hoffman wore a simple checked tunic and cloak with only a gold belt and a leather moneybag representing his wealth.

Shylock was listening in the dark shadows at the back of the stage when the 'news on the Rialto' (3.1.1) brought word of Antonio's lost ship. Insisting that 'my daughter is my flesh and blood' (34), he put his hands over his eyes, his raw emotion compelling Solanio to change the topic to Antonio's losses. Shylock paused here before redirecting his grief to anger: 'let him look to his bond' (43) he said slowly, darkly, fingering his handkerchief. The grieving, lost father was now cruel and resolute as if Shylock had found a way to cope with the loss of fatherhood by immersing himself in revenge against Antonio, and through him the world. Hoffman stretched the emotional range of the part as he ranted. 'Hath not a Jew eyes', he said, almost crying. 'If you prick us,' he said quietly, 'do we not bleed.' 'If you tickle us', he said wistfully. Then he paused, 'and if you wrong us,' he put his hand up and spoke firmly, 'shall we not revenge' (54–62). He continued in the same assertive tone: on 'it shall go hard' (67) he folded his arms to his body as if suddenly feeling the cold. Finally, Shylock covered his face with his hands as Solanio and Salerio backed away, frightened by Shylock's madness. When Tubal told Shylock that he could not find Jessica, Shylock sank to the floor, his face in his hands, then stood and hugged Tubal, crying as he lamented 'loss upon loss' (85).

At the start of the trial scene (4.1), Shylock sat on a block in the middle of the stage, sharpening a knife on the sole of his shoe and holding his bond. When he saw Antonio, he spat in his face, quick revenge for the abuse he suffered in his first scene. Shylock's moment did not last long: once Portia had pronounced her judgement and he realized he could not take his bond, Shylock knelt and asked for the bond to be paid thrice. Those onstage laughed at him. Shylock was once more the object of scorn and abuse. Portia took his knife and teased him with it, daring Shylock to take his pound of flesh. Shylock took it, hesitated, weighing up whether it would be worth his life to take his revenge, and then slammed the knife down. His anger turned inwards, Shylock put his hand over his mouth, then crossed his arms as if cold, hugged himself, paced the stage and begged for mercy. Gratiano (Michael Siberry) forcefully pushed Shylock to the floor so that he hit his head on the stage and Shylock then pulled his cloak over himself, cried, then knelt and crossed his arms again. When Portia sentenced Shylock to renounce his faith, Antonio snatched Shylock's skullcap. Shylock tried to grab it, still kneeling, and, failing to find it, instead felt his skull, as if for the first time. Looking broken, he shook his head and put his arm up, said 'I am content' (4.1.392) with a sardonic smile, finally accepting his fall. He picked up his skullcap and kissed it, put his hand onto the top of his head, stood up and walked off stage with his hand still there. It was a thorough, humiliating defrocking, violent and cruel.

By contrast, Hall's next production, *Twelfth Night* at the Playhouse Theatre (1991) was 'exquisite' and 'visually beautiful' (*Guardian* 21 May 1991), returning him to a pared down, autumnal version of his SMT style with one of the plays that most defined his early period. The production lacked the political edge of *The Merchant of Venice* but still mixed mortality and sexuality. His SMT *Twelfth Night* had been melancholic, but he was now self-consciously exploring his own 'late' period with a sense of mortality and the retreat of sexuality to the fore of his interpretation of Shakespeare. The production was sensuous, set in a Caroline world in a design by Timothy O'Brien that called to mind Lila De Nobili's rich stage set. He hung a large chandelier over dark, seventeenth-century-style floorboards; a painted backdrop showed an orchard in autumn, behind which was a pond covered in mist (*Spectator* 9 May 1991). Hall made the sea and water a keynote of the production, with the far-away sound of the sea lapping a shore playing every time Viola talked of Sebastian. Billington admired Hall's 'sea-dominated magic realism' which he interpreted as a reflection on 'the way our lives are permeated by memories of human loss' (*Guardian* 21 May 1991). Hall again cast Eric Porter as Malvolio as a direct connection between the past and present productions. For Viola, he cast Maria Miles, a young actress who was enjoying a reputation as an up-and-coming talent thanks to her well-received performance in Hall's production of Ibsen's *The Wild Duck* in 1990. Dressed in male costume, Miles looked like a toy Cavalier. For Billington, Miles was one of the highlights of the production, he particularly admired the 'amused awareness of the erotic havoc she is causing with Olivia' (*Guardian* 21 May 1991). Other reviewers thought her 'joyless' (*Chicago Tribune* 12 May 1991). Hall shifted the play's focus from Malvolio to Feste, played by David Ryall. He was a 'dry, wry, philosophical Feste' whose performance embodied the production's melancholic mood. His final song 'is rendered with sardonic asperity as if to imply there is a Beckettian absurdity about the endless cycle of human affairs' (*Guardian* 21 May 1991). Not all reviewers were convinced by Hall's return to the pastoral beauty of his SMT years. Peter Holland found only 'ordinariness and banality' and thought the performance 'desperately unfunny' (Holland 1997: 81), a view shared by the *Chicago Tribune*, whose reviewer mocked Hall's plodding approach to the text (12 May 1991).

The politics of combining death and sexuality were better explored in Hall's next production, with these themes almost inevitably leading to *All's Well That Ends Well*, which he directed for the RSC in 1992. Although Hall had directed modern drama in Stratford, this was his first Shakespeare since his resignation from the company. Staged in the new Swan theatre (constructed in the old conference hall where Hall had rehearsed many of his classic RSC productions), *All's Well That Ends Well* was performed in a year of turbulent politics. All was not well in Britain. An unexpected Conservative victory in a general election frustrated Hall's ambition for more public subsidy. A recession, compounded by a run on the pound, which led to crippling interest rates and the UK's dramatic departure from the European Exchange Rate Mechanism, cast a gloomy shadow over the nation. Rising unemployment hit the working classes, while the middle classes faced redundancy, negative equity on their property and repossession of their homes. The country was indeed sick and Hall's 'dark, disturbing and challenging' *All's Well* reflected that mood (Fraser 1985: 9). This was apparent in the stage design, which cast distorted reflections of the stage through a 'tilted, twisted mirror' (*Guardian* 3 July 1992) which loomed at the rear, with 'architectural models of the Rossillion country pile, the Parisian palace and the Tuscan churches' (*Observer* 5 July 1992) suspended from it. The property of the rich and the powerful framed the elongated reflections of the actors, a reminder perhaps of the inequalities which the economic crisis had exposed. The designer John Gunter created a simple mid-seventeenth-century setting. Gunter's minimalist sensibilities, his ability to create vivid but simple stage pictures, was in harmony with Hall's textual fundamentalism. For the next decade, Gunter was Hall's main designer on his Shakespeare productions, taking John Bury's place as Hall's most longstanding collaborator in the theatre.

In this strangely mirrored world, the Caroline elegance of the costumes barely concealed hidden sexual desires, obsession and incipient violence. The central character for Hall was Helena, played by Sophie Thompson with 'the air of a retiring schoolgirl' (*Evening Standard* 3 July 1992). In her first scene, she was demure, head bowed, awkward under the scrutiny of the court. On her own, she addressed the audience in slow and measured verse, her voice sounding naïve and full of dreams of love, her hands kept politely clasped in front of her. She only moved when she had a chance to see Bertram: her arms fell to her side briefly, and she came to the side of the stage as if admitting a guilty secret. These were flashes of passion which hinted at something deeper than a demure 'retiring schoolgirl'. Helena's offstage 'cure' – a piece of magic laden with unforced innuendo – was rewarded with a game. The Lords walked around her in a circle as music played, stopping so that she could inspect her potential prizes. Each time she talked to a Lord, the music stopped, and the rejected Lord retired from the game – this was courting by musical chairs. With only a miserable looking Bertram left, Helena continued the game, but the game was now tense, awkward. Bertram ended with his back to Helena as the music stopped. Helena fell to the ground and stayed there, silent, as Bertram objected. Helena's moment of control over her sexual destiny was over, the illusion of power dissipated by Bertram's refusal, which even the King's anger could not restore. Potency quickly changed to impotence. When Bertram finally capitulated, he refused to look at Helena. The scene brought out the dark turn, the complex mix of power and sexuality on display, and Bertram's angry denial of sex destroyed the fairy-tale illusion.

The connection between violence and sexual desire was represented vividly by the clown, Lavache, played by Anthony O'Donnell as a grotesque counter-foil to Barbara Jefford's stern Countess. He was an obese man dressed in faded red motley, extraordinary shoes and smeared clown make-up, his face 'covered in sores' (Fraser 1985: 9). As Fraser observed, 'his fool's bauble' was 'a phallus used for aggression, not comedy' (Fraser 1985: 9). In Act 1, Scene 3, Lavache began his ballad by imitating a cuckoo, literalizing the Clown's line 'your cuckoo sings by kind' (1.3.63), and then declaimed the lyrics, without melody, stamping his feet aggressively.

This sense of a world where sexual desire goes hand in hand with cruelty and anger was also explored in the duping of Parolles (4.3). Michael Siberry played a nuanced Parolles, a character who was outlandish and extrovert, but also 'wreathed in anxieties and evasions' (*Observer* 5 July 1992). His mock trial was 'not funny but cruel and painful' (Fraser 1985: 9) and for Michael Coveney, it was 'the most powerful sequence in the play' (*Observer* 5 July 1992). For Sheridan Morley, Siberry turned Parolles into a 'new center for the piece', a Malvolio-like 'alternative hero despite his own self-delusions' (*New York Times* 3 November 1993). Siberry spoke the part with a 'resonant drawl' (*Evening Standard* 13 October 1993), at first bringing out Parolles' charm but by the end of the performance, he was 'transformed into a ragged but unashamed misanthrope' (*Evening Standard* 3 July 1992). For his first scene (1.1), when he debates virginity with Helena, Parolles wore a white scarf and a large, floppy red hat topped extravagantly with a feather. His banter with Helena was playful but had a dangerous undertone, he growled suggestively on 'away with't' (1.1.133), followed Helena as she sat away from him and leaned close to her. The scarf was used later to bind his arms when he was captured and led off stage blindfolded to the ominous sound of a drum beating. When brought back for interrogation, Parolles was thrown violently to the floor, still bound and blindfolded, and he stayed like this as his captors questioned him. He stood once the letter had been taken from him and stumbled about the stage, still blind, then laughed madly as the letter was read out. Parolles was finally reduced to begging for his life, the blindfold was taken off, and he turned about, looking at the familiar faces about him, the cruel realization sinking in over a long pause. Bertram and the other soldiers left Parolles alone. This was not a game but a violation, a nasty humiliation. A soldier undid the scarf binding Parolles' hands, and he fell forward to the stage on all fours, like an animal. As he spoke his soliloquy, he stood slowly at 'Captain I will be no more' (4.3.325) as if regaining his humanity through renouncing his rank and his colleagues.

Hamlet 1994, *Julius Caesar* 1995 and *King Lear* 1997

The mid-1990s saw Hall return to Shakespearean tragedy with his third *Hamlet* in 1994, followed by his return to the Roman plays with *Julius Caesar* in 1995 and his production of Shakespeare's darkest play, *King Lear* in 1997. The political situation was changing, and culture was becoming an essential part of the political narrative again as young politicians such as Tony Blair, who was elected with a landslide majority in 1997, set the tone for a new generation unburdened by the past. Hall was not persuaded, and his cynicism about government failure to invest in the arts only increased under Blair, turning into a deep hostility towards his government. *Julius Caesar*, a play about leadership, was a first broadside against the coming 'new Labour' approach to culture and society, and he marked Blair's eventual election with *King Lear*.

Sexuality and mortality continued to preoccupy Hall, so it was natural that he would turn back to *Hamlet* in a production which was strikingly different from his previous attempts at the play. In preparing *Hamlet*, which went on an international tour before a residency at the newly named Gielgud Theatre in London, Hall found himself reflecting on modern sexuality in the wake of the AIDS crisis. He felt that society had 'started to evaluate our sexuality in the most honest terms since classical times', in particular, he thought, in negotiating between heterosexuality and homosexuality (*Times* 2 November 1994). Hall had recently been energized by a performance of Tony Kushner's play *Angels in America*, subtitled 'A Gay Fantasia on National Themes'. Kushner's two-part play centres on Prior Walter, a gay man who is diagnosed with AIDS and then visited by ghosts and angels, although he does not know if they are real or part of his disease. The parallels with *Hamlet* were not foregrounded but, clearly, they sparked Hall's imagination. *Angels in America* cast a huge shadow over Hall's *Hamlet*, not least because Hall cast the actor he saw playing Prior, Stephen Dillane, in the title role. The play inspired Hall to think about how Hamlet functions post-AIDS: 'There is a real bisexuality in Hamlet, and he has not come to terms with it,' he told *The Times* (2 November 1994). In his first talk to the cast (reproduced in the theatre programme), Hall expanded on the theme, reflecting on the play's 'shifting sexuality, uncertain sexuality' which is 'at the heart of the play'. As with his previous work, a sense of history framed Hall's assessment. Homosexuality was a modern construct, he argued: 'for the Renaissance', he said, 'there was just sexuality' (quoted in Holland 1996: 237).

These ideas about sexual ambiguity drove the production. The sets and costumes, designed by Hall's daughter Lucy Hall, drowned Elsinore in sensuous red velvet. Louise Doughty described it as a setting 'sick with sexuality' (*Mail on Sunday* 13 November 1994). The stage was divided by a curtain of red ropes which Billington thought invoked the neo-fascist politics of the far-right Ukrainian party Svoboda (*Guardian* 7 November 1994). They combined ideas about bloodlines and voyeurism, for a world where nothing is truly concealed, with a sense of violent restraint: the rope curtain was imprisoning and revealing, its striking colour suggesting violence and passion. With a few exceptions, Hamlet among them, most characters wore Edwardian-style red costumes. To some critics, the production called to mind the Mad Hatter's Tea Party: Nightingale, for example, described the actors as 'Dickensian coachmen redesigned for Alice's Adventures in Wonderland' (*Times* 7 November 1994).

This bohemian sensuousness spilled out into the characterization of Claudius' court. Claudius, played by Michael Pennington in a red velvet frock coat and waistcoat, was a drunkard, 'always reaching for a glass of whiskey', as Holland observed, and 'aggressively male'. Gertrude, played by Gwen Taylor in a white dress streaked with red, spent the first act besotted with Claudius' sexual charisma, acting with 'inappropriate girlishness' until the closet scene, when Hamlet pushed her face into her bed, slashed a portrait of Claudius, and finally opened her eyes to her folly (Holland 1997: 219). For the rest of the play, she wore mourning black and became ever more distant from Claudius. As Gertrude's sexuality retreated, Ophelia's erupted. Her rejection by Hamlet was, as Fay noted, 'unusually harsh' (Fay 1995: 353). After Polonius' death, Ophelia, played by Gina Bellman, arranged his clothes on the stage and then 'obscenely rode on them, like a parody of sex'. Later, she tried to French-kiss Laertes (Holland 1996: 237). After dragging Polonius' body about the castle, Hamlet, now covered in blood, stripped his clothes off. For many critics, Hamlet's nudity was the most memorable part of the performance but, for Holland, this at least was not meant to be sexual: 'his naked body became a comic robot, the residual flesh almost a machine' (Holland 1996: 237).

In many respects, Hamlet was the least overtly sexual character in the play. He may have simulated sex during the closet scene, but Hamlet was the character who was least like the play that Hall described in his programme note. Fay, for example, thought Dillane was 'far from the bisexual Hamlet

Hall said he had in mind' (Fay 1995: 353). Critics focused instead on Dillane's wry, sardonic humour, a 'bitter jokiness' that signalled 'a harsh modernity' (Holland 1996: 235). He played an unusually downbeat Hamlet, 'sometimes to the point of slovenliness' (*Times* 7 November 1994), particularly in early scenes where Hamlet seems to accept his disempowerment. In contrast to the bohemian velvets of Claudius' court, Hamlet wore baggy clothes like a modern student. Dillane was an alt-Hamlet, his use of humour casting him as a contemporary alternative comedian. Billington described him as a 'hawk-faced joker ... who uses protective irony', arguing that '[m]ockery as a mask for disillusion' was the keynote of Dillane's performance rather than unexplored sexuality as Hall had originally envisaged (*Guardian* 7 November 1994). Hall was alive to the success of Dillane's thoroughly modern, out of his time Hamlet: 'For me one of the most exciting things about the way Dillane approaches it is that he asks questions upon question. He is not seeking the answers, and still less consistency' (*Times* 2 November 1994). However, Dillane turned that questioning inwards as well as outwards: as one critic noted, he was 'ironically and bitterly self-critical' (*Sunday Times* 13 November 1994) and his callousness was brutally displayed in his overly cruel rejection of Ophelia which, as Billington observed, implied that 'he never had that much feeling for her in the first place' (*Guardian* 7 November 1994).

Julius Caesar returned Hall to the world of power politics – and, for the last time, to the Royal Shakespeare Company. His reputation for political manoeuvring seemed to bleed into the production. At its centre were two flawed leaders unable to match their reputations. Christopher Benjamin played Caesar as a man almost crippled by self-doubt, a 'great man prey to human vanities' according to Jack Tinker (*Daily Mail* 6 July 1995), who was 'less than the pretense', as Nightingale put it (*Times* 7 July 1995). When Caesar faced the soothsayer, he was full of genuine nerves, fearing the future he claimed to disdain. The real focus of the production was John Nettles' Brutus, whom Billington thought a 'tormented liberal'

(*Guardian* 7 July 1995) caught between his sense of historical and moral duty. He genuinely loathed killing Caesar. Nettles played him as calm on the outside but 'internally troubled' (*Times* 28 May 1996). Reflecting later on his performance, Nettles described Brutus as a man of contradictions: 'He is a political disaster – and yet he is not without a certain nobility ... He is a man who thinks much, but none too well' (Nettles 1998: 185). In rehearsal, Hall and Nettles elected to foreground Brutus' internal contradictions: 'The point of Brutus is precisely the contradiction he embodies ... Brutus appears a noble Roman ... The reality is that Brutus is that most dangerous of men, a misconstruer of events and men' (Nettles 1998: 187). The world these characters inhabited was a 'living nightmare': as Billington put it, Hall captured 'both the edgy apprehensiveness of conspiracy and the Shakespearean ambiguity of character' (*Guardian* 7 July 1995).

A striking set anchored Hall's directorial vision. Gunter created a world that brought together the angled Modernism of Hall's 1959 *Coriolanus*, the unforgiving steel of *The Wars of the Roses*, the mirrored darkness of Hall's 1965 *Hamlet* and the epic sweep of his *Antony and Cleopatra*. It was a 'greatest hits' stage set, a fitting and triumphal setting for what would prove to be Hall's RSC swansong. Reviewers compared the set design to 'the architect Speer' (referring to the Nazi Albert Speer) and the 'artist David' (*Times* 7 July 1995). In other words, it was a world that conjured from the past images of political ambition. The colour scheme was predominantly black and red – the colours of mourning and blood. The set was dominated by a gigantic bust of Caesar, which, as Holland witheringly noted, 'seemed to have been carved out of a giant bar of white chocolate' (Holland 1997: 232). The bust overshadowed the later action, often upstaging the actors, who were caught between the giant head of Caesar looming behind them, and the imagined head of Peter Hall beating out the frenetic pace in front of them. Blood increasingly washed through the play-world. A bucket of blood was thrown across the stage after Cinna's murder; the bust of Caesar wept 'rivers of blood' during the final battle scene (*Daily Mail* 6 July 1995). Political theatre drowned in horrific gore, Brecht trumping Artaud, the arc of blood shooting out of Caesar's body invoking Artaud's play *Jet de Sang* (Spurt of Blood).

Hall took the production first to the Barbican, a space he had helped to design but never worked in, and then to the newly built Globe in London. The International Shakespeare Globe Centre wanted Hall to workshop scenes from *Julius Caesar* as the last in a series of events designed to show off the new playhouse ahead of its official opening (Nelsen 1997: 324). The stage was still rudimentary and undecorated, but the basic layout was fixed, giving Hall and his actors the opportunity to try out the stage space. Hall was frank about its limitations. He came onto the stage at the start of the rehearsal and immediately pronounced it to be 'frightfully wrong'. When he finished the workshop, Hall expressed his frustration in an act of stage violence, furiously kicking one of the stage pillars 'as if intending to boot it into oblivion'. In between, Hall demonstrated how poor the sightlines were. Nevertheless, Hall was alive to the theatrical energy of the thrust stage and the open-air audience: 'the justification of Caesar's assassination becomes a debate in which the audience is involved too' (*Times* 13 September 1995). Hall's final work for the RSC bled into the foundation of a new Shakespeare stage space for London, one that in many respects fulfilled the ambitions Hall had for the London arm of the company back in the 1960s. Hall bridged this gap with typical forthrightness, his physical attack on the stage gaining headlines and overshadowing his more thoughtful exploration of the social dynamics of the stage space and the auditorium.

This physical assault on the stage turned into an assault on modern British culture with his next Shakespeare production when he directed *King Lear*, which he played in repertoire with his first revival of *Waiting for Godot* by Samuel Beckett – the play which had made Hall's career. Both are plays about the disappointments and failures of middle-aged and old men. A single blue box set designed by Gunter highlighted the thematic similarities between the plays. Actors played on a mainly bare stage, with simple set pieces highlighting the barren world against which elderly men pitted themselves in frustration and anger. A small withered tree served as a set for both Godot and Lear's blasted heath. For *Lear*, Gunter added a back wall with jagged lightning bolts that were lit for storm scenes and could be widened to reveal stark ruined landscapes. In some scenes, shadow puppets represented battles, and a 'mounting cacophony' suggested the play's final battle (*Plays International* November 1997).

Hall explored the relationship between Shakespeare and Beckett, something he had been talking about since the 1960s. Denis Quilley played both Pozzo in *Godot* and Gloucester in *Lear*. Reviewers were quick to pick up on the resonance between the two performances: Charles Spencer wrote, '[i]t's impossible to watch Denis Quilley's deeply moving, humane performance as the blinded Gloucester, for instance, without remembering him as the blind Pozzo' (*Daily Telegraph* 26 September 1997). Greg Hicks played Lucky and Edgar, and it appeared to some reviewers as if the characters of Pozzo and Lucky had been reimagined for Hall's staging of Gloucester's attempt to end his life. Billington called this 'tragedy transmuted into farce' and praised Hall for coming close to 'the play's tragi-comic heart' in a way which revealed 'man's Beckettian solitude in a hostile universe' (*Guardian* 26 September 1997). Alan Howard, in the title role, gave a measured performance, slowly unveiling Lear's madness. He began as 'an imperious, majestic Lear' because Howard insisted that there 'has got to be somewhere for Lear to fall from' (Croall 2015: 89). Yet by the end of the play, Lear was no longer aloof but a 'tender, tactile Lear' who, after his madness reached its peak, descended into a primal sense of compassion, growling 'like an aggrieved wolf' over the bodies of his daughters and gently comforting the blind Gloucester (*Times* 26 September 1997).

Now approaching seventy, his dream of a publicly funded theatre decimated by nearly two decades of monetarism, his hope for a different government shattered by the Blair administration, Hall was an aggrieved wolf, looking ahead only to mortality and the impotence of age. Magazines such as *Vanity Fair* talked about London swinging again, for the first time since the 1960s, and 10 Downing Street threw parties for artists, actors and pop stars. Culture was being turned over for political purposes, and with hindsight, Hall's grim, absurdist vision of the nation disintegrating, of an older generation betrayed by the young, was prescient. In interviews, he talked with bitterness and disenchantment about the lack of government investment in the arts. He did not direct another Shakespeare production in Britain for six years and instead decamped to America for a world elsewhere.

6

Playing Shakespeare in America

As the millennium approached, Hall directed several plays in America, including four Shakespeares. Two of these trod very familiar territory: *A Midsummer Night's Dream* and *Troilus and Cressida* revisited his work with the RSC and although in some respects they were modern productions, both recycled ideas from those early works. He also staged *Romeo and Juliet* and directed *Measure for Measure* for the first time, a play which was unexpectedly resonant in the wake of a sex scandal at the White House involving the President. Hall was, as ever, busy in America. Alongside these works, he re-formed his old partnership with John Barton to direct *Tantalus* (2000), Barton's ambitious ten-play cycle based on Greek myths, in Denver. Hall worked coast to coast, simultaneously directing *Romeo and Juliet* in Los Angeles and *Troilus and Cressida* in New York in 2001. He talked about his hope to found an American ensemble company on the model of the Royal Shakespeare Company. He gave interviews, held workshops, taught theatre at the University of Houston, spoke constantly about the importance of rhythm in verse speaking, reflected on the untapped possibilities of the American accent, and criticized from afar the arts policies of the Labour government led by Tony Blair in the UK. He continued to direct modern drama and opera in the UK, but between 1999 and 2001, he directed only four plays in London: his main focus was America.

This brief American interlude started when Gordon Davidson, the long-serving Artistic Director of the Center Theater Group (CTG) in Los Angeles, invited Hall to direct a season in 1999. Hall remembers that Davidson had been trying to get him there for several years. Hall was intrigued by the invitation: 'I have always wanted to see Shakespeare done by American actors in America, but with them strictly observing the form' (Hall 1993: 425). The CTG started life as a theatre company run by John Houseman at the University of California. Davidson had taken it over in 1964 when he was thirty-two (just two years younger than Hall) and finally launched it as a major theatre company in 1967 when he moved it into the Mark Taper Forum and the cavernous Ahmanson Theatre, where he quickly built up a reputation by inviting international companies such as the RSC and later the National (Bartow 2009: 14). In Davidson, Hall found a sympathetic figure whose own attempts to set up a theatre on the RSC/National Theatre model mirrored Hall's ambitions. Davidson was in many respects an American version of Hall who 'somehow managed to chart a course between the Scylla of wealthy patrons on one side and the Charybdis of operating a publicly owned building on the other' and had 'a nose for the kind of theatre that attracts heated debate' as well as an 'earnest vision of a theatre' (London 2013: 350). The RSC was one of the first companies that Davidson brought to the CTG in 1967, and he worked with them on *Catch my Soul*, a musical adaptation of *Othello* with the rock'n'roll star Jerry Lee Lewis as Iago.

Hall travelled to Los Angeles in early 1999 and within a few weeks had a company of twenty-five American actors ready to work with him (Hall 1993: 426). Initially, Davidson commissioned Hall to produce one play, but following an anonymous $250,000 donation, the season was expanded to allow Hall to direct two plays (*Playbill* 3 June 1999) and extend the rehearsal period to eight weeks. This was just what Hall needed for his American experiment. He now had the opportunity to workshop for two months with a single ensemble. For Hall, exploring the American accent was in many ways more important than the actual plays. For two months, he was a one-person academy of classical acting, coaching his American cast in Shakespeare's rhythms which he believed 'essential to any remotely authentic production' (*Independent* 30 August 1999). Hall told the American media that 'American actors lack technique but have plenty of temperament and a great sense of rhythm and musicality.' Hall's theatrical background may have been English, but as a jazz musician, his sense of rhythm was American. He saw no contradiction between the two, noting that in some respects the American tradition was closer to Shakespeare's culture than modern England (*Playbill* 3 June 1999).

Much of the rehearsal time was spent teaching the actors the rhythms and 'correct' delivery of Shakespeare's iambic pentameters – which Hall believed essential to any remotely successful production (*Independent* 30 August 1999). As usual, Hall was not short of vision or ambition for his new venture, as he told the media he aimed 'to develop a bit of a Shakespeare tradition' at the Ahmanson (*Variety* February 1999). By the summer, once the plays had opened, Hall's vision had coalesced into something even grander. He told the *Independent* that he aimed at no less than a 'semi-permanent company of stage actors in a town where the theatre is traditionally seen as a stop-gap pursuit between jobs on television or the big screen'. He wanted to create 'an American-flavoured Shakespeare company, in which everyone would be trained into performing in a uniform style' and 'offer Los Angeles some of Shakespeare's most challenging plays and so disprove once and for all that the city is uneducated, superficial and interested only in big money' (*Independent* 30 August 1999).

Hall and Davidson found it harder than they thought to bring together an ensemble. Hall tested the water by holding two actor workshops in Los Angeles (*Playbill* June 1999). He attracted a starry workshop group, among them Kevin Kline, Christopher Plummer, Dustin Hoffman and Minnie Driver (*LA Times* 13 March 1999), all keen to learn from the master. However, Hall was disappointed that none of these Hollywood names wanted to commit to a full production. Hall formed the first company around Kelly McGillis and Richard Thomas. McGillis had been a Hollywood star in the 1980s with notable lead performances in blockbusters such as *Witness* (1985) and *Top Gun* (1986), but by the 1990s she was mainly working on television movies. Thomas was an Emmy-award winning theatre and television actor best known for playing John-Boy in the popular television series *The Waltons*.

Measure for Measure and *A Midsummer Night's Dream* 1999

Hall took Davidson's advice and paired a safe play with a more left-field choice. Alongside *A Midsummer Night's Dream*, Hall directed *Measure for Measure*. The company rehearsed for six hours a day, three spent on *A Midsummer Night's Dream*, three on *Measure for Measure* (*LA Times* 13 June 1999), so that the ensemble could explore the different ways that Shakespeare developed ideas about sexuality and power. The productions were premiered on the same day. However, reviewers missed the potential resonances between the two plays. If Hall wanted to use *Measure for Measure* as a way of 'reading' *A Midsummer Night's Dream* differently, none of his reviewers picked that up. Instead, responses focused on *Measure for Measure*'s contemporary relevance. As Hall noted in several interviews, the times were certainly right for a play like *Measure for Measure*. Davidson told *Playbill* that 'you can't do it and not think about what has just gone on in Washington' (*Playbill* 3 June 1999). The *Independent* noted that America was peculiarly receptive to the play's 'themes of over-zealous prosecution, uncontrollable sexual urges, puritanical hypocrisy and abuse of the power' and quoted Hall, who said, 'There was really evil humour operating, with the audience picking up things in the play that I doubt English audiences would' (*Independent* 30 August 1999). From Hall's point of view, the play's focus on obsessive and transgressive sexuality was a natural development of his work on, for example, *Hamlet*, but he found in America an audience receptive to exploring the hidden role of sexual desire in politics. In 1998, American politics was dominated by a sex scandal at the White House. The *Drudge Report* published a story claiming that President Clinton had had an affair with an intern, Monica Lewinsky, in the White House. Clinton denied the allegations, but when clear evidence emerged that they were true, he was impeached. Clinton had been dogged by rumours of sexual infidelity and abuse for some years, but he was also being aggressively pursued by what his wife, Hillary Clinton, called a 'vast right-wing conspiracy' (*Washington Post* 28 January 1998): a puritanical backlash not so much against Clinton as a sexual predator but against the sexually liberal generation which Clinton represented. *Measure for Measure* does not work as an allegory of the Clinton scandal: Clinton was no Angelo, in that he was never a hypocritical puritan, nor was Lewinsky an Isabella. But the mixture of politics, sexual abuse, aggressive puritanism and abusive liberalism are all there in ways which can transform the play, for American audiences, into a very contemporary, dark satire.

Hall and his designer, John Gunter, made the connection explicit by including on the stage a nine-foot model based on the Capitol building in Washington DC. The shadow of Clinton's impeachment loomed over the performance, firmly anchoring Shakespeare's exploration of sexual exploitation and political hypocrisy in a specifically American context. The stage was otherwise bare, save for simple furniture and prison bars. Recalling his work with Hall on *Hamlet*, Gunter created a stage box out of blue wool serge and steel tubing, a deliberately minimalist set intended to put the 'the emphasis on the actors and the text', as Gunter told *Entertainment Design* in 1999. The framing walls, he explained, 'were done in perspective to enclose the space and bring the action downstage to the audience'. This sense of enclosure was reinforced during prison scenes when metal bars stretched across the full length and height of the stage, creating a powerful image of entrapment which added to the production's claustrophobia. Hall originally wanted to set the play during the Enlightenment, but Gunter persuaded him to set it in the nineteenth century to give more of a sense of a world in the grip of rapid progress. Gunter contrasted the extravagant costumes of Mistress Quickly, Pompey Bum and the other 'low-life' characters with the puritanical, dark costumes of the court (*Entertainment Design* 1999), whose characters wore 'knee-length overcoats and stovepipe hats' (*LA Times* 22 June 1999). There was some sense of modernity as well, signalled by three virtually naked sex workers 'looking as though they had come from Sunset Strip rather than Stratford' (*Guardian* 22 June 1999). Reviewers praised the production's 'menacing charm' and the 'ashen palette' which 'beautifully heightens a morally complex play and production' (*LA Times* 22 June 1999), although Charles Marowitz found it 'curiously unaffecting' (Marowitz 2002: 7).

A Midsummer Night's Dream was a hybrid of Hall's 1950s and 1990s work. Visually, it belonged clearly to his late period with few (and significant) stage props and a design emphasis on costume rather than sets as a way of foregrounding the text over spectacle. Trees were moved across the stage to denote the forest world, with the court world represented by Shaker-style furniture. Otherwise, production ideas emerged through costume, which contrasted a stylized Elizabethan aesthetic with a romantic sense of earthy otherness. The lovers wore simple pastel gowns 'with a slight shimmer to catch the light' (Slingerland 1999: 6), courtiers wore elaborate Elizabethan-style costumes. Hippolyta was distinctly exotic and martial, her Elizabethan dress complemented with armour over her right arm and leopard skin on her left shoulder, which one reviewer described as 'a poetic marriage of period costuming with stylized mythological flavour' (Slingerland 1999: 6). The outlines of Titania (McGillis) and Oberon's (Peter Francis James) costumes deliberately echoed those of Theseus and his court, but the material was made from 'ethereal black sheers and brocades with metallic threads and different textured weaves' (Slingerland 1999: 6). The fairies were heavily made-up and looked like they had emerged from the earth and hedgerows. Puck, played by Richard Thomas, was naked from the waist up, his bare chest and biceps seemingly brushed with mud. He wore a garland around his neck and left wrist. To make him look more inhuman, he was given long, elf-like ears; his hair was brushed upwards and died white and black to look like flames jumping off his head. Thomas was an impish, mischievous Puck with a sparkle of danger and a whiff of pantomime.

However, in other respects, this production was safe ground for Hall. He found surprisingly little new to say about the play and even in his interviews he focused on *Measure for Measure* as the play which was of most interest to him as well as his audiences. Marowitz may have been too harsh when he called it '*Dream*-by-numbers' but he was right to note that the production recalled the 'twenties romanticism of Max Reinhardt', especially as Thomas' half-naked Puck looked like a grown-up version of Mickey Rooney's famous performance of the part in Reinhardt's 1935 Hollywood film (Marowitz 2002: 7). In 1959, Hall was keen to rescue the play from the style of production that Reinhardt's film epitomized, but his 1999 version reflected the lessons he had learned from recording an audio version of the play in 1992, set to Mendelssohn's score, and his 1981 production of Britten's opera. The *LA Times* (22 June 1999) called the 1999 production 'pretty and pretty conventional' and compared Puck to the David Bowie persona Ziggy Stardust 'reincarnated as a demonic puppy'.

Romeo and Juliet 2001 and *Troilus and Cressida* 2001

Despite mixed reviews, Hall's 1999 season at the CTG was popular with audiences, and *Measure for Measure* was well-received for bringing an unfamiliar Shakespeare play into a distinctly American political environment. In interviews at the time, Hall was enthusiastic about creating a permanent ensemble to stage Shakespeare in America. Once again, Hall was not just looking for opportunities to stage plays, but for a home where he could develop his distinctive theatrical vision of well-spoken Shakespeare in repertoire with modern plays. For the millennium, Hall planned to return to the CTG with *King Lear*, starring Christopher Plummer, and *As You Like It*. In the event, neither production made it to the rehearsal room, with a transfer of his London revival of *Amadeus* marking Hall's spot for the next season at the Ahmanson. The year 2000 was one of the few in Hall's career when he directed no Shakespeare: instead, Shakespeare, Davidson, and Plummer all had to give way to another American project which consumed Hall through the year: an epic staging of John Barton's ten-play Trojan cycle *Tantalus* at the Denver Center for the Performing Arts, followed by an international tour.

In 2001, Hall returned to his American Shakespeare work with two productions: *Romeo and Juliet* at the CTG and, curiously, *Troilus and Cressida* in New York for Theatre for a New Audience. There was no more talk of an American experiment or an American repertory company – these would be Hall's final Shakespearean works for the United States. He had learnt some lessons from his two-year US sabbatical. His 1999 casts had been mostly white in a country where race is one of the defining notes of national politics. Now both plays had mixed-race casts with African Americans (or in *Troilus and Cressida*'s case, a British black actor, Idris Elba) taking lead roles.

At the CTG, Hall directed *Romeo and Juliet*, a play he had not attempted since 1961. The *LA Times* dismissed the production as 'stolid, dogged, two 1/2-star Shakespeare': '[i]t is not overwhelming and it is not underwhelming,' Michael Phillips wrote, adding, '[y]ou leave the production feeling merely whelmed' (6 February 2001). This time, Hall was unable to attract any Hollywood stars: one reviewer called it 'a bit like *Hamlet* without the Dane' (Hornby 2001: 311) although veteran actor James Avery (Capulet) and British actor Miriam Margolyes (Nurse) were familiar faces and both had played the roles before. Hall and Gunter created a standard late-Hall bare stage set on a 'sharply raked stage' with (unusually for Hall) a thrust stage breaking the proscenium arch (Hornby 2001: 311), once again putting the play into a vaguely nineteenth-century setting, this time in a sun-drenched Mediterranean past but with a mixed-race cast that summoned the 'theatrical never-neverland of multicultural America' (*Variety* 5 February 2001). The set, designed to look like a European palazzo overlooked by oval windows reminded one reviewer of a continental Renaissance theatre (Hornby 2001: 311). The production was beautiful: Richard Hornby called it 'one of the most gorgeous productions I have ever seen' (Hornby 2001: 311) and even Phillips admired the 'pretty pictures', in particular, 'the golden-hued entrance of the masked ball attendees' (*LA Times* 6 February 2001). Hall filled the large Ahmanson stage with big fight scenes and dances and, in keeping with his late style, kept a fast pace through the whole production. Flamenco music and ragged gypsy costumes (for Romeo and his friends) added extra colour.

Hall followed his usual practice of starting with text and voice workshops, driving his cast through his version of the Play Way. Margolyes recalls, 'Peter literally had text classes for the first two weeks. We didn't get off our chairs.' For example, 'Peter taught me to notice that there are words that begin with the same letter: "will you speak well ... " And to use that to push the emotion of the line forward: "that killed your cousin?" I have to punch that out. Those words start with the same letter for a reason' (*Backstage* 21 February 2001). Hall steered his cast away from Hollywood naturalism towards a more Brechtian approach to theatre: 'Don't act it, tell it,' he told his cast, and 'Act on the line': Avery recalls learning, 'Everything in that line has all the emotional feeling you need to know if you just do the line' (*Backstage* 21 February 2001).

The production was overshadowed by memories of Baz Luhrmann's 1996 film of the play, also set in Los Angeles with a multi-racial cast that reflected the city's ethnic mix and added British actors, including Margolyes as the Nurse. Hall avoided the drugs, drag queens and guns that characterized that film, but he did make more concessions than he usually would to audience expectations. Jesse Borrego's Mercutio was 'just another contempo-compendium of crotch-grabs and pumping motions' (*LA Times* 6 February 2001); Lynn Collins' flame-haired Juliet was a forthright, confident Juliet for the 'MTV generation' (*LA Times* 4 March 2001) struggling with the demands of 'teen vulnerability and womanly sensuality' (*Variety* 5 February 2001); and D.B. Woodside's Romeo was 'a highly credible now-centered youth' (*Curtain Up* 30 January 2001). Hall's biggest concession – and most controversial decision – was to try to replicate Luhrmann's mixture of white, African American and Hispanic casting. Having made the choice, Hall was quick to distance himself from making any kind of theatrical statement about race: '[The choice] was born very much out of the wonderful racial mix of Los Angeles,' he told the *LA Times*: 'what I'm trying to say is that you need the energy and the vitality and the passion and the danger of that mixture, and protecting ourselves from that mixture leads to a kind of death'. But then he added, rather airily: 'But I don't want to push the point because then you end up making a thesis. You can understand the metaphor if you wish to.' For someone who had been so vocal about Shakespeare's contemporary relevance in his past works, Hall was reticent to 'push' any sense that his casting choices arose from anything other than the talent pool around him. No doubt Hall was nervous about intervening, as a white British director, into an extraordinarily sensitive political issue, but his reticence frustrated his actors who broke all protocol by publicly criticizing him before the production even premiered. Collins reacted against Hall's refusal to challenge audiences, telling the *LA Times* that they should 'make them understand'. She insisted, 'Racism does not end. The world is mixing when it comes to race and even gender, yet it's still an issue, it just is.' Woodside was even more direct: 'I know Sir Peter's point of view, that people will pick it up on perhaps a subconscious level ... I really think that perhaps we missed the mark here; I think that we have a chance to say something really, really special – not just about human beings and love, but about race and class' (*LA Times* 4 March 2001). For some reviewers, this incomplete gesture towards a theatrical statement on race was a misfire: 'racial antagonism isn't a subtext of the play,' complained Lawrence Christon, so 'the background element of family wrath tends to shrivel, despite a certain amount of expository finger-pointing, and with it the sense of alarm we feel at watching these kids play with fire' (*Variety* 5 February 2001).

With *Romeo and Juliet* just opened in Los Angeles, Hall went straight to New York to rehearse *Troilus and Cressida*, which opened in April at the American Place Theatre. Having spent the previous year working on *Tantalus*, on a set that recalled his 1960 *Troilus and Cressida*, it was a natural step for Hall to return to Shakespeare's sardonic take on the Trojan War. Hall directed the play for Theatre for a New Audience, a classical theatre company set up by Jeffrey Horowitz in 1979 on the model of the RSC, with a repertoire rooted in Shakespeare and modern drama. There was little talk this time of an American experiment. Although the actors spoke with American accents, many were British, including Idris Elba as Achilles, Hall-era RSC veteran Terence Rigby as Agamemnon, and Tony Church as Pandarus, a part Church had played for the RSC in 1976. The designer was Douglas Stein: for the first time in years, Hall did not have Gunter realizing his ideas for a Shakespeare play. The play was performed in the round on a stage 'turned into a sandbox' (*New York Times* 16 April 2001), recalling his earlier RSC production as well as *Tantalus*.

The production opened with lights revealing four skeletons, two of them copulating in what the *New York Times* thought 'a chilling depiction of Shakespeare's bile-filled connection between lust and battle' (*New York Times* 16 April 2001). Andrew Weems, playing Thersites, came onstage to clear the skeletons away, replacing them with bits of armour, and spoke the prologue, reading from a copy of the most recent Arden

Shakespeare edition, pulled out of a bag. The 'prologue' was an edited version of the epistle included in the 1609 Quarto, which claims that *Troilus* has never been staged before, 'neuer clapper-clawd with the palmes of the vulgar'. The irony was deliberate: Thersites read 'the smoaky breath of the multitude' while dragging on a cigarette. When he came to the part of the Epistle that calls the play a comedy, Thersites 'looked at the book's cover as if to question the authority of the statement' (Apfelbaum 2004: 59). For Roger Apfelbaum, Hall 'conflated textuality with performance' (59). There was perhaps an element of self-parody here, as the text which Hall fetishized in his working methods was brought on stage and subjected to the scrutiny of the multitude. But it was also a way of signalling the distaste many readers and audiences have had for the play through its history. Hall told Ron Rosenbaum, 'there's nothing bleaker ... in the whole canon than *Troilus*' (*Observer* 2 April 2001): 'Troilus is ... a fool,' he continued, 'Cressida a manipulative tart, Ulysses a very scheming, amoral politician ... Agamemnon's a fool; Ajax is a dope; Achilles is a narcissistic, irresponsible queen.' Reviews of the production were mixed. Bruce Weber thought it 'thick-limbed and trudging' (*New York Times* 16 April 2001), but Charles Isherwood rated it as 'overall one of the better Bard productions to be seen in New York in several seasons' (*Variety* 15 April 2001). Brooke Pierce sat in the middle, admiring Hall's 'solid, fluid, and tight' direction but feeling that he 'doesn't quite raise the level of action to the fever pitch that it should reach' (*Theatre Mania* 20 April 2001).

Having worked with the picture frame, proscenium arch theatre of the Ahmanson for the past two years, Hall was finally able to stretch out into a more flexible theatre space. As well as putting his actors in the round, he directed the stage action around the auditorium, to balconies behind the audience and corridors through the stalls, creating a sense of the audience immersed in a world rather than separated from it. Stein dressed the Trojans in clean, Middle Eastern-style maroon costumes that made them seem 'exotically sexy' (*Variety* 15 April 2001), the Greeks wore ragged and dusty leathers making them look like a 'shabby medieval motorcycle gang' (*New York Times* 16 April 2001). For Elyse Sommer, the relevance to modern conflicts such as 'Vietnam, the Balkans, Northern Ireland and the Israeli-Palestine conflict' (*Curtain Up* 14 April 2001) was palpable: Hall captured a world locked in a cycle of exhausting and pointless warfare typified by the production's 'relentless parade of entrances and exits' (*New York Times* 16 April 2001). At the centre of all this, Joey Kern played Troilus as a young lover full of hope and ardour and ended the performance a 'blood-soaked, vengeful warrior' (*Theatre Mania* 20 April 2001). In the Greek camp, Elba combined 'physical prowess' and 'graceless egomania,' lounging about the camp with a wine goblet, a 'controlling arm' over the 'doting' Patroclus (*New York Times* 16 April 2001).

For the final battle, fight director B.H. Barry created a scene 'with enough vigor and grunts to make you wonder if you're at a live showing of [the film] *Crouching Tiger, Hidden Dragon*' (*Curtain Up* 14 April 2001), the actors kicking sand into the faces of the front row audiences (*Theatre Mania* 20 April 2001). Scott Zielinski, the Lighting Designer, added a special lamp to create a harshly lit stage, which was unforgiving in battle scenes (Zielinski n.d.). In one of the production's most compelling images, Elba, as Achilles, stood with legs wide apart, sword in hand, over Hector's body spread out half-naked and bloody, like a hunter triumphant over his prey. The production ended as it began with Weems' 'lavishly repellent' (*Variety* 15 April 2001), 'pugnacious' (*New York Times* 16 April 2001) Thersites, which suggested to Isherwood that 'the worst of humanity, like cockroaches, will be here long after the best has been defeated' (*Variety* 15 April 2001).

Hall's vision of an American Shakespeare company, trained in his methods, never took root. In 2002, Hall returned to the National Theatre to direct a major production of *The Bacchai* and after that the focus of his professional life was in the UK, with only two more works in America, neither of them Shakespeare (although he did bring his *As You Like It* to the CTG – this will be discussed in the next chapter). His American interlude had mixed results: *Tantalus* was the most ambitious production Hall ever undertook, but he and Barton had a bitter falling-out over Hall's treatment of Barton's text. Looking back on his American Shakespeare productions, we can see some typical Hall themes. His militant classicism led him to an overly conservative production of *A Midsummer Night's Dream*, whilst his refusal to engage with race stunted his *Romeo and Juliet*'s ability to make a real impact. Yet his *Measure for Measure* showed him still able to make striking political comments about power and sexuality. *Troilus and Cressida* captured the darkening mood of a country about to be set on course for two major wars following terrorist attacks on New York in September 2001, four months after *Troilus and Cressida* finished its short run in the same city.

7

National Stages

Hall's final decade as a director saw him return to Britain where he embarked on one last attempt to establish a theatre with a permanent ensemble. He had lost none of his ambition for making either theatres or theatre, and he continued to work to the end of his career at a fast pace. The public funding of the arts, the cause Hall had long championed, suffered after the global financial crash in 2008, and the idea of national culture was itself put under pressure after the attack on New York's World Trade Center in 2001. Hall was as ever sensitive to the big narratives in the world and his productions of Shakespeare reflected the darkening mood of the Western world as it went to war in Afghanistan and Iraq. Hall stayed away from the tragedies: except for his indifferent *Romeo and Juliet* in LA, his 1997 *King Lear* was his final major statement about Shakespearean tragedy. Instead, he ended his career where he began, with mature interpretations of the comedies, including two major comedies that he had never directed before. He returned to *Love's Labour's Lost* and *A Midsummer Night's Dream* to help establish the Rose theatre in Kingston. However, he made one final, unexpected epic statement about Shakespeare, the nation and the nature of power in the post-9/11 age with the two *Henry IV* plays in 2011.

As You Like It 2003– 2005, *Much Ado about Nothing* 2005 and *Measure for Measure* 2006

Hall's 2003 *As You Like It* was the pivotal work of his late period, bridging the gap between his American sabbatical and the final large theatre project of his career, the establishment of the Rose at Kingston, a suburban indoor theatre space inspired by the Elizabethan theatre space that staged Shakespeare's earliest known productions. *As You Like It* launched two important careers, that of Dan Stevens, who made his theatrical debut as Orlando (from 2004 onwards) and later found fame as the lead actor in the television series *Downton Abbey*; and Hall's daughter Rebecca, who quickly buried charges of nepotism with a remarkable performance as Rosalind. Hall first directed the play at the Theatre Royal, Bath, in the summer of 2003, starting a relationship with that theatre that would last until his final production, *Henry IV*, in 2011. This was the first time Hall had directed Shakespeare in Britain since his acclaimed 1997 *King Lear*. In 2004, Hall revived the production, with a few casting changes, to draw press attention to the Rose theatre, which was still unfinished: the company performed the play there, even though it was still a building site, with a stage that was little more than breeze blocks. The production was revived once more for a 2005 American tour which included an extended run at the Ahmanson, concluding Hall's relationship with the CTG and, as it turned out, with America.

As You Like It was Hall's Shakespeare production for his inaugural season at the Theatre Royal in Bath. The season started with Hall's typical energy but also showed him broadening his directorial sensibilities away from the usual formula of Shakespeare and modern drama to encompass the nineteenth and early twentieth centuries. He directed seven plays in Bath, three of which transferred to London, among them plays by Harold Pinter, George Bernard Shaw, Samuel

Beckett, and Georges Feydeau. Although Hall did not keep this pace up, his summer seasons at Bath continued until his retirement from the stage in 2012, making this one of the longest residencies of his career. The theatre was not the home he had been looking for, though; it was more like a flat share as the Theatre Royal had its own artistic director (Laurence Boswell) and staged productions by other directors.

The Theatre Royal was not a subsidized theatre but had ambitions to be more than a typical regional theatre hosting pre-West End work and touring productions. In 1998, the theatre set up Theatre Royal Bath Productions as a commercial subsidiary with the remit to produce profitable productions for its main house as well as commercial tours and West End transfers, with the revenues ploughed back into the theatre's artistic programme. Hall's relationship with the theatre went back to his days at the National when he had supported the renovation of the eighteenth-century theatre, which relaunched with the National's *A Midsummer Night's Dream* (directed by Bill Bryden with Paul Scofield leading the cast) in 1982 (Lowndes 1982: 76–82). After a career spent campaigning for the subsidized theatre, Hall was now in the ironic position of being the source of subsidy for the Theatre Royal. Hall's tenure in Bath never seems to have satisfied his longing for a theatrical home: the Rose was his focus through these years. As Hall subsidized the Theatre Royal, they, in turn, allowed him the opportunity to commit his time to the Rose. Despite his extraordinarily prolific output in Bath (twenty-six productions in eight years), he refrained from setting out an artistic vision comparable to the ones he had set out for his ventures in America and at the Old Vic. He directed all his artistic energy towards the Rose.

Hall became Artistic Director of the Rose in 2003, although the theatre then was little more than a shell. A local project to establish a theatre in Kingston had been bubbling since 1986. Hall's ambition to have a residency at the Rose was frustrated by lack of funds (*Daily Telegraph* 16 January 2008), and when the Rose was finally complete and open, he stepped down as Artistic Director to be replaced by Stephen Unwin. Two ideas appealed to Hall. As there was no Arts Council funding available for the Rose, and funding from the local council was insufficient, the project relied on an innovative partnership with Kingston University, where Hall was a professor and was also its Chancellor. The university proposed creating a Masters of Fine Art (MFA) with students spending their final year working in the company. Hall found this 'very exciting'. He told the *Daily Telegraph*: 'There is nowhere in this country where somebody can train to be an actor and then, on the result they've achieved, move into a professional situation as part of the course' (16 January 2008). Hall had always approached directing in the manner of a Cambridge don leading a seminar. His Perse days when learning and theatre were intertwined still cast its shadow. He had brought academics like John Barton and John Russell Brown into the theatre as directors, but here, at the end of his career and in his eighth decade, Hall finally had a chance to bring academia directly onto the stage.

As You Like It was a strange choice of play to launch these projects (as well as concluding his time at the Ahmanson). Hall had never directed it before: in the past, he had tended to play it safe when launching new residencies but *As You Like It* was a risk for a summer season that demanded a sure-fire hit. The play can be among Shakespeare's sunniest plays, but Hall found in it a restless world tormented by unfulfilled desire and frightened of love rather than seduced by it. For the *New York Times*, Hall 'never entirely erases the air of apprehension that hovers over his Arden' (*New York Times* 20 January 2005). John Gunter created a simple but vivid design, for a sombre looking production set in a winter-bound forest which one American reviewer found to be as 'forbiddingly cold and windswept as New York is at the moment' (*New York Times* 20 January 2005). Although the second half saw the world turn into spring, the predominant note of the production was signalled by the dark tones of the first half: 'I have also never seen a production of *As You Like It* that so insists on keeping in mind how harsh and capricious the world can be' (*New York Times*

20 January 2005). The Duke and his courtiers wore charity-shop overcoats to protect them from the winter, looking out of place in the forest. Dark chords heralded opening scenes of 'nasty physical violence and familial animosity' (*New York Times* 20 January 2005), the 'oppressive' court of the usurping Duke wearing black shirts and military berets (*Financial Times* 3 December 2004) that several reviewers recognized as a reference to Oswald Mosley's black-shirt fascists from the 1930s. Indeed, the whole production felt like a dark memory from Hall's pre-war childhood. The production did not present a world full of gentle comedy, but one beset by dark change, overshadowed by fascism and populated by refugees, on the brink of either brutal totalitarianism or absolute chaos. For one reviewer, the bleak setting called to mind the Great Depression of the 1930s, although the anxious mood and the frenetic pace also seemed to resonate with the contemporary 'era of invasions, evictions and bankruptcies' (*Curtain Up* 13 February 2005). Gunter created a simple forest with 'enormous, looming trees' (*Variety* 8 February 2005) which some found atmospheric (*Variety* 8 February 2005) and others 'acceptable but utterly uninspiring' (*Independent* 25 August 2003). The set was not even simple enough for the Rose performances, as the unfinished theatre had no backwall as such: instead, back projections and fabric backcloths marked the seasons (*Financial Times* 3 December 2004).

Most reviews focused on Rebecca Hall's remarkable performance as Rosalind. Hall had cast his daughter in a West End production of Shaw's *Mrs. Warren's Profession* in 2002, which he revived for his first summer season in Bath. Rebecca Hall had shone then and once again pulled much of the attention away from her father with an original interpretation of the character which was at turns witty and anguished. Michael Billington admired Rebecca Hall's 'profound sadness', a quality he had never seen in the character before. He wrote that it seemed as if 'her inability to declare her love was a source of spiritual frustration' (*Guardian* 20 August 2003). The *Financial Times* also noted 'the sadness and romantic torment' that took the performance away from conventional interpretations of the character (*Financial Times* 3 December 2004). As Ganymede, Rebecca Hall wore a fake thin beard, and an overcoat with the collar turned up rakishly and overlong unbuttoned sleeves that sometimes hid her hands; her hair was concealed by a tattered wide-brimmed trilby, and a scarf was draped loosely about her neck. She looked like an adolescent in oversize clothes, trying to look grown up but not sure how to wear them: 'gracefully gawky', as the *New York Times* reviewer put it (*New York Times* 20 January 2005). Hall gave Rosalind 'not only the restless vigour and romanticism of youth but also its trepidation as her character braces herself for the leap into dangerous adulthood' (*New York Times* 20 January 2005). Yet she could also display what Billington called a 'touching bashfulness', casting her gaze downwards when Orlando won his wrestling match, indicating that he had 'overthrown more than his enemies' (*Guardian* 20 August 2003). Her mock-courtship scenes with Orlando later in the play were unusually tense, full of risk and 'melancholy sadness' (*Guardian* 20 August 2003). Billington later admitted he was 'smitten' by Rebecca Hall's performance (*Guardian* 6 December 2004). The *Financial Times* praised her 'native genius' for making Rosalind seem 'luminously human' (*Financial Times* 3 December 2004). Not all reviewers were so smitten: *The Independent* thought she injected 'too much contemporary drawl into her delivery' (25 August 2003) while *Variety* worried that her 'register can rise and remain uneasily high' (*Variety* 8 February 2005). In an interview for *SFGate*, Hall explained that he had avoided the play before because he had not been able to find a Rosalind as enchanting as Vanessa Redgrave (*Financial Times* 3 December 2004). Hall and his daughter worked together on discovering why Rosalind stays in disguise once she reaches the forest, where she could have reverted to being herself: 'The answer, we realized together, is because Rosalind's frightened of love. She feels its danger.'

Joseph Millson played Orlando in Bath, but Hall cast Dan Stevens for the Rose revival and subsequent tour. Stevens played the part with 'fury and despair' (*Curtain Up* 13 February 2005). He was an 'angry-young-man' from the 1950s (*Variety* 8 February 2005) whose 'roaring aggression' in the opening gave the production 'a searingly intense edge' (*Variety* 8 February 2005). Stevens' 'riveting' performance contrasted with Rebecca Hall's psychologically complex Rosalind. Stevens took 'risks with every line and gesture ... discovering material rather than simply reciting it' (*Variety* 8 February 2005). There was tenderness in his performance: as he sung 'Song blow thou winter' mournfully, Stevens gently fed Adam with a large spoon from a bowl. In the forest, he wore a bohemian coat and bag: the *New York Times* noted his 'loopy' change from 'virile firebrand into tongue-tied, love-addled fool' (*New York Times* 20 January 2005). For Billington, reviewing the production a second time when Hall revived it at the Rose, Stevens presented an Orlando 'in whom fraternal anger competes with tongue-tied love' (*Guardian* 6 December 2004).

Aside from the revival of *As You Like It* at the Rose, Hall did not direct Shakespeare again until 2005, when he produced *Much Ado about Nothing* at the Theatre Royal, Bath. In his autobiography, reflecting on the plays left in the canon that he had yet to direct, he wrote that *As You Like It* and *Much Ado* 'still beckon me', so it was fitting that he should move from one to the other (Hall 1993: 412). Once again, Hall searched for the melancholy within the comedy, darkening the hues of a normally sunny play. Hall had a new designer to work with: Kevin Rigdon, an American theatre designer who also taught at the University of Houston, where Hall was an honorary professor and occasionally gave seminars. Hall and Rigdon worked together on *Man and Superman* and *Galileo's Daughter* at the Theatre Royal in 2004, but this was their first Shakespeare collaboration. Rigdon was Hall's main designer for the following two years. (Hall's long-term designer John Gunter retired from the stage after being diagnosed with Alzheimer's in 2007.) Hall's new partnership marked a step away from the simple blue boxes and sparse sets which characterized most of his post-National Shakespeare work.

Instead, Rigdon created more scenic, naturalistic stages. He set *Much Ado about Nothing* in the 'mellow, sun-weathered Sicilian courtyard' (*Guardian* 8 July 2005) of a medieval castle dominated by imposing stone walls and a huge, fifteen-foot arched doorway in the centre of the stage. For some scenes, rows of tall candleholders ringed the performance area. Garlanded bowers and sweeping staircases were wheeled on for key scenes. The actors wore elegant Regency costumes, which several reviewers compared to those worn in film adaptations of Jane Austen's novels. The costumes jarred with the medieval setting. The *Financial Times* thought 'the multi-historical layers enrich the play to marvellous effect' (8 July 2005) but other reviewers were less convinced: 'this story of Mediterranean intrigue and romance isn't done any favours by being set in the Jane Austen era. The chaps are all dressed like Lord Nelson and the women like Bo Peep' (*Independent* 9 July 2005). Either way, this was a more ambitious and operatic use of theatre design than Hall had applied to Shakespeare for some time.

Hall paired the production with Noël Coward's *Private Lives*, directed by Thea Sharrock with many of the same actors. For the press performance, the plays were staged on the same day to enhance the sense that the repertoire was a coherent exploration of (as the *Telegraph* put it) 'love second time around' (8 July 2005) or, as *The Guardian* more directly put it, 'two famous sex-war comedies' (8 July 2005). However, Hall struggled to create the same kind of ensemble engagement that he had achieved with similar pairings at the RSC and the National. Charles Edwards, who played Don Pedro, remembers flitting between rehearsal rooms without gaining much sense of the plays: 'my daily rehearsals would be shared out between the two rehearsal rooms. You just tend to pop in to do your bit, and then rush off to the other room' (Shuter and Edwards 2011: n.p.).

For the lead roles, Hall cast Janie Dee and Aden Gillet. In 2003, Hall had worked with both actors on a similarly themed suite of productions which combined Noël Coward's *Design for Living* with Pinter's *Betrayal*. Dee and Gillet played the lead roles in those plays about tortured love, so it was a natural step for Hall to cast them as Beatrice and Benedick to renew (as the *Telegraph* put it) their 'sparky stage partnership' (*Daily Telegraph* 8 July 2005). Dee played a 'sumptuously vivacious' Beatrice (*Guardian* 8 July 2005) with 'an ache of vulnerability' (*Daily Telegraph* 8 July 2005) who was left 'giddy' when Benedick finally kisses her (*Daily Telegraph* 8 July 2005). Gillet was 'acidly perplexed' (*Guardian* 8 July 2005). He played Benedick as an army officer who is 'starchy and benign' (*Independent* 9 July 2005). However, the actors' lack of experience in acting Shakespeare was picked up by some reviewers. The *Financial Times* thought they were 'undercast' (8 July 2005) and even Billington, who wrote the most positive review, thought that other actors overshadowed the pair, notably Philip Voss as Leonato, who underwent 'an astonishing transition from benign host to manic father' in a performance that Billington compared to Lear; and Charles Edwards as Don Pedro, who had a 'homosexual fixation with Claudio'. Billington wrote that, after Hero's restoration, Don Pedro 'realises he has been duped, snarls angrily at the dancers and is left, at the curtain, in splenetic, vengeful isolation' (*Guardian* 8 July 2005).

Reviews were largely positive. The *Daily Telegraph* judged it a 'splendidly assured production' that 'captures the pain at the play's heart' and offered 'rare emotional depth' (*Daily Telegraph* 8 July 2005). For Billington, the 'shock lies in discovering that Hall's production of the Shakespeare is far more radically revisionist than Thea Sharrock's of Noël Coward' (*Guardian* 8 July 2005). Once again, Hall had looked for the darker themes in Shakespeare's comedy, revealing *Much Ado* to be a 'tragedy manqué, filled with bitterness and anguish'. In the *Financial Times*, Alastair Macaulay also recognized the way Hall mixed 'dark cruelty and brightly joking romance'. Macaulay compared Hall to a 'master-conductor' who possesses 'a complete grasp of the right tempi, the right dynamics and the true significance of the shifting harmonies'. Macaulay wrote that he had seen many better productions of the play, but none 'where I have been so sure that the director has a shortcut to Shakespeare's mind' (*Financial Times* 8 July 2005).

Macaulay had it right: this was expert, impeccable Shakespeare, but no more. The production lacked the ambition and intellectual power which typified most of Hall's work. For once, Shakespeare was not at the forefront of Hall's mind. In 2005, his creative energies lay elsewhere, partly in the ongoing saga of the Rose, which remained incomplete, but mainly in the fiftieth anniversary of his production of *Waiting for Godot*. This renewed attention to Hall, whom the nation was finally recognizing as one of the great figures of British theatre. He was the subject of a *South Bank Show* documentary which includes footage of the *Much Ado* rehearsals. The centrepiece of the anniversary year was his third and final *Godot*, which opened in Bath that August, for which he received, by his own account, 'the best notices' of his life (Knapper 2007: 580). The celebrations were overshadowed by a rather squalid rights issue which meant that Hall could not take the production to London. The Beckett estate assigned the London rights jointly to the Barbican and the Gate in Dublin for a production directed by Walter Asmus, effectively shutting Hall out of the celebrations of his pioneering achievement (*Observer* 28 August 2005). The issue was finally resolved the following year when Hall's *Godot* transferred to the New Ambassador's theatre. The anniversary year was capped by another celebration when Pinter was awarded the Nobel prize for literature. Hall told the press it was 'a great prize for a great and original poet of the theatre' – but it was also an indirect recognition of Hall's daring as the director who discovered Pinter (BBC News 13 October 2005). Hall was still full of energy and youthful mischief. When Stephen Knapper sat in on the *Godot* rehearsals, he found Hall tinkling a tune on the piano to 'summon up the spirit' while talking about clowns (Knapper 2007: 579).

In 2006, Hall produced *Measure for Measure*, which played a summer season in Bath before transferring to the RSC's new, temporary main stage, the Courtyard Theatre, in Stratford-upon-Avon. The return to Stratford should have been a significant event as it was the fiftieth anniversary of Hall's first production at the SMT. Neither this nor Hall's return was celebrated. The choice of play was apt: *Measure for Measure* is a dark and twisted play about a Duke 'of dark corners' who moves between the world of power and the quotidian worlds of the streets, much in the same way as Hall divided his working life between management offices and the rehearsal room, somehow always the outsider in both settings. Here, Hall was returning as the outsider, performing under his own company's name rather than the RSC's: he was more of a disguised monarch than a Duke returning to cast judgement on his deputies. The then current artistic director, Michael Boyd, had embarked on a massive rebuilding project which rendered the main RST building unusable. Partly to offset the risk to the RSC's business by this long-term capital project, Boyd launched some ambitious theatrical projects, the highlight of which was his 2006 Complete Works season. Companies from all over the world were invited to help the RSC stage all thirty-seven plays, and this was how Hall came to Stratford once more, this time with his own company. The bulldozers were busy razing the theatre building, leaving only the façade and front corridor. With his past shielded by a builder's fence and turned into a hardhat only area, the stage on which he had directed Laughton and Olivier dismantled, the offices where he had planned the birth of the RSC gone, the box office where scores of young people camped overnight for tickets to see *Hamlet* turned to rubble, Hall returned for what would prove to be his final theatrical statement in Stratford.

He put *Measure for Measure* on a mostly bare stage with the actors in Puritan-style seventeenth-century costumes. A large throne dominated the set during court scenes, iron bars descended from the flies to suggest a prison, but the whole set had a prison-like feel, a 'stark prison background' as the reviewer for *The Stage* put it (13 July 2006). Benedict Nightingale observed that 'iron bars' were 'everywhere' (*Times* 14 July 2006). In prison, inmates wore sacking with their crimes written on them, identifying them as 'Bawd' or

'Fornicator'. Nightingale read this as a way of denoting 'that this is a society that severely criminalises sexual sin'. At the rear of the stage, there was a 'massive reflective wall' with hidden, secret doors (Kirwan 2006: n.p.). The world was 'stark' and 'sombre' according to *The Stage*, 'soberly beautiful' for *The Guardian* (14 July 2006).

For Hall, the play was about the Duke, and in interviews before and during the production, he ruminated on the complexities of this 'extraordinary long part and an extraordinarily tortured part' (Neill 2006: n.p.). He cast James Laurenson, who was also playing Vladimir in Hall's third *Waiting for Godot*. Although only sixty-six, Laurenson looked older: tall, gaunt, greying and wizened, he played an unusually old and haunted Duke, 'struck in years', as Billington put it, whose head was buried in his huge monk's habit. He played the Duke as a 'shrewd, self-controlled figure' (*Guardian* 14 July 2006) who behaved with the compassion and sympathy of a 'country doctor' (*Daily Telegraph* 14 July 2006) but was ultimately the most problematic character of them all. Laurenson's Duke knew from the beginning that Angelo would turn out to be a hypocrite. Hall and Laurenson treated the Duke as the play's central character. This was a shift away from recent theatrical tradition which, since John Barton's 1970 production, has tended to focus attention on Isabella. For Hall, Isabella is not a sympathetic part at all. He saw her as a fanatic, and under his direction, Andrea Riseborough played her as a 'young woman with the glib certainty and closed, tight face of the untested, born-again Christian' (*Daily Telegraph* 14 July 2006). She was 'rather strident' (*The Stage* 13 July 2006) and 'impetuous' (*Guardian* 14 July 2006). For Billington, the production was 'partly about the gradual corruption of Isabella' although this was not through Angelo's actions but her 'complicity in the Duke's dirty tricks' (*Guardian* 14 July 2006). By taking a less sympathetic approach to Isabella, argued Charles Spencer, Hall highlighted the play's 'contradictions and ambiguities' (*Daily Telegraph* 14 July 2006). In the production's final scene, the Duke stunned his onstage audience with his unexpected proposal to marry Isabella, who does not respond 'in any way' (Womersley 2006: n.p.). After an awkward silence, the Duke walked slowly offstage alone, those left staring after him in shocked disbelief (Kirwan 2006: n.p.).

Love's Labour's Lost 2008 and *A Midsummer Night's Dream* 2010

For his 2008 season, Hall returned to *Love's Labour's Lost*. The first play he had produced for the Shakespeare Memorial Theatre now became the first play he directed exclusively for the Rose, although by this point he had semi-retired with the title Director Emeritus. He recruited a new designer, Christopher Woods and a mostly new cast with only Susie Trayling (playing Rosaline) and Peter Bowles (Don Adriano de Armado) having any history of working with Hall. In some respects, it was an odd choice of play with which to launch a new theatre. *Love's Labour's Lost* was an uncharacteristically low-key production with a practically bare set (the only thing on stage apart from the actors was a lectern) and a focus on the text that baffled some critics and apparently bored some audiences, as several reviews commented on the lack of audience laughter. Hall was also in competition with the RSC's production of the same play, starring David Tennant who was at the height of his fame as the eponymous lead actor in the popular television show *Doctor Who*. It was a competition he could not possibly win. *Love's Labour's Lost* was not even a particularly easy or safe play for Hall to direct. True, he had directed it before, but the last time he had done so was over fifty years before, a production which Hall barely remembered: 'That first production doesn't exist anymore so I can't really compare the two,' he told the *Telegraph*. 'I have no idea if I have taken a radically different approach this time around. I am a different person' (23 November 2008).

He had taken a radically different approach. In contrast to the highly pictorial 1956 production, this time Hall stripped everything away to show off the new theatre – and show off the fundamental idea Hall had for this theatre as a place where the text would be dominant. The only piece of scenery, a lectern was a challenge to the actors to use the bare space of the theatre to create the play. The theatre, then, was in effect the set. However, the lectern also signalled the didactic nature of the work, as if Hall was himself invisibly there, giving a lecture on the importance of the text over directorial design. Peter Kirwan described the set as 'conscious of its own learnedness' (Kirwan 2009: 315) in a production which 'took on a truly academic air'. Billington compared it less elegantly to a 'denuded swimming pool' (*Guardian* 30 October 2008). Some reviewers complained that the stage action was 'inert' with actors often standing around on the stage.

But this stillness of performance allowed Hall and his company to foreground the play's language. Among Hall's least visual productions, *Love's Labour's Lost* gave full reign to his iambic fundamentalism. Hall told the *Telegraph* that the 'interesting thing about *Love's Labour's Lost* is that it's all about words. All the characters are obsessed with words. Am I saying the right word? Have I got the right words in my mouth?' (23 November 2008). There were distant echoes, buried memories, of the Perse and his first introduction to verse-speaking and the pedagogic power of language: '[w]hile the performers provided a feast for the ears, the staging almost exclusively consisted of characters standing around, talking, giving the audience little to engage with other than the words' (Kirwan 2009: 316). As Charles Spencer observed, the supporting cast often stood 'mutely around the edge of the stage as the linguistic fireworks exploded' (*Daily Telegraph* 30 October 2008). Kirwan complains that the staging killed the comedy of the overhearing scene, usually an easy win for productions of the play. Here, the Lords simply retreated to either end of the play, with Berowne climbing a ladder to a balcony so that 'the scene became a straightforward and rather dull progression of poetry readings, with the occasional comment from above' (Kirwan 2009: 316). Hall avoided any concessions to the audience, any stage business which did not naturally arise from the language. For some reviewers, this approach tended to expose the play's weaknesses. For the *Financial Times*, 'the production inadvertently brings out the paucity of actual narrative' (30 October 2008), and John Thaxter commented that the play exhibited 'minimal character development or plot continuity' (*The Stage* 29 October 2008). For other reviewers, though, Hall, by refusing to concede to audience expectations, revealed an exercise in language. For Billington, the production confronted and delighted in 'the play's sophisticated verbal games' (*Guardian* 30 October 2008). Kirwan noted that Holofernes, played by William Chubb, approached 'wordplay' as 'a form of self-challenge', applauding himself 'as the words formed witty conclusions' (Kirwan 2009: 316). Chubb performed Holofernes 'with much angular fingerwork and some brilliant tics and changes of speed' (*Daily Mail* 30 October 2008). Kevin Trainer, as Moth, gave a performance that was 'exceptional in its verbal dexterity' (Kirwan 2009: 316). Meanwhile, Finbar Lynch played Berowne as a 'melancholy thinker' with an 'aptitude for speaking in sonnets' that was 'more impressive than his susceptibility to what they might actually mean' (*Independent* 30 October 2008). By contrast, Bowles found comedy in the part of Armado by exaggerating gestures for comic effect while at the same time subtly suggesting at a deeper romantic dimension to his relationship with Moth (Kirwan 2009: 316).

Hall's purpose revealed itself in the production's melancholic ending, when, as Spencer put it, '[d]eath suddenly arrives in this sunlit arcadia'. Spencer admired the way that Hall found in the final act a 'deeper, darker emotion' as Berowne comes to understand that 'honest plain words best pierce the ear of grief' (*Daily Telegraph* 30 October 2008). Having celebrated and indulged in the play's verbal dexterity and language games, Hall now foregrounded a different approach to language. The production became 'a critique of the very linguistic playfulness it had earlier exemplified' which, for Spencer, revealed *Love's Labour's Lost* as 'a surprisingly moving work about the glibness of youthful certainty' (*Daily Telegraph* 30 October 2008). It was as if Hall was looking back on his Marlowe days and his education at the Perse where language was always supreme. But perhaps he was looking forward too. Hall was in the last phase of his career, and the shadow that death cast over the end of this production was a shadow he could also feel. One reviewer picked up on this resonance: '[i]t almost felt as though veteran Sir Peter was bringing a close to his own glorious career' wrote one journalist (*Daily Mail* 30 October 2008).

Hall's final production at the Rose was *A Midsummer Night's Dream* in 2010, with Judi Dench reprising the role of Titania. Like much of Hall's late work, this was a production which looked both backwards and forwards. Hall was undoubtedly on safe ground returning once again to *Dream*, the Shakespeare play that he spent the most time with and productions of which book-ended his career. His strong partnership with Dench secured the production, and her star power ensured that critics and audiences came to Kingston. Rachael Stirling, daughter of Diana Rigg, was cast as Helena, the same role that her mother had played for Hall when he made his 1969 film of the play. The cast included many regulars from the Peter Hall Company, among them Oliver Chris (Bottom), Charles Edwards (Oberon), William Chubb (Egeus and Starveling) and James Laurenson (Quince). There were familiar faces behind the scenes too. Hall had been without a regular designer since John Gunter retired, but for this production, he hired Elizabeth Bury, a 1960s veteran of the RSC and wife of John Bury. Hall celebrated his eightieth birthday a few months after the production's run, leading to a minor flurry of press interest in his career.

A Midsummer Night's Dream was also a restless production, underpinned by a sense of urgency about the Rose Theatre, which risked being affected by the global financial crisis of 2008 during which the UK government's budget deficit had ballooned to an unsustainable level. The year 2010 would see a general election as the sitting parliament was coming to the end of its five-year term. Hall had been a vocal critic of the Labour government, but the years from 1997 to 2010 had been more sympathetic to arts funding than any other government since the 1960s. Both major political parties were standing on platforms of deficit reduction with severe cuts in public funding inevitable whatever the outcome of the forthcoming election (in the event, that June the British people voted for a hung parliament, which resulted in a coalition of the Conservatives and Liberal Democrats). Hall's first *Dream* was produced at the end of a period of post-war austerity and on the eve of a new phase of economic confidence, of which the arts was a major beneficiary. Now a new era of austerity was beginning.

Dench's casting influenced Hall's interpretation. At seventy-five, she was playing the same role she had first performed in her early thirties in Hall's 1962 revival. Some critics thought Dench too old to play Titania, but Hall justified her casting in an intriguing induction scene in which Dench, dressed as Elizabeth I, silently rehearsed with a group of aristocrat actors before leaving the stage with her 'part'. Bury's sparse, mainly black set, dressed with cardboard trees, reinforced the idea that the audience was watching a play-within-a-play. The idea cemented Hall's approach to the play as a courtly wedding performance, making explicit an idea that was never far from his mind in his SMT production and his film. Wrapping *Dream* in an extra layer of meta-theatricality, turning the aristocrats into Bottoms and Quinces, added to the sense of fantasy. But the real theatrical coup was Dench's costume, recognizably an interpretation of Elizabeth I's white dress and ruff and recognized as such by almost every press reviewer. In a pre-performance interview, Hall told an audience that Elizabeth probably would have taken part in plays (Heijes 2010: 683).

On one level, these metatheatrical layers and temporal recursions were merely Hall being a little bit mischievous, but they also conveyed something significant about Hall's sense of who Shakespeare was and what he thought Shakespeare was trying to do. Dench played a melancholic Titania who, as Susannah Clapp put it, 'mourns the fact that everything is slipping'. There was 'frost on the rose and buds on the ice' and 'crops rotting in the fields and massive floods'. For Clapp, Dench and Hall revealed *Dream* as a play that was prescient about climate change: 'A comedy which, flickering between conscious and unconscious, has long seemed to be a pageant of the twentieth-century imagination now appears wired directly into the crises of the twenty-first century' (*Observer* 21 February 2010). As Coen Heijes notes, Hall located the play in an 'earthier and very English setting' (Heijes 2010: 683). The England that Hall surveyed at the end of his career was not just being blown about by carbon-fuelled rough winds: looming cuts to arts funding and regional development funding threatened to bring about the end of his career-long dream to run an ensemble company freed of financial concerns.

Reviewers focused their attention on Dench, with Clapp cheekily commenting that 'it's not so much a production as a coronation' (*Observer* 21 February 2010). Sam Marlowe quipped, 'what surrounds her onstage feels like little more than scanty window-dressing for Dench's performance' (*ArtsDesk* 16 February 2010). Dench was 'bewitching, by turns statesmanlike, flirtatious, magisterial and sensual' (*ArtsDesk* 16 February 2010). Her voice, 'with its rustles and shivers' sounded like 'shaken foliage' (*Observer* 21 February 2010). Even when showing some vulnerability when enchanted by the transfigured Bottom, Dench's performance had a steeliness which reminded audiences that she was Elizabeth playing Titania. Clapp saw the whole production as 'the fantasy of an elderly monarch with her eye on younger men': in other words, the dream of the title was Elizabeth's (*Observer* 21 February 2010). Bottom and Oberon were both played by unusually young actors – Chris was in his early thirties, Edwards in his early forties. They were young suitors to the old queen, yet there was little in the way of erotic tension. As Heijes put it, 'this was not a lovesick forest queen speaking to a brutish ass, but a mature and experienced woman snuggling with an adored pet and remembering a life filled with love' (Heijes 2010: 683). Paul Taylor in the *Independent* also noted that Hall downplayed the play's eroticism, comparing Titania's relationship with Bottom to a childish devotion to a pet: 'She hugs him tight as one might want to embrace, say, Lassie' (*Independent* 16 February 2010).

Twelfth Night 2011 and *Henry IV, Parts 1 and 2* 2011

Hall's final two productions took him back to the national stage. Nicholas Hytner wanted to mark Hall's eightieth birthday by persuading him back to the National for what would prove to be a valedictory production. Given a free choice of play, Hall opted for *Twelfth Night* which, along with *A Midsummer Night's Dream*, was one of the plays he had directed the most often over the course of his career. Shortly afterwards, Hall returned to the *Henry IV* plays, which he had in his autobiography called his favourite plays, for a more intimate, low-key production at the Theatre Royal, Bath. With typical maverick style, Hall divided himself between a small chamber comedy on the national stage and a national epic on the provincial stage. Even with the garlands of the National Theatre crowning his career on the South Bank, Hall's final work marked him out as a perpetual outsider.

Hall had once said that *Twelfth Night* was a play 'about growing up' (Hall 1993: 146), so it was both fitting and typically contrarian of Hall to use it to mark his birthday. There may also have been a sense of unfinished business: he had never tackled any of Shakespeare's mid-period comedies at the National. Nevertheless, Hall continued to develop the autumnal feel of his recent comedies. Reviewers noticed that it has a 'dusky twilit feel' (*New York Times* 25 January 2011), and 'a valedictory feel, rather than a celebratory one' (*Arts*

Desk 20 January 2011). The cast had a family feel to it, with his daughter Rebecca Hall playing Viola and Finty Williams, Judi Dench's daughter, cast as Maria. In keeping with his late style, Hall focused in on the language and avoided complicated stage business.

Hall worked for the first and last time with the designer Anthony Ward, who created a 'golden autumnal' set (*Arts Desk* 20 January 2011) with an 'overhanging canopy' which in the second scene unfurled to 'reveal the shipwrecked Viola and a sea captain' (*Guardian* 19 January 2011). The reveal covered the set 'with a pattern of leaves past their prime' (*New York Times* 25 January 2011). Ward and Hall dressed the cast in Caroline costumes. Ward dressed the stage in 'russet and ochre' tones (August 2011: n.p.). At the back of the stage, Ward constructed a Jacobean skyline of houses surrounding a large hall and its gardens (*Curtain Up* 20 January 2011). Eavesdropping on Malvolio, Fabian and Aguecheek hid behind transparent screens decorated with leaves (*Curtain Up* 20 January 2011). Later, Malvolio was imprisoned in a bird cage, 'his tall frame squashed as if sitting on a perch' (*Curtain Up* 20 January 2011). Joining the cast onstage and in an elevated gallery, 'doubleted musicians' played period instruments, mixing music and action. Hannah August quipped that Hall might have been better off taking the production down river to the reconstructed Globe (August 2011: n.p.).

David Ryall, as Feste, wore 'muddy, funereal black' with only a few 'half-hearted' gestures to motley (*Arts Desk* 20 January 2011). Ryall was, as one reviewer put it, a 'scrofulous, sardonic' Feste, 'more festering than festive' (*Arts Desk* 20 January 2011) or as Billington put it, 'a wry, weathered observer of human folly' (*Guardian* 19 January 2011). Ryall had played the part in Hall's 1994 production. Now reprising it in his late seventies, Ryall did nothing to hide his age but made a virtue of it by playing Feste as a 'wizened presence' (*New York Times* 25 January 2011) weighed down by an unspoken past. His Feste was decrepit, and although it was never made explicit, Ryall based his performance on the idea that 'Feste might have been a defrocked priest in a former life' (*Guardian* 28 December 2014). Many reviewers saw Ryall as a surrogate for Hall himself: 'the actor seems to be standing in for a director who knows full well about the march of time but isn't prepared to lessen his step any time soon' (*New York Times* 25 January 2011). Several reviewers wondered if Feste's final song, 'The Wind and the Rain,' which is about growing from 'a little tiny boy' to an old man 'in his beds' was meant to be 'a kind of valedictory from Mr. Hall himself' (*New York Times* 25 January 2011). He began by lightly tapping his fingers on his tabor 'in imitation of the rain' (August 2011: np). As he sang 'But that's all one, our play is done' to a melancholy tune by Mick Sands, 'a canopy of dead leaves descends upon him slowly like a shroud' (*Arts Desk* 20 January 2011).

The heart of the production was to be found not in big theatrical moments but in small details or, as Billington put it, 'simple moments' that 'anchor the play in a world of human truth' (*Guardian* 19 January 2011). In Act 1, Scene 2, Rebecca Hall made a 'characteristically luminous' entrance as Viola (*New York Times* 25 January 2011), dripping wet from the shipwreck, and her initial hope that her brother has not drowned was undercut by the reality of a seaman's corpse on the stage. When Viola offered the Captain a reward, he refused it 'with a gentle shrug as if to point up the irrelevance of reward in the face of marine tragedy' (*Guardian* 19 January 2011).

Charles Edwards played Aguecheek as 'an aristocratic manic depressive' (*Guardian* 19 January 2011) and 'a deliciously twitchy fop, his eyes forever swivelling insecurely' (*Independent* 20 January 2011); Simon Callow gave a 'booming, fruity' performance (*Independent* 20 January 2011) of Sir Toby as 'a genuine rural blueblood' who is 'capable of insensate cruelty' (*Guardian* 19 January 2011); Marton Csokas was 'languorously self-indulgent' (*Guardian* 19 January 2011) as a 'long-maned' and 'sleazy' Orsino (*New York Times* 25 January 2011) and Simon Paisley Day as Malvolio caught 'all of the character's narcissistic self-love' but also solicited sympathy for his imprisonment (*Guardian* 19 January 2011).

Spencer thought Rebecca Hall played 'one of the finest Violas I have seen' and Taylor said she was a 'modern-sounding, intriguingly understated heroine' who 'retains throughout an amused ironic reserve' (*Independent* 20 January 2011). However, other reviewers were more reserved. Billington wrote that Hall 'misses some of Viola's growing mischief and allows her hands to hang limply from her sides for much of the evening' (*Guardian* 19 January 2011). For Billington, the production caught 'perfectly the play's melancholy and preoccupation with time, transitoriness and loss' with an 'awareness of the still, sad music of humanity' (*Guardian* 19 January 2011). Other reviewers thought it 'sluggish' and 'flat' (*Independent* 20 January 2011), embracing an autumnal sadness at the expense of the play's 'madcap' comedy (*New York Times* 25 January 2011). Even Spencer worried that the production's lack of an overarching concept made it 'dull' and 'puritanically stark', but he praised the production's 'bittersweet mixture of laughter and pain' (*Daily Telegraph* 19 January 2011).

In his final productions, Hall turned back to the history plays, the genre on which his reputation for cutting-edge political theatre had been founded in the 1960s but which he had left entirely alone since 1965. All his late work had been comedies – even his US productions of *Romeo and Juliet* and *Troilus and Cressida* were a decade behind him and the last time that the British stage had seen a Hall production of Shakespeare that was not a comedy was his 1997 *King Lear*. His comedies seemed increasingly personal, twilight works marked by an iambic fundamentalist commitment to the text, a minimum of stage business, Elizabethan dress and a foreboding sense of the gathering darkness. David Ryall's decrepit Feste, singing his final plaintive song as the autumn leaves gathered around him like a shroud, seemed as fitting a metaphor for Hall's retirement from the stage as any. With characteristic stubbornness, Hall turned his back on the comedies and stared at the contemporary world head on for a final epic of English history. In his autobiography, Hall wrote, 'I yearn to return to the two *Henry IV*s' because they 'remain my favourite plays' (Hall 1993: 412). When he was a teenager, Hall had seen Olivier in the plays at the Old Vic, using a camping stool to reserve his place in the box office queue in the early morning and then taking either the cheapest seats or standing in the gallery to watch Olivier play Hotspur (Hall 1993: 56). Seeing both productions in one day convinced Hall of the importance of big theatrical events (Hall 1993: 113). A decade later, when he was still at Cambridge, Hall was entranced by Richard Burton's Hal and Henry V in Anthony Quayle's history play cycle at the SMT in 1951, which would inspire him to stage his own cycle. He saw the productions many times and spent the train journeys between Cambridge and Stratford 'doing bad imitations of Harry Andrews, the definitive Henry IV' (Hall 1993: 89–90).

Hall had refrained from making direct comments on the modern world since turning his back on Blair's Britain in the late 1990s. The world he faced in 2011 was very different, scarred by the post-9/11 wars in Iraq and Afghanistan and the worst financial crisis since the Great Depression. Although Hall had been a fierce critic of arts funding under Blair's government, even that was now being ruthlessly slashed by a Conservative-led coalition government committed to drastic cuts in public spending to address the ballooning budget deficit. A new age of austerity had begun. For Hall, it must have felt as if the clock was resetting to the 1940s before the creation of the welfare state. Michael Billington saw Hall's Henries as his 'search for order in a divided, burning land' (*Guardian* 28 July 2011).

The cast wore Victorian costumes, hardly a radical idea for a twenty-first-century Shakespeare production, but for Hall, it was a rare move away from the early modern costumes that typified his late work. It all looked dangerously like a directorially imposed idea of the kind he had been zealously avoiding for decades. The iambic fundamentalist was unexpectedly returning to the big ideas and national sweep of the Hall of the 1960s. The Victorian period shunted the plays into something recognizably modern. By looking back to the nineteenth century, Hall positioned the plays as a founding narrative of the twentieth-century world order, an origin myth about the formation of empire and the hope for a stable, ordered future. The period is roughly equivalent to Shakespeare's relationship with the Wars of the Roses: Shakespeare was looking back roughly two centuries from his own time to a story that would, eventually, describe how his world had come into being. Now Hall was shunting that narrative forward to 150–200 years before the present as if to say, this is a story that belongs to us. Shakespeare was once more our contemporary. Tom Mison played Prince Hal, David Yelland was Henry IV, Ben Mansfield (one of the few actors to have been in all three of Hall's recent Shakespeare works) was Hotspur, Lizzie McInnerny played Mistress Quickly, and Desmond Barrit played Falstaff in a performance that Billington hailed as 'the best Falstaff since Robert Stephens' in 1991 (*Guardian* 28 July 2011).

Simon Higlett designed the set. Hall had worked with Higlett several times since 2006 but never on a Shakespeare play. Higlett's set was again a radical departure for a late Hall production and harked back to Hall's 1960s work when the set was an elaborate expression of his directorial vision, a setting for a production out to make a statement rather than a minimalist canvas on which to paint Shakespeare's words. The set was principally a wooden frame set against a grimy, fire-damaged brick wall with some bricks missing: the interior of a barn perhaps or a ruined castle, somehow medieval and industrial at the same time, a tired and destroyed feudal world. Stairs gave Hall an upper level to work with, and a curtain underneath the alcove that the stairs created gave a place for concealment. For Spencer, the set evoked 'castles and brothels, staterooms and battlefields' (*Daily Telegraph* 28 July 2011). Unusually for Hall, backdrops were flown in to mark scene changes when the brick wall opened, sometimes to 'provide a panorama of English life' (*Guardian* 28 July 2011), at other times to represent the empty contested spaces of battlefields. In some scenes, a single withered tree, echoing Beckett, suggested a barren landscape beyond: this was Gadshill, but it also became the scene of the Battle of Shrewsbury, fought against a blood orange-washed backdrop. By the end of 2 *Henry IV*, the tree had started to blossom as a final message of hope and reconciliation. The backdrop was now a ruined wall, the remains of a damaged, bombed-out world that called to mind wars such as Afghanistan or Iraq – but for Hall perhaps also evoked the memory of post-Blitz London.

Against this panoramic sweep of history, somehow Elizabethan, Victorian and modern all at the same time, Hall turned the production on Hal's complicated relationship with Falstaff, the father figure he both loved and knew he must reject. As Billington observed, Hal's promise to banish 'plump Jack' was played first in his father's voice – 'I do' – and then, ominously, his line 'I will' was delivered 'in his own steely register', interrupting and undercutting the scene's comedy. Mison was alert to Hal's affection for the fat knight: finding the old knight on the battlefield, apparently dead, Hal gave him a tender kiss. When Hal became Henry V and rejected Falstaff, Mison made it clear 'that the dismissal of Falstaff exacts its own personal cost' (*Guardian* 28 July 2011).

Although in many ways a different kind of production to Hall's late works, the Henries were nevertheless autumnal works, meditations on ageing and the cycle of history in which the supremacy of the young rests on the ruin of the old. Hall could once easily have been Hal, the young pretender eagerly snatching the crown and sweeping away an old guard. However, now Hall was more of a Falstaff, a character that he was beginning to resemble, whose constant hopes for preferment are thwarted, his sense of his importance not matched by those he helps into power. But there was Henry IV as well, a dark and complex figure who was weighed down by the crown he wears, whose physical illness is evident in his first appearance in 2 *Henry IV*, dark drums scoring his soliloquy and pain affecting his voice. Later, he writhed in pain and collapsed, a bed was brought out, and he was put into it, his crown laid on the pillow. When Hal entered, the first thing he noticed was the crown, which he approached with an over-eager, greedy eye. Mison's movements were locked to the crown – that became his focus, the thing that both drew and repelled him as he considered the situation. Believing his father dead, Hal put his hand to the crown, trembling, then withdrew, walked around to the back of the bed to crouch by the crown and then stood upright quickly. Finally, he took the crown and put it on, then ran off the stage. Hal was brought back on to face his father to find Henry bitter, angry and unaccepting. When Henry finally gave Hal the crown, the old man cried. It was a moving, complex performance of a man angry with history, unwilling to pass his burden on but also unable to continue. He was walked offstage to the sound of Parry's Jerusalem, an appropriate keynote for a production that managed to be both dark and full of national spirit.

With *Twelfth Night* and his *Henry IV* cycle, Hall brought his career as a Shakespeare director to a close in suitably epic style, pointing to the absurdity of authority figures who misunderstand history and its capacity to betray those who try to control it. He had of course been such a figure himself: most of his professional life had been devoted to creating cultural institutions whose power had been diminished by government policy. The irony was not lost on Hall, and his exploration of authority in the Henries worked both on a personal and political level. In early 2011, he told an audience for a live platform event at the Cottesloe that he feared for the future of Shakespeare and the theatre because 'we are still in a situation where the government doesn't understand what culture is and why it needs any hope, why it needs any help' (Hall 2011: n.p.). He had lost none of his capacity for trenchant political comment in defence of the arts, yet in the same interview he hesitates in places, mishears questions, and stops anecdotes in the middle of telling them: early signs, perhaps, of the dementia which compelled him to retire.

The Henries were a fitting capstone to Hall's long career and seemed to gather together its different threads without ever feeling elegiac. The cycle was on the one hand as political and forthright as anything he had done since the 1960s, addressing questions of national culture and the nature of history in ways which called attention to the changed context of nationhood since the invasion of Iraq in 2003. At the same time, the production's aesthetic drew on both Brecht and Beckett, mixing cruel absurdity with naïve hope. In the final scene between Hal and his father, Hall found proto-Pinteresque notes in the cruel silences between them, that which is not said being, in the end, more important, more meaningful, than the words themselves.

Against the grain of his late work, Hall ended the production, and his career as a Shakespeare director, not with Shakespeare's words, but with silence and an unscripted image: Henry V presenting himself to the stage, to the world, in an iconic image of power that deliberately resembled the first appearance of Henry IV at the start of the cycle. Military drums broke the silence: power, Hall implied, is a trap, and a joke that history plays on those who aspire to be king.

LIST OF PRODUCTIONS

Several of Hall's productions went on tour, most of his RSC productions transferred to London and some of his National productions played in more than one of its auditoriums. In the list below, I have only noted the year and venue of each play's first production.

Shakespeare Memorial Theatre

1956 *Love's Labour's Lost*
1957 *Cymbeline*
1958 *Twelfth Night*
1959 *A Midsummer Night's Dream*
1959 *Coriolanus*
1960 *Two Gentlemen of Verona*
1960 *The Taming of the Shrew* (uncredited – co-directed with John Barton)
1960 *Twelfth Night*
1960 *Troilus and Cressida* (co-directed with John Barton)
1961 *Romeo and Juliet*

Royal Shakespeare Company

1962 *A Midsummer Night's Dream*
1962 *Troilus and Cressida* (co-directed with John Barton)
1963 *The Wars of the Roses: Henry VI, Edward IV* and *Richard III* (co-directed with John Barton and Frank Evans)

1964 *Richard II* (co-directed with John Barton and Clifford Williams)
1964 *1 and 2 Henry IV* (co-directed with John Barton and Clifford Williams)
1964 *Henry V* (co-directed with John Barton and Clifford Williams)
1965 *Hamlet*
1967 *Macbeth*
1968 *A Midsummer Night's Dream* (Film, CBS)

National Theatre – all Olivier Theatre unless otherwise stated

1974 *The Tempest* (Old Vic)
1975 *Hamlet* (Old Vic)
1978 *Macbeth* (co-directed with John Russell Brown)
1980 *Othello*
1984 *Coriolanus*
1987 *Antony and Cleopatra*
1988 *Cymbeline* (Cottesloe)
1988 *The Winter's Tale* (Cottesloe)
1988 *The Tempest* (Cottesloe)

Various companies

1989 *Merchant of Venice* (Phoenix Theatre, Peter Hall Company)
1991 *Twelfth Night* (Playhouse Theatre, Peter Hall Company)
1992 *All's Well that Ends Well* (Swan Theatre, Royal Shakespeare Company)
1992 *A Midsummer Night's Dream* (Audio Performance for CD, Peter Hall Company)

1994 *Hamlet* (Gielgud, Peter Hall Company)
1995 *Julius Caesar* (Barbican and tour, Royal Shakespeare Company)
1997 *King Lear* (Old Vic, Peter Hall Company)
1999 *Measure for Measure* (Ahmanson Theatre, Centre Theatre Group)
1999 *A Midsummer Night's Dream* (Ahmanson Theatre, Centre Theatre Group)
2001 *Romeo and Juliet* (Ahmanson Theatre, Centre Theatre Group)
2001 *Troilus and Cressida* (American Place Theatre, Theatre for a New Audience)
2003 *As You Like It* (Theatre Royal Bath, Peter Hall Company)
2005 *Much Ado about Nothing* (Theatre Royal Bath, Peter Hall Company)
2006 *Measure for Measure* (Theatre Royal Bath, Peter Hall Company)
2008 *Love's Labour's Lost* (Rose Theatre Kingston)
2010 *A Midsummer Night's Dream* (Rose Theatre Kingston)
2011 *Twelfth Night* (National Theatre)
2011 *1 and 2 Henry IV* (co-directed with Richard Beecham and Cordelia Monsey, Theatre Royal Bath, Peter Hall Company)

REFERENCES

Addenbrooke, David. 1974. *The Royal Shakespeare Company*. London: William Kimber.
Apfelbaum, Roger. 2004. *Shakespeare's Troilus and Cressida: Textual Problems and Performance Solutions*. Newark: University of Delaware Press.
Aris, Stephen. 1964. 'The Royal Shakespeare'. *New Society London* 3, no. 76 (12 March): 12–14.
August, Hannah. 2011. '*Twelfth Night* at the National Theatre'. *STET*. 23 January. Accessed 31 October 2017. http://www.stetjournal.org/blogs/theatre/twelfth-night-at-the-national-theatre/#more-1417.
Barton, John and Peter Hall. 1970. *The Wars of the Roses*. London: BBC.
Bartow, Arthur. 2009. 'Controversy and Gordon Davidson: An Interview with Arthur Bartow, May 1988'. In *The American Theatre Reader: Essays and Conversations from American Theatre*, edited by Sarah Hart, 414–424. New York: Theatre Communications Group.
Bate, Jonathan, Eric Rasmussen and Will Sharpe, eds. 2011. *Cymbeline*. London: Macmillan.
Beacock, D.A. 1943. *Play Way English for To-Day: The Methods and Influence of H. Caldwell Cook*. London: Thomas Nelson and Sons.
Beauman, Sally. 1982. *The Royal Shakespeare Company: A History of Ten Decades*. Oxford: Oxford University Press.
Bedford, S.K. 1992. *Coriolanus at the National: Th' Interpretation of the Time*. London and Toronto: Associated University Presses.
Bennett, Susan. 1996. *Performing Nostalgia: Shifting Shakespeare and the Contemporary Past*. London and New York: Routledge.
Billington, Michael. 1988. *Peggy Ashcroft*. London: John Murray.
Blakemore, Michael. 2013. *Stage Blood: Five Tempestuous Years in the Early Life of the National Theatre*. London: Faber & Faber.
Brown, John Russell. 1961. 'Directions for *Twelfth Night, or What You Will*'. *Tulane Drama Review* 5, no. 4 (June): 77–88.

Brown, John Russell. 1974. *Free Shakespeare*. London: Heinemann Educational.
Brown, John Russell. 1982a. *Focus on Macbeth*. London and New York: Routledge.
Brown, John Russell. 1982b. 'Troilus and Cressida, 1960'. In *Aspects of Shakespeare's Problem Plays*, edited by Kenneth Muir and Stanley Wells, 149–152. Cambridge: Cambridge University Press.
Bryden, Ronald. 1969. *The Unfinished Hero and Other Essays*. London: Faber & Faber.
Cribb, Tim. 2007. *Bloomsbury and British Theatre. The Marlowe Story*. Cambridge: Salt.
Croall, Jonathan. 2015. *Performing King Lear: Gielgud to Russell Beale*. London: Bloomsbury.
David, Richard. 1978. *Shakespeare in the Theatre*. Cambridge: Cambridge University Press.
Dawson, Anthony B. 1997. *Shakespeare in Performance: Hamlet*. Manchester: Manchester University Press.
Dunbar, Judith. 2010. *Shakespeare in Performance: The Winter's Tale*. Manchester: Manchester University Press.
Evans, Gareth Lloyd. 1967. 'Shakespeare, the Twentieth Century and "Behaviorism"'. In *Shakespeare Survey 20*, edited by Kenneth Muir, 133–142. Cambridge: Cambridge University Press.
Evans, Gareth Lloyd. 1968. 'Shakespeare and the Actors: Notes towards Interpretations'. In *Shakespeare Survey 21*, edited by Kenneth Muir, 115–126. Cambridge: Cambridge University Press.
Eyre, Richard. 2003. *National Service: Diary of a Decade at the National Theatre*. London: Bloomsbury.
Farber, Donald C. 2014. *I Had to Do it: Stories of a Life*. New York: Rosetta Books.
Fay, Stephen. 1995. *Power Play: The Life and Times of Peter Hall*. London: Hodder & Stoughton.
Fraser, Russell, ed. 1986. *All's Well That Ends Well: The New Cambridge Shakespeare*. Cambridge: Cambridge University Press.
Friedman, Michael D. 2015. '"Let Me Twine/Mine Arms about that Body": The Queerness of Coriolanus and Recent British Stage Productions'. *Shakespeare Bulletin* 3, no. 3 (Fall): 395–419.
Frost, Robert James. 1983. 'The Shakespearean Performances of John Gielgud'. PhD. University of Birmingham.
Goodwin, John, ed. 1964. *Royal Shakespeare Theatre Company 1960–63*. London: Max Reinhardt.

Greenwald, Michael L. 1985. *Directions by Indirections: John Barton of the Royal Shakespeare Company*. Newark: University of Delaware Press.

Hall, Peter. 1964. 'Shakespeare and the Modern Director'. In *The Royal Shakespeare Theatre Company, 1960–63*, edited by John Goodwin, 41–48. London: Max Reinhardt.

Hall, Peter. 1983. *Peter Hall's Diaries: The Story of a Dramatic Battle*, edited by John Goodwin. London: Hamish Hamilton.

Hall, Peter. 1993. *Making an Exhibition of Myself*. London: Sinclair-Stevenson.

Hall, Peter. 1999. *The Necessary Theatre*. London: Nick Hern.

Hall, Peter. 2003. *Shakespeare's Advice to the Players*. London: Oberon.

Hall, Peter. 2011. Interview, 'In Conversation with Nicholas Hytner'. National Theatre Discover. Accessed 1 October 2018. https://www.youtube.com/watch?v=bUZq2vDcqaU.

Hall, Peter. 2014. Interview. Muse of Fire. Accessed 1 October 2018. https://globeplayer.tv.

Hampton-Reeves, Stuart. 2013. 'Peter Hall'. In *Great Shakespeareans XVIII: Hall, Brook, Ninagawa, Lepage*, edited by Peter Holland, 47–78. London: Bloomsbury.

Hampton-Reeves, Stuart and Carol Chillington Rutter. 2006. *Shakespeare in Performance: The Henry VI Plays*. Manchester: Manchester University Press.

Hankey, Julia. 1987. *Plays in Performance: Othello*. Bristol: Bristol Classical Press.

Heijes, Coen. 2010. '*A Midsummer Night's Dream*. By William Shakespeare. Directed by Sir Peter Hall. Rose Theatre, Kingston, London. 16 February 2010'. *Theatre Journal* 62, no. 4 (December): 683–684.

Hodgdon, Barbara. 1972. '*The Wars of the Roses*: Scholarship Speaks on the Stage'. *Shakespeare Jahrbuch* 108: 175.

Holland, Peter. 1996. 'Shakespeare Performances in England, 1994–1995'. In *Shakespeare Survey 49*, edited by Stanley Wells, 235–268. Cambridge: Cambridge University Press.

Holland, Peter. 1997. *English Shakespeares: Shakespeare on the English Stage in the 1990s*. Cambridge: Cambridge University Press.

Holm, Ian. 2004. *Acting My Life: The Autobiography*. London: Corgi.

Holmberg, Arthur. 1981. '*Othello* by William Shakespeare'. *Theatre Journal* 33, no. 2 (May): 259–260.

Hornby, Richard. 2001. 'Death in the Mall'. *The Hudson Review* 54, no. 2 (Summer): 305–312.
Huntley Film Archive. 1960. *'View of the Royal Shakespeare Theatre'*. Accessed 1 June 2018. https://www.huntleyarchives.com/preview.asp?image=1093527.
Jackson, Russell. 2002. *Romeo and Juliet: Shakespeare at Stratford Series*. London: Arden Shakespeare.
Kenny, Sean. 1993. 'The Building of the Theatre'. In *Scenographic Imagination*, 3rd edition, edited by Darwin Reid Payne, 98–101. Carbondale and Edwardsville: Southern Illinois University Press.
Kirwan, Peter. 2006. '*Measure for Measure* (Theatre Royal Bath/Peter Hall Company) @ The Courtyard Theatre'. 14 September. Accessed 30 October 2017. http://blogs.nottingham.ac.uk/bardathon/2006/09/14/measure-for-measure-the-courtyard-theatre/.
Kirwan, Peter. 2009. 'Love's Labour's Lost'. *Shakespeare Bulletin* 27, no. 2 (Summer): 315–319.
King, Ros. 2005. *Cymbeline: Constructions of Britain*. Aldershot: Ashgate.
Knapper, Stephen. 2007. 'Peter Hall in Rehearsal'. *Contemporary Theatre Review* 17, no. 4: 578–581.
Lewis, Peter. 1990. *The National: A Dream Made Concrete*. London: Methuen.
Loehlin, James N. 1997. *Shakespeare in Performance: Henry V*. Manchester: Manchester University Press.
Loehlin, James N. 2002. *Shakespeare in Production: Romeo and Juliet*. Cambridge: Cambridge University Press.
London, Todd. 2013. *An Ideal Theatre: Founding Visions for a New American Art*. New York: Theatre Communications Group.
Lowen, Tirzah. 1990. *Peter Hall Directs Antony and Cleopatra*. London: Methuen.
Lowndes, William. 1982. *The Theatre Royal at Bath: The Story of a Georgian Playhouse*. Bristol: Redcliffe Press.
McKellen, Ian. 2003. 'Coriolanus: Words from Ian McKellen'. Accessed 12 July 2018. http://www.mckellen.com/stage/coriolanus/index.html.
Madelaine, Richard. 1998. *Shakespeare in Production: Antony and Cleopatra*. Cambridge: Cambridge University Press.
Maher, Mary Zenet. 2003. *Modern Hamlets and Their Soliloquies*, 2nd edition. Iowa: University of Iowa Press.

Marowitz, Charles. 1973. *Confessions of a Counterfeit Critic: A London Theatre Notebook, 1958–1971*. London: Methuen.

Marowitz, Charles. 2002. 'Cue for Passion: On the Dynamics of Shakespearean Acting'. *New Theatre Quarterly* 18, no. 1: 3–9.

Miles, Patrick. 1995. 'Chekhov, Shakespeare, the Ensemble and the Company'. *New Theatre Quarterly* 11, no. 43 (August): 204.

Mitchell, S.J.D. 1976. *Perse: A History of the Perse School 1615–1976*. Cambridge: Oleander Press.

Mullin, Michael. 1975. 'Peter Hall's *Midsummer Night's Dream* on Film'. *Educational Theatre Journal* 27, no. 4 (December): 529–534.

Myers, Wayne. 2010. *The Book of 'Twelfth Night, or What You Will': Musings on Shakespeare's Most Wonderful (and Erotic) Play*. Tucson, AZ: Wheatmark.

Neill, Heather. 2006. 'Peter Hall Directs Measure for Measure at Last!: Interview with Sir Peter Hall'. *Theatre Voice*, May. Accessed 31 October 2017. http://www.theatrevoice.com/audio/shakespeare-measure-for-measure-heather-neill-talks-to-sir/8th.

Nelsen, Paul. 1997. 'Positing Pillars at the Globe'. *Shakespeare Quarterly* 48, no. 3 (Autumn): 324–335.

Nettles, John. 1998. 'Brutus in *Julius Caesar*'. In *Players of Shakespeare 4*, edited by Robert Smallwood, 177–192. Cambridge: Cambridge University Press.

O' Connor, Gary. 2002. *Paul Scofield: The Biography*. London: Sidgwick & Jackson.

Ormsby, Robert. 2014. *Shakespeare in Performance: Coriolanus*. Manchester: Manchester University Press.

Pearson, Richard. 1990. *A Band of Arrogant and United Heroes: The Story of the Royal Shakespeare Company Production of The Wars of the Roses*. London: Adelphi Press.

Potter, Lois. 1992. 'A Brave New Tempest'. *Shakespeare Quarterly* 43, no. 4 (Winter): 450–455.

Ripley, John. 1998. *Coriolanus on Stage in England and America, 1609–1994*. Vancouver: Fairleigh Dickinson Press.

Rosenberg, Marvin. 1997. *The Adventures of a Shakespeare Scholar: To Discover Shakespeare's Art*. Newark: University of Delaware Press.

Rosenthal, Daniel. 2013. *The National Theatre Story*. London: Oberon.

Seldon, Anthony and Daniel Collings. 2013. *Britain under Thatcher*. London and New York: Routledge.

Shaughnessy, Robert. 2018. *Shakespeare in the Theatre: The National Theatre 1963–1975*. London: Bloomsbury.
Shuter, Paul and Charles Edwards. 2011. 'Pre-rehearsal Interview: Transcript'. *Shakespeare's Globe*. Accessed 30 October 2017. http://www.shakespearesglobe.com/discovery-space/adopt-an-actor/archive/benedick-played-by-charles-edwards/pre-rehearsal.
Sinfield, Alan. 1994. 'Royal Shakespeare: Theatre and the Making of Ideology'. In *Political Shakespeare: Essays in Cultural Materialism*, 2nd edition, edited by Jonathan Dollimore and Alan Sinfield, 182–205. Manchester: Manchester University Press.
Slingerland, Amy L. 1999. 'LA does Shakespeare, and it's not a Movie'. *Entertainment Design* 33, no. 9 (October): 6.
Speaight, Robert. 1961. 'The Old Vic and Stratford-upon-Avon 1960–61'. *Shakespeare Quarterly* 12, no. 4 (Autumn): 425–441.
Speaight, Robert. 1965. 'Shakespeare in Britain'. *Shakespeare Quarterly* 16, no. 4 (Autumn): 320.
Speaight, Robert. 1966. 'Shakespeare in Britain'. *Shakespeare Quarterly* 17, no. 4 (Autumn): 389–398.
Speaight, Robert. 1967. 'Shakespeare in Britain'. *Shakespeare Quarterly* 18, no. 4 (Autumn): 389–297.
Speaight, Robert. 1973. *Shakespeare on the Stage: An Illustrated History of Shakespearian Performance*. London: Collins.
Thompson, Ann and Neil Taylor, eds. 2006. *Hamlet*. Arden 3rd Series. London: Bloomsbury.
Walker, Roy. 1986. 'Peter Hall's Production of *Twelfth Night*'. In *Twelfth Night: Critical Essays*, edited by Stanley Wells, 83–88. Cambridge: Cambridge University Press.
Wardle, Irving. No date.'Interview with Peter Hall'. Irving Wardle Tapes (c. 1966).
Warren, Roger. 1986. 'Shakespeare in Britain, 1985'. *Shakespeare Quarterly* 37, no. 1 (Winter): 114–120.
Warren, Roger. 1989. *Shakespeare in Performance: Cymbeline*. Manchester: Manchester University Press.
Warren, Roger. 1995. *Staging Shakespeare's Late Plays*. Oxford: Clarendon Press.
Warren, Roger. 2013. 'Staging *A Midsummer Night's Dream*: Peter Hall's Productions, 1959–2010'. In *Shakespeare Survey 65*, edited by Peter Holland, 146–154. Cambridge: Cambridge University Press.
Wells, Stanley. 1977. *Royal Shakespeare: Four Major Productions at Stratford-upon-Avon*. Manchester: Manchester University Press.

Womersley, David. 2006. 'Review of Peter Hall's *Measure for Measure*'. 21 September. Accessed 31 October 2017. http://www.socialaffairsunit.org.uk/blog/archives/001117.php.

Zielinski, Scott. No date. 'Single Source Downlight for Harsh Lighting for Troilus and Cressida'. Accessed 27 October 2017. http://www.seleconlight.com/index.php?option=com_content&view=article&id=844&Itemid=15&lang=en.

INDEX

Addenbrooke, David 49
Aeschylus 109
   Oresteia 109
Afghanistan War 131, 163, 185, 187
Agutter, Jenny 94
Ahmanson Theatre 150, 151, 157, 160, 164, 166
AIDS epidemic 132, 142
Aldermaston March 25
American Place Theatre, New York 159
An Anointed King (BBC radio programme) 71–2
Andrews, Harry 20, 185
Anouilh, Jean 2, 6, 14
Apfelbaum, Roger 160
Apocalypse Now (film) 83
Aris, Stephen 62
Aronson, Boris 35–6
Artaud, Antonin 146
   Jet de Sang 146
Arts Council 56, 108, 111–12, 114, 166
Arts Theatre 9, 14
Ashcroft, Peggy 15, 21, 23, 40, 44, 54–5, 67–8
Asmus, Walter 172
August, Hannah 182
Aukin, David 124
Austen, Jane 170
Avery, James 157

Badel, Alan 20
Bailey, James 19–20
Banqueting House, Whitehall 92
Barber, John 116, 119
Barnett, Barbara 40
Barrit, Desmond 186
Barry, B. H. 161
Barton, John 4, 17, 19, 20, 24, 30, 40, 44, 46, 47, 56, 58–61, 66, 70, 71, 73, 75, 149, 156, 162, 166, 174
   adapting Shakespeare 59–61
   dir. *Measure for Measure* 1970 174
   'Shakespeare and the Dramatic Critics' (debate) 17
   dir. *Taming of the Shrew* 1960 40, 44
   Winterlude (play) 44
Bartow, Arthur 150
Bate, Jonathan 127
Bayreuth 110
BBC 43, 71
BBC Radiophone Workshop 84
BBC Shakespeare 120
Beacock, D. A. 3
Beatles, the (rock band) 51, 88
   'Lucy in the Sky with Diamonds' 83
Beauman, Sally 49

Beckett, Samuel 2, 6, 14, 35, 44, 146–7, 164–5, 172, 187, 189
Bedford, S. K. 112–14, 115, 117–18
Bellman, Gina 143
Benjamin, Christopher 144
Bennett, Susan 16
Benthal, Michael 28
  dir. *Twelfth Night* 1958 28
Berliner Ensemble 13, 39
Berry, Chuck 51
Berry, Cicely 5
Bilk, Acker 55–6
Billington, Michael 11, 21, 68, 99, 105–6, 114, 116, 118, 124, 127, 128–9, 133–4, 137, 142, 144, 145, 147, 167, 171, 174, 176–7, 182–5, 187
  Peter Hall – Work in Progress (television programme) 124
Birmingham Repertory Theatre 58, 67
Blair, Tony 131, 141, 147, 149, 185
Blakemore, Michael 34, 90, 94, 96
Bogdanov, Michael 116
Bolt, Robert 126
Bond, Edward 51
Borrego, Jesse 158
Boswell, Laurence 165
Bowie, David 155
Bowles, Peter 175, 177
Boyd, Michael 173
Brecht, Bertolt 35, 46, 65, 112, 146, 157, 189

Brenton, Howard 8, 115
  The Romans in Britain (play) 8, 115–16
Brien, Alan 36, 45–6, 73–4, 78, 82
British Library 11
British Pathé 54
Britten, Benjamin 110
Broadway 29, 133, 135
Brook, Peter 17, 21, 23, 25, 45, 84
  Love's Labour's Lost 17, 25, 28
  dir. Theatre of Cruelty Season 84
  dir. *Titus Andronicus* 23
  dir. *U.S.* 84
  dir. *Venice Preserv'd* 45
Brown, Douglas 3
Brown, John Russell 4, 27, 85–7, 100–2, 104, 166
  Free Shakespeare 95–6, 101
Bryant, Michael 104, 129
Bryden, Bill 165
  dir. *A Midsummer Night's Dream* 1982 165
Bryden, Ronald 80, 82
Buller, Francesca 7
Burton, Richard 73–4, 185
Bury, Elizabeth 178–9
Bury, John 65–6, 77, 82–6, 93–4, 97, 102, 105, 107, 110, 112, 139

Callow, Simon 90, 183
Campaign for Nuclear Disarmament 25
Cardboard City 133–4

Carroll, Lewis, *Alice in Wonderland* 42
Cavalli 92
Center Theatre Group 150, 155–6, 162, 164
Che Guevara 112
Chitty, Alison 120, 123, 126–7
Chris, Oliver 178, 180
Christon, Lawrence 159
Chubb, William 177–8
Church, Tony 45, 159
Churchill, Winston 76
Civil Rights Movement 76
Clapp, Susannah 180
Clinton, President 132, 149, 153
Clinton, Hillary 153
Clouet, Jean 42
Cocteau, Jean 23
Cold War 63
Collings, Daniel 133
Collins, Lynn 158
Comédie Française 39
Cook, Henry Caldwell 3
  The Play Way 2–3
Coveney, Michael 140
Coward, Noël 170–1
Cribb, Tim 14
Crouching Tiger, Hidden Dragon (film) 161
Csokas, Marton 183
Cushman, Robert 99, 106

Darlington, W. A. 11, 19–22, 28, 32, 47, 54, 75, 82–3
David, Richard 99
Davidson, Gordon 150–2, 156
Dawson, Anthony 76–7
Day, Simon Paisley 183
Dean, James 13
Dee, Janie 170–1

Dee, John 92
De Jongh, Nicholas 101
Democrazia Proletaria 112
Dench, Judi 10, 57, 85, 87, 90, 119, 120–3, 178–80, 182
De Nobili, Lila 15, 22, 25, 27, 32–3, 42, 46, 57, 137
Denver Centre for the Performing Arts 156
De Souza, Edward 35
Dillane, Stephen 142–4
Doctor Who (television series) 175
Donmar Warehouse 71
Dotrice, Roy 71, 73–4
Doughty, Louise 142
Downs, Jane 28
Downton Abbey (television series) 164
Driver, Minnie 151
Drudge Report 153
Dunbar, Judith 124
Dyer, Chris 134

Edwards, Charles 170–1, 178, 180, 183
Edwards, Christopher 128
Eisenhower, Dwight D. 44
Elba, Idris 159, 161
Elizabeth I 179–80
Elizabeth II 13
  coronation 14
Elizabethan Stage Company 9, 14
Elliot, Denholm 42, 47
Elsom, John 93
Engel, Susan 64
Epidaurus Theatre 109, 113
Evans, Edith 29, 37–8, 54–5
Evans, Frank 58

Evans, Gareth Lloyd 11–12, 45, 47, 54–5, 81
Eyre, Richard 124, 126, 130

Falklands Crisis 114
Farber, Donald 54
Fay, Stephen 19–21, 24, 40, 63, 73, 99, 105, 126, 143–4
Feast, Michael 94
Fernald, John 14
Festival of Britain 15, 58
Feydeau, Georges 165
Finney, Albert 11, 34, 89, 98–100, 102–3
Fleetwood, Susan 98
Flower, Fordham 28–9, 34
Flynn, Errol 86
Forster, Peter 19–20
Fraser, Russell 138, 140
Friedman, Michael D. 117
Frost, Robert James 92–3

Gainsborough, Thomas
  The Blue Boy (painting) 26
Gardner, Edmund 43, 46
Gascoigne, Bamber 73–4
Gate Theatre, Dublin 172
General Election (UK)
  1959 30
  1979 100
  2010 179
Gerhard, Roberto 36
Gielgud, John 15, 76, 89, 91–2, 93–5, 99
Gielgud Theatre 142
Gillet, Aden 170–1
Gillet, Eric 43
Gilliatt, Penelope 78–9
Global Financial Crisis 178
Glyndebourne Festival 110

Godfrey, Derek 56, 85
Goodwin, John 62
Granville-Barker, Harley 120
Greater London Council 111
Greenwald, Michael L. 44–5, 47, 58–9, 65–7
Griffith, Hugh 73–4
Gryphon (rock band)
  'Midnight Mushrumps' 93
Gulbenkian Foundarion 5
Gunter, John 139, 145–47, 153–4, 157, 159, 166–7, 169, 178
Guthrie, Tyrone
  dir. *All's Well that Ends Well* 29–30
  dir. *Coriolanus* 117

Hailey, Bill 13
Hall, Jennifer 126
Hall, Lucy 142
Hall, Peter
  dir. *All's Well that Ends Well* 1992 133, 138–41
  dir. *Amadeus* 1979 105–6, 110
  dir. *Amadeus* 2000 156
  dir. *A Midsummer Night's Dream* 1959 10, 29–35, 38–9
  dir. *A Midsummer Night's Dream* 1962 56, 179
  dir. *A Midsummer Night's Dream* 1969 57, 84–8, 115
  dir. *A Midsummer Night's Dream* 1981 (Britten) 110
  dir. *A Midsummer Night's Dream* 1992 (CD) 155

dir. *A Midsummer Night's Dream* 1999 149, 152, 154–5, 162
dir. *A Midsummer Night's Dream* 2010 163, 178–81
dir. *Antony and Cleopatra* 90, 111, 119–23, 145
as Artistic Director of the Rose 165
dir. *As You Like It* 161, 164, 166–9
dir. *The Bacchai* 161
dir. *Betrayal* 2003 170
dir. *Coriolanus* 1959 11, 29–31, 35–9, 43, 47–8, 53, 123, 145
dir. *Coriolanus* 1984 7, 90, 111–19
dir. *Cymbeline* 1957 16–17, 21–4
dir. *Cymbeline* 1988 125, 127
dir. *Der Ring des Nibelungen* 110
dir. *Design for Living* 170
as Director of NT 1, 8, 89
dir. *Edward IV* 59, 61, 67–8
as founder of RSC 1
dir. *Galileo's Daughter* 169
dir. *Gigi* 14
dir. *Hamlet* 1965 10, 43, 50, 75–80, 84, 88, 97–8, 145, 173
dir. *Hamlet* 1975 11, 89, 96–100, 105, 109
dir. *Hamlet* 1994 132, 141–4, 153
dir. *Henry IV* plays 1964 70, 73–4
dir. *Henry IV* plays 2011 9, 10, 163–4, 181, 184–9
dir. *Henry V* 70, 74–5
dir. *Henry VI* 59
dir. *The Homecoming* 80
dir. *Il Ritorno d'Ulissein Patria* 92
dir. *Julius Caesar* 141, 144–6
dir. *King Lear* 146–8, 163
dir. *La Calisto* 92
dir. 'Late Plays' trilogy 90, 123–30, 133
dir. *Love's Labour's Lost* 1956 16–21, 23
dir. *Love's Labour's Lost* 2008 163, 175–8
dir. *Macbeth* 1967 6, 11, 50, 80–4, 86, 88–9, 97, 102
dir. *Macbeth* 1978 89, 101–3, 105, 108
dir. *Man and Superman* 169
dir. *Measure for Measure* 1999 132, 149, 152–5, 162
dir. *Measure for Measure* 2006 172–5
dir. *Merchant of Venice* 7–8, 132–7
dir. *Mrs. Warren's Profession* 167
dir. *Much Ado About Nothing* 169–72
dir. *Othello* 90, 101, 103–8
dir. *Richard II* 70–3
dir. *Richard III* 59, 61, 63, 65–70
dir. *Romeo and Juliet* 1961 50–6
dir. *Romeo and Juliet* 2001 149, 156–9, 162–3, 184

Shakespeare's Advice to the Players 4, 7
dir. *Tantalus* 149, 156, 159, 162
dir. *The Tempest* 1974 89, 91–5
dir. *The Tempest* 1988 126–7, 129 97, 130
dir. *Troilus and Cressida* 1960 39–41, 43–8, 97, 133, 159
dir. *Troilus and Cressida* 1962 56
dir. *Troilus and Cressida* 2001 149, 156, 159–61, 162, 184
dir. *Twelfth Night* 1958 16, 24–9, 88, 132, 137
dir. *Twelfth Night* 1960 40, 43
dir. *Twelfth Night* 1991 133, 137–8, 182
dir. *Twelfth Night* 2011 181–4, 188
dir. *The Two Gentleman of Verona* 39, 40–3, 46, 48,
dir. *Waiting for Godot* 1955 6, 14, 20, 27, 44
dir. *Waiting for Godot* 1997 146–7
dir. *Waiting for Godot* 2005 172, 174
dir. *The Wars of the Roses* 4, 43, 50, 55, 57–71, 75, 77, 88, 95, 109–10, 119, 145
dir. *The Wild Duck* 137
dir. *The Winter's Tale* 124, 127–8

Hall, Rebecca 164, 167–9, 182–4
Hampton-Reeves, Stuart 67
Hankey, Julia 106
Hardwick, Paul 46, 57
Harrison, Tony 109
Haygarth, Tony 129
Heijes, Coen 179–80
Hicks, Greg 115–16, 147
Higlett, Simon 186
Hobson, Harold 78, 92–3
Hodgdon, Barbara 65
Hoffman, Dustin 7–8, 133, 135–7, 151
Holland, Peter 138, 142–5
Holm, Ian 24, 34, 56–7, 68–9, 70, 74–5, 85
Holmberg, Arthur 104, 106
Hope-Wallace, Philip 11, 19–20, 23, 33–4, 53–5, 66–9, 82
Hopkins, Anthony 90, 119, 120–3
Hornby, Richard 156–7
Horowitz, Jerry 159
Houseman, John 150
Howard, Alan 147
Huntley Film Archive 41
Hurren, Kenneth 125
Hurry, Leslie 45
Hytner, Nicholas 181

Ibsen, Henrik 137
International Shakespeare Globe Centre 146
IRA 91
Iraq War 131, 163, 185, 187, 189
Isherwood, Charles 160

Jackson, Glenda 78
Jackson, Russell 52–3, 55
James, Geraldine 31, 126–7, 135
James, Peter Francis 154
Jefford, Barbara 85, 140
Johnson, Richard 24, 26
Jones, Inigo 92

Kendal, Felicity 105–7
Kennedy, John F.
  assassination 63–4
Kenny, Sean 52–3
Kern, Joey 161
King, Francis 127
King, Ros 125
Kingston University 166
Kirwan, Peter 174–7
Kline, Kevin 151
Knapper, Stephen 172
Knights, L. C. 77
Kohler, Estelle 78
Kott, Jan 62–3
  Shakespeare our Contemporary 62
Kushner, Tony
  Angels in America 142

Lansbury, Angela 98, 100
Laughton, Charles 10, 18, 29, 32–4, 57, 173
Laurenson, James 174, 178
Lawson, Leigh 134
Leigh, Vivien 15, 26
Leppard, Raymond 15, 31
Levin, Bernard 30, 66, 69, 100
Lewinksy, Monica 153
Lewis, Jerry Lee 150
Lewis, Peter 90–1, 127, 129
Littlewood, Joan
  Oh! What a Lovely War 65

Livingstone, Ken 111
Locke, Philip 98
Loehlin, James N. 75
London, Todd 150
Lord Chamberlain 51
Los Angeles 149, 151
Lowen, Tirzah 119–20
Lowndes, William 165
Luckham, Cyril 27
Luhrmann, Baz 157
Lynch, Finbar 177
Lyric Theatre, London 45
Lyttelton, Oliver 100

Macaulay, Alastair 171–2
McEwan, Geraldine 20, 24, 26, 28, 40
McGillis, Kelly 152, 154
McInnerny, Lizzie 186
McKellen, Ian 6, 90, 113, 115–18
Macmillan, Harold 61–2, 64
Madelaine, Richard 121
Maher, Mary Zenet 78
Mansfield, Ben 186
Margolyes, Miriam 157
Mark Taper Forum, LA 150
Markle, Fletcher
  dir. *A Midsummer Night's Dream* (film) 32–3
Marlowe Dramatic Society 4, 14, 26, 44, 178
Marlowe, Sam 180
Marowitz, Charles 78, 154–5
  dir. *Hamlet* 59
Martin, George 49
Mason, Brewster 77
Mayo, Janet 115
Mendelssohn, Felix
  A Midsummer Night's Dream (score) 31, 155

Merchant, Vivien 80, 82
Miles, Maria 137–8
Miles, Patrick 48
Miles, Sarah 125–6
Miller, Jonathan
    dir. *Antony and Cleopatra* 120
Millson, Joseph 168
Miners' Strike 114
Mirren, Helen 85–6
Mison, Tom 186–7
Mitchell, S. J. D. 3
Mohyeddin, Zia 53–4
Moiseiwitsch, Tanya 30
Monck, Nugent
    dir. *Cymbeline* 17
Mongiardino, Renzo 42
Monteverdi, Claudio 92
Morgan, Priscilla 35
Morley, Sheridan 140
Moscow Arts Theatre 39
Mosley, Oswald 167
Mullin, Michael 85, 87
Murray, Brian 54–5
Mussolini, Benito 38
Myers, Wayne 26

national anthem 13
national service 41
National Theatre (NT) 1, 8–11, 15–16, 18, 34, 38, 48, 50, 58, 65, 89, 90, 92, 94–5, 100–1, 105, 112, 114–15, 118–19, 123–4, 130, 131, 133–4, 150, 161, 165, 169–70
    Cottesloe Theatre 110–11, 126, 130, 188
    Lyttelton Theatre 100
    Olivier Theatre 94, 100, 102, 105, 109, 113–14, 119, 130

NBC 32–3
Neill, Heather 174
Nelsen, Paul 146
Nettles, John 144–5
New Ambassador's Theatre, London 172
New York 149, 156, 159–60, 166
New York Public Library 133
Nightingale, Benedict 106, 113, 116, 143–4, 173–4
Nixon, Richard 90–1, 98
Northern Broadsides (theatre company) 109
Nunn, Trevor 9

O'Brien, Timothy 137
O'Connor, Gary 17, 104–6
O'Donnell, Anthony 140
Old Vic 15, 28, 52, 90–1, 93, 165, 185
Olivier, Laurence 15, 18, 26, 29–30, 34–8, 69, 73–6, 89, 99, 123, 173, 185
Orgel, Stephen 92
Ormsby, Robert 111–12, 114
Osbourne, John
    Look Back in Anger (play) 13
O'Toole, Peter 40, 44, 47

Parker, Nathanial 134
Parry, Hubert 188
    'Jerusalem' (hymn) 188
Pearson, Richard 59–60, 64–5
Pennington, Michael 143
Perse, The (school) 3, 166, 176, 178
Peter, John 124, 128
Peter Hall Company (theatre company) 7, 9, 131, 178

Phillips, Michael 156–7
Phoenix Theatre, London 133
Pierce, Brooke 160
Piggot-Smith, Tim 127–8
Pinter, Harold 6, 44, 51, 80, 96, 110, 164, 170, 172, 189
 The Birthday Party (play) 44
Playhouse Theatre, London 137
Plummer, Christopher 151, 156
Poel, William 3, 115
Porter, Eric 73, 137
Potter, Lois 129
Presley, Elvis 13, 25
Pryce-Jones, Alan 41, 42
Pryce-Jones, David 65
Punch (magazine) 42
'Purple Haze' (song) 83

Qualye, Anthony
 dir. History Plays 73, 185
Queen Mary 15
Quilley, Denis 94, 98, 147

Ranson, Malcolm 118
Rasmussen, Eric 127
Redgrave, Vanessa 34–5, 168
Reinhardt, Max 155
 dir. *A Midsummer Night's Dream* (film) 31
Revill, Clive 20, 23
Richardson, Ian 80, 85
Richardson, Tony 17, 30
Rigby, Terence 159
Rigdon, Kevin 169–70
Rigg, Diana 34, 85, 178
Ripley, John 115
Riseborough, Andrea 174
Robeson, Paul 29–30, 104
Rogers, Paul 73, 85, 87

Rooney, Mickey 155
Rosenbaum, Ron 160
Rosenberg, Marvin 81
Rosenthal, Daniel 14, 90, 108
Rose Theatre, Kingston 9, 57, 164–5, 167, 169, 172, 175, 178
Roud, Richard 86
Royal Court Theatre, London 13
Royal Opera House, London 89
Royal Shakespeare Company 1, 5, 6, 8–10, 15–16, 18, 20–1, 24, 28, 34, 38, 40–1, 43, 48–51, 54–8, 63, 65, 69–71, 84–5, 88–9, 124, 138, 144–6, 149, 159, 170, 171–2
 Aldwych Theatre, London 39, 56, 71, 75, 77
 Barbican Theatre, London 172
 Catch my Soul (musical) 150
 Complete Works season 173
 Courtyard Theatre, Stratford 172
 Royal Shakespeare Theatre, Stratford 74
 Swan Theatre, Stratford 10, 138
Rudkin, David 51, 63
 Afore Night Come 63
Rutter, Barrie 109
Rutter, Carol Chillington 67
Ryall, David 138, 182–4
Rylands, George 3
 dir. *Twelfth Night* 26

Saint-Denis, Michel 5
Sands, Mick 183

Schoenberg, Arnold 36
Scofield, Paul 6, 11, 17, 40, 80–2, 84, 90, 103–8, 165
Seale, Douglas 58, 60
Second World War 1, 41, 76
Seldon, Anthony 133
September 11 attacks 1, 131, 162–3, 185
Shakespeare, William
   A Midsummer Night's Dream 10, 16, 181
   All's Well that Ends Well 10
   Antony and Cleopatra 9
   As You Like It 156
   Coriolanus 7, 11, 16, 115
   Cymbeline 16
   Hamlet 3, 7, 10–11, 156
   Henry IV plays 9, 10, 29
   Henry VI plays 4, 64, 67
   Julius Caesar 4
   King John 64
   King Lear 130, 141, 156
   Love's Labour's Lost 16, 18, 23
   Macbeth 3, 6, 10, 63
   Measure for Measure 129
   The Merchant of Venice 7
   Othello 150
   Richard II 3
   Romeo and Juliet 52
   The Taming of the Shrew 3
   The Tempest 125
   Titus Andronicus 23
   Troilus and Cressida 16
   Twelfth Night 16
   The Two Gentleman of Verona 16, 39
Shakespeare Memorial Theatre, Stratford 9, 13, 15–18, 20, 22, 28–9, 30, 33–4, 36, 38–41, 43, 48, 50, 55–6, 58, 84–5, 88, 130, 137–8, 173, 175, 179, 185
   Russian tour 28–9
Shakespeare Recording Society 55
Shakespeare's Globe, London 146
Shakespeare Summer School, Stratford 23, 38
Sharpe, Will 127
Sharrock, Thea 170–1
   dir. *Private Lives* 170
Shaughnessy, Robert 93, 100
Shaw, George Bernard 164, 167
Shaw, Glen Byam 15, 21, 29, 54
   dir. *King Lear* 29
Shorter, Eric 69
Shuter, Paul 170
Sibbery, Michael 136, 140
Sinden, Donald 68
Sinfield, Alan 2, 49–51, 56–7, 69, 70, 80, 88
   Political Shakespeare 49
Slade (rock band) 93
Slingerland, Amy L. 154
Sommer, Elyse 161
South Bank Show (television series) 7, 124, 172
Soviet Presidium 63
Speaight, Robert 23, 43, 52–4, 77, 79–80, 83
Speer, Albert 145
Spencer, Charles 147, 174, 176, 178, 184, 186
Stein, Douglas 159
Stephens, Robert 186
Stevens, Dan 164, 168–9
Stirling, Rachael 178
Stott, Ken 128
Strong, Roy 92

Suez Crisis 14, 30, 63
Suzman, Janet 68, 78
Svoboda 142
Swift, Clive 85

Tanfield, John 3
Tate, Sir Jeffrey 31
Taylor, Gwen 143
Taylor, Neil 79
Taylor, Paul 181, 184
Tennant, David 175
Tenniel, John 42
Thatcher, Margaret 8, 100, 108, 111, 114, 131, 133
Thaxter, John 177
Theatre for a New Audience 156, 159
Theatre Royal, Bath 10, 164–5, 167, 169, 181
Theatre Workshop, London 65
Thomas, Richard 152, 154
Thompson, Ann 79
Thompson, Sophie 139
three-day week 91, 97
Tillyard, E. M. W. 57
Tinker, Jack 144
Top Gun (film) 152
Toynbee, Polly 104
Trainer, Kevin 177
Trayling, Susie 175
Trevellick, Jill 115
Trewin, J. C. 26, 81
Tutin, Dorothy 24, 26, 47, 54–6, 103
Tynan, Kenneth 12, 23, 25, 37, 53–7

United Nations 115
University of California 150

University of Houston 149, 169
Unwin, Stephen 166
Ure, Mary 32

Vanity Fair (magazine) 148
Verdi, Giuseppe
    Macbeth (opera) 102
Vermeer, Johannes 55
Veronese, Paolo
    Mars and Venus Bound by Cupid (painting) 120
Vian, Boris
    The Empire Builders (play) 63
Vietnam War 76, 81, 83–4, 91
Voss, Philip 171

Wagner, Richard 110
Wain, John 26–7
Walker, Roy 27
Wannamaker, Sam 30
Ward, Anthony 182
Wardle, Irving 2, 11, 82, 114, 116, 119
Warhol, Andy 88
Warner, David 10, 66–7, 69–70, 72–3, 75–6, 78–80, 85, 98
Warren, Roger 4, 22, 32, 114, 116–18, 124, 127–8
Washington DC 152
Watergate 91, 98
Watson, Cecil 27
Watteau, Jean-Antoine 25
Weber, Bruce 160
Weems, Andrew 159, 161
Wells, Stanley 29, 35–8, 77–9
West Side Story (film) 52
Wheatcroft, Geoffrey 101

Whiting, John 2, 6, 14
Williams, Clifford 70–1, 73
Williams, Finty 182
Williams, Tennessee 6
Wilson, Cecil 32
'winter of discontent' 101
Witness (film) 152
Wolfenden, Guy 84
Womersley, David 175
Wood, Peter 70
   dir. *The Winter's Tale* 39–40

Woods, Christopher 175
Woodside, D. B. 158
Worsley, T. C. 66
Worth, Irene 117
Wymark, Patrick 24, 27

Yelland, David 186

Zeffirelli, Franco 55
   dir. *Romeo and Juliet* 52
Zielinski, Scott 161

www.ingramcontent.com/pod-product-compliance
Lightning Source LLC
Chambersburg PA
CBHW051810230426
43672CB00012B/2682